U0113237

中国能源政策解读

能源革命与"一带一路"倡议

许勤华 钟兆伟 ◎著

石油工业出版社

内 容 提 要

本书从国内和国际两个层面全面解读了中国能源政策的发展过程，比较了中国与其他国家的能源文化，阐述了中国开展能源革命的前因后果，剖析了"一带一路"倡议下能源合作的机遇与风险。

图书在版编目（CIP）数据

中国能源政策解读：能源革命与"一带一路"倡议 / 许勤华，钟兆伟著.
北京：石油工业出版社，2017.5
（读点石油财经丛书）
书名原文：China's Energy Policy from National and International Perspectives: The Energy Revolution and One Belt One Road Initiative
ISBN 978-7-5183-1893-3

Ⅰ.①中… Ⅱ.①许… ②钟… Ⅲ.①能源政策–研究–中国 Ⅳ.①F426.2

中国版本图书馆CIP数据核字（2017）第085801号

©2016香港城市大学
本书原由香港城市大学出版社发行全世界。
本书中国大陆英文版由香港城市大学授权石油工业出版社有限公司在中国大陆（台湾、香港及澳门除外）出版发行。

中国能源政策解读：能源革命与"一带一路"倡议
许勤华　钟兆伟　著

出版发行：石油工业出版社
　　　　　（北京市朝阳区安华里二区 1 号楼　100011）
网　　址：http://www.petropub.com
编 辑 部：(010) 64523602　图书营销中心：(010) 64523633
经　　销：全国新华书店
印　　刷：北京晨旭印刷厂

2017年5月第1版　2017年5月第1次印刷
740×1060 毫米　开本：1/16　印张：24
字数：340千字

定　价：98.00元
（如发现印装质量问题，我社图书营销中心负责调换）

版权所有，翻印必究

前　言

中国能源发展的基本情况

　　环境问题不仅是中国能源政策的一个制约因素，也正成为其三个重要方面之一。这三个方面是能源安全，环境和气候。三者之间互为相关，彼此支持，共同维持中国经济的可持续发展。

　　自 2012 年年底，中国已成为全球最大的能源生产国之一。随着其经济地位的大幅提升，中国已成为世界的焦点，在应对气候变化挑战的同时更加强烈地感受到国民对环境安全的渴求。

　　在"十一五"期末，中国能源产业得到了实质性的发展。一次能源总产量从 2005 年的 21.6 亿吨标准煤增加到 29.7 亿吨标准煤，能源自给率达到了91%。可再生能源在一次能源中所占比例从 2005 年的 7.4% 增加到 2010 年的9.4%，非化石燃料能源由 6.8% 增加到 8.6%。中国与中亚、俄罗斯、中东、非洲、南美以及亚太地区开展海外油气合作，海外股权石油生产逐渐增加。能源强度下降了 19.1%。

　　至于煤炭产业，中国面临的难题是煤田往往位于离消费区域较远的位置。交通是能源安全的一个巨大挑战。中国也已开始从东南亚进口煤炭，并从澳大利亚大量进口，加强了海外合作。因此，中国已更加依赖海外煤炭。就供电行业而言，电力投资额已达到 1.2 万亿元，且完成了从山西经河南到湖北653.8 千米的特高压电网模型建设。然而其安全性、经济价值、技术障碍以及可靠性有待进一步检测。在石油和天然气行业，原油依靠海外供给率已占近

60%。根据国家统计局的数据，2015年中期石油储备二期工程结束后，目前的石油储备能力已经增加到2860万立方米。由此而来的石油储备虽然增加到了近40天，仍然离国际能源署提出的90天的安全标准线相差甚远。中国于2006年开始进口天然气，于2007年变成天然气净进口国。应对气候变化、环境保护和以市场为导向的能源产业刺激中国开拓天然气的进口（包括液化气）和减少煤的使用。对天然气进口的日益依赖已引起国内煤炭产业以及那些倡导核能和页岩气持续发展以此来减少对海外天然气的依赖的人的关注。

各国的经济状况、能源产业发展程度、能源利用方式有所不同，文化及历史背景多样丰富，生活和生产环境、外交策略及政治经济体制又各具特色，因此多种能源文化并存于世。中国对一些关键术语及概念拥有特殊解释，如能源安全、能源效率、能源法、能源独立性、能源进口依赖度、能源外交政策、国有企业、国际能源合作、能源短缺等，这些都充分展现了中国的特色能源文化。

1993年至2011年期间，中国能源结构的实质没有改变，国内绿色能源的总产量无明显提高，其中石油和天然气的供给安全成为一个突出的问题。"十二五"期间出台的能源政策有望解决这一问题。"十二五"期间，低油气价格、能源结构的优化、新能源及可再生能源（NRE）使用比例的增加短期内缓解了能源供给的安全问题，但就长期而言，中国仍有待一场真正的能源革命。

中国的能效变化具有地区差异，碳排放量亦是如此。能效的提高确实有利于环境的改善。中国政府在发电方面实施了四条政策。第一，电厂减少燃煤发电，提高天然气使用率；这会带来石油消耗的持续下降，刺激其他燃料的需求。这一趋势在中国的中、东、南部尤为明显，北部却收效甚微。第二，倡导电厂采用节能减排技术，如烟气脱硫等。第三，鼓励建设60万千瓦以上规模电厂代替小型低效电站。第四，制定激励措施，如碳排放税。能效的提高和能源结构的优化有效降低了碳排放量，这一比例从2004年的10.7%下降到2010年的10.41%。在温室气体减排方面，交通部门的贡献度最高，各类交通运输（海运、空运、陆运、铁运）的有关当局出台了多项法律以提高能效，减少排放；东部比中、西部人口稠密，所以东部成效较小，西部交通基础设施又欠发达，因而中部的实施效果最佳。

能效的整体改善主要体现在发电行业上，采矿、化工、钢铁、非金属产业能效提升较小。"十二五"期间，中国计划较 2010 年实现二氧化硫减排 8%，一氧化氮减排 10% 和碳强度下降 17% 的目标。各行业能耗中，交通部门的减排潜力最大。官方数据表明这些减排目标超额完成：二氧化硫减排 18.0%，一氧化氮减排 18.6%，碳强度下降了 20%[①]。

① http://news.xinhuanet.com/local/2016-02/19/c_128732113.htm

中国政府计划未来能源发展分三个阶段。到 2030 年，能源消耗主要来源于化石燃料，其次是新能源和可再生能源，并越来越接近化石燃料能耗。到 2050 年，可再生能源和化石燃料消耗持平，各占能源消耗总量的一半。2050 年之后，能源消耗主要来自可再生能源，其次是化石能源。中国政府要完成这一宏伟计划，关键要优化能源结构，提高能源效率，提倡使用清洁能源。

中国在能源发展方面多年来一直面临三个主要矛盾：可持续能源需求同人均能源严重不足之间的矛盾，煤炭导向型能源结构同低碳发展之间的长期矛盾，以及化石燃料高能源强度同生态环境高要求之间的矛盾。"十二五"规划是中国政府调整经济发展模式的重要时期。中共十八届三中全会公告指出，在"市场起决定性作用"的经济转型过程中，这些矛盾会更加突出。

中国能源发展"十二五"规划于 2013 年 1 月 1 日正式印发，规划明确指出能源发展的主要目标和首要任务是使用清洁能源，提高能源利用效率，计划到 2015 年，单位 GDP 能耗比 2010 年下降 16%，能源消耗总量 40 亿吨标准煤，其中国内生产 36.6 亿吨标准煤。计划总用电量 6.15 万亿千瓦时，能源利用效率提高 38%。非化石燃料占一次能源消耗比重增加到 11.4%，天然气占到 7.5%。碳排放量比 2005 年减少 17%，污染物排放减少 10%。

2015 年中国实现可再生能源生产大幅提高并不容易，因为中国大部分可再生能源都用于发电。其结果就是，可再生能源生产提高 11.4%，可替代能源生产如核能、风能、生物质能、太阳能就需要提高 200%。完成单位 GDP 能耗下降 16% 这一计划,不但要求地方政府有效贯彻落实中央政策,还需要 GDP 增长维持在 8% 左右。在不久的将来,中国能源结构依然以煤为主,大约占中国能源结构份额的一半。能源政策带来的环境效益取决于政策的实施。然而有报道称,2015 年中国的太阳能和风能发电容量分别提高了 74% 和 34%[①]。

① https://cleantechnica.com/2016/03/06/china-renewable-growth-soars-fossil-fuel-use-declines/

中国的石油及天然气长期以来处于供不应求的状态。中国在 1993 年及 1996 年先后成为成品油及原油的净进口国。自 20 世纪 90 年代以来,中国企业就响应"走出去"战略,并积极打造了一项具有前瞻性的全球计划,以满足中央政府围绕"充分利用好两种资源、两个市场"所规定的各项要求。目前,已有超过 100 个石油及天然气国际合作项目在 33 个国家间开展,并大致分为了五大国际石油及天然气合作区域。一个关于石油、液化天然气、天然气、煤和铀的进出口贸易体制已初步形成,并以油轮运输为主,管道及铁路运输为辅。国际市场有多种业绩指标,其中包括了现货、期货及长期采购协议。中国的国有能源企业已大大提升了自身的国际竞争力。

中国对外能源政策的制定经历了若干根本性的转变,这些转变在政府颁布的官方能源安全政策中有迹可循。同时,我们从能源企业的经济活动及其国际合作的参与中也可看出种种变化。能源安全方面的观念转变引发了多方位的能源合作。这使得中国的能源企业在对外能源合作中发挥了重要作用并摒弃了"政府打头阵,企业随后跟"的形式套路。

中国实行积极的对外能源政策,在某种程度上保证了其能源安全,并履行了保护全球能源安全的责任并缓解了部分地缘政治冲突,而这一切都带来了积极影响。然而,随着"走出去"战略逐步实施,中国面临着更多风险。这可能会使正常的双边关系被贴上"能源"标签,进一步强化他国关于"中国掠夺资源"的猜测,对双边外交关系造成消极影响。在参与国际能源合作

20 年后，中国首次正视了其在国际能源秩序中的地位和重要性，并在此基础上对其对外能源政策进行了重新定位。

　　鉴于石油、天然气及国家安全等多方面的考虑，中国在其对外能源政策上将继续实行全球能源政策，坚持重视与中亚及俄罗斯的双边关系，加大中东地区投资，加强中非合作，推动南美发展以及巩固亚太地区发展。

PREFACE

Basic Information about China's Energy Development

The introduction of a carbon trading market in China shows that environmental concerns are not only a restraint on Chinese energy policy, but they are becoming one of the three key aspects in energy policy. These aspects are energy security, environment and climate and foreign relations. The three are interrelated and mutually supportive of each other with the main purpose of maintaining the sustainable development of the Chinese economy.

Since the end of 2012, China has been one of the world's largest energy producer. As its economic status rises dramatically, China has become the focus of the world, feeling more strongly its citizens' yearning for environmental safety while experiencing the challenges of coping with climate change.

By the end of the Eleventh Five-Year Plan in 2010, China's energy industry had seen substantial development: total production quantity of primary energy had increased from 2.16 billion tons of standard coal in 2005 to 2.97 billion tons. The energy self-supply rate had reached 91%. The proportion of new and renewable energy in primary energy had risen from 7.4% in 2005 to 9.4% in 2010, and non-fossil fueled energy from 6.8% to 8.6%. China had developed its overseas oil and gas cooperation with Central Asia, Russia, the Middle East, Africa, South America and the Asia-Pacific region, and gradual growth had been seen in overseas equity oil production. Energy intensity had decreased by 19.1%.

Regarding the coal industry, China's difficulty is that the coalfields are located far away from the consuming areas. Transportation has been a great challenge for energy security. China has also started to import coal from Southeast Asia and in significant amounts from Australia, which improves overseas cooperation. As a result, China has become more dependent on overseas coal. With regard to the power supply industry, investment in electric power has reached 1200 billion yuan, with the completion of a 653.8 kilometer extra-high-voltage model electric network from Shanxi to Hubei via Henan. However, further testing of its safety, economic value, technical obstacles and reliability is required. In the oil and gas industry, dependence on overseas supply of crude oil has reached nearly 60%. The present petroleum reserve capacity is 28.6 million cubic meters (National Bureau of Statistics of the People's Republic of China) (from 16.4 million cubic meters) after the second construction phase was finished in mid-2015. The resulting net import of petroleum has been increased to approximately forty days, still far from the ninety days suggested by the International Energy Agency. China started to import natural gas in 2006 and the year 2007 saw its net import of natural gas. Coping with climate change, environmental protection and a market-oriented energy industry motivated China to develop natural gas imports, including liquid natural gas (LNG), and reduce coal use. The growing dependence on natural gas imports has caused concern from the domestic coal industry, and from those who advocate continuous development of nuclear power and shale gas to reduce the dependence on overseas natural gas.

A variety of energy cultures exist in the world due to the different development levels of economies and energy industries, ways of using energy, diverse cultural and historic backgrounds, living and production environments, foreign strategies, and political and economic systems. China has its own special interpretation of some key terms and concepts like energy security, energy efficiency, energy law, energy independence, dependence on overseas supply, foreign policy on energy, state-owned company, international energy cooperation and energy shortage etc., which display a profoundly distinct Chinese energy culture.

There was no change in the nature of the Chinese energy structure from 1993 to 2011, and no obvious increase in total production of domestic green energy. The security of supply of petroleum and natural gas became a prominent issue, which was to be resolved by the energy policies of the Twelfth Five-Year Plan (FYP). With the aid of low oil and gas prices and the optimization of energy mix with the increased ratio of NRE (new and renewable energy) during the Twelfth FYP period, the problem of supply security was alleviated in the short-term, however, for long-term security, China is still awaiting the real energy revolution.

There are regional differences in the changes in Chinese energy efficiency, which are also reflected in the different levels of carbon emissions. The improvement of energy efficiency has indeed had a positive influence on the environment. Regarding power generation, the Chinese government has implemented four policies. The first is to reduce thermal coal use in power plants and increase natural gas use, leading to a continuous decrease in oil power generation and a rapid increase in other fuels. This trend is clearly evident in the central, eastern and southern parts of China but is less obvious in the northern part. The second is to advocate energy-saving and emission reduction technology in power plants, such as the use of smoke and gas desulphurization etc. The third is to encourage the building of power plants over 600,000 kilowatts (kW) in scale, to replace small and low efficiency generating units. The fourth is to impose incentives like emissions taxation. Increased energy efficiency and energy-mix change reduced carbon emissions by 10.7% and 10.41% respectively from 2004 to 2010. The transport sector has played the most important role in reducing greenhouse gases.

The authorities responsible for different types of transportation (sea, air, road and railway) have issued various laws to improve efficiency and decrease emissions. These laws are less effective in the eastern region due to its denser population than in the central and western regions, and in particular more effective in the central region than the western region whose transportation infrastructure is less developed.

The greatest overall improvement in energy efficiency has been in power generation, and less improvement has been made in mining, chemical, steel, iron and non-metal industries. In the Twelfth FYP, China aimed to achieve an 8% decrease in sulphur dioxide emissions, 10% in nitrogen monoxide and 17% in carbon intensity compared with 2010. Of all the areas of energy consumption, transportation has the greatest potential for emissions reduction. According to official data these aims were fulfilled: 18.0% decrease in sulphur dioxide; 18.6% decrease in nitrogen monoxide; 20% decrease in carbon intensity[1].

[1] http://news.xinhuanet.com/local/2016-02/19/c_128732113.htm

The Chinese government plans three phases for future energy development. Up to 2030, energy consumption will be mainly derived from fossil fuels with new and renewable energy sources playing an increasingly close second. From 2030 to 2050, consumption will be split evenly between fossil fuels and renewable energy sources. After 2050, renewable energy will prevail while fossil energy will play a secondary role. To fulfil this grand plan, optimizing energy structure, improving energy efficiency and advocating clean energy use will be key strategies of the Chinese government.

For many years now, China has faced three types of structural conflicts in energy development, namely the conflict between sustainable energy needs and severe shortage of resources per capita, the long-term conflict between coal-oriented energy and low carbon development, and the conflict between the high energy intensity of fossil fuel usage and the more demanding requirements of the ecological environment. The Twelfth FYP was considered as an important phase for the Chinese government to adjust economic development patterns. These conflicts will be more prominent in the process of economic transition in which "the market plays the decisive role", as stated in the proclamation of the Third Plenary Session of the 18th Central Committee.

The Twelfth FYP of Chinese Energy Development issued on January 1, 2013 confirmed the key goals and gave priority to clean energy use and increased energy efficiency: energy intensity was planned to be reduced by 16% from 2010 to 2015. Energy consumption was planned to be 400 million tons of standard coal, 366 millions of which was for self-supply. Power consumption was planned to be 6150 billion kilowatt hours (kWh). Energy efficiency was planned to increase by 38%. The proportion of non-fossil fuels in primary energy was planned to grow to 11.4%, with natural gas accounting for 7.5%. Carbon emissions were planned to be reduced by 17% compared with 2005, and pollutant emissions to fall by 10%.

It was hard for China to achieve its ambitious increase of renewable energy production by 2015, for most of the renewable energy is used in power generation. As a result, 11.4% growth in renewables requires an increase of 200% in alternative sources such as nuclear, wind power, bioenergy and solar energy. The planned 16% decrease in energy not only required local governments' efficient enforcement of the central government policies but also for GDP growth to remain around 8%. In the near future, coal will still dominate, representing approximately half of the Chinese energy structure. Environmental profits from the energy policy will depend on the implementation of the policy. However, it was reported that China's solar and wind energy capacity increased by 74% and 34%, respectively, in 2015 [1] .

① https://cleantechnica. com/2016/03/06/china-renewable-growth-soars-fossil-fuel-use-declines/

The supply of China's petroleum and natural gas has, for a long time, been insufficient to meet consumption demands. China became a net importer of refined oil products in 1993 and of crude oil in 1996. Since the 1990s, Chinese enterprises have followed the Going Out strategy and proactively developed a global plan in order to fulfil the requirements of "making full use of two kinds of resources and two markets" imposed by the central government. Over 100 international cooperation projects in oil and gas have been carried out in thirty-three countries, broadly organized into five large international oil and gas cooperation zones. A preliminary import and export trading system was built for petroleum, LNG, natural gas, coal and uranium. Transportation is mainly by oil tankers, assisted by pipelines and railway freight. Multiple financial measures like spot, futures and long-term purchase agreements exist in international markets. Chinese state-owned energy companies have greatly increased their international competitiveness.

There have been fundamental changes in the formulation of China's external energy policy. Changes can be seen in the official energy security policy issued by the government, in the economic activities of energy companies and in their involvement in international cooperation. The change in the conception of energy safety has caused a series of multilateral trends in energy cooperation. It has helped that Chinese energy companies play an important part in external energy cooperation, and have abandoned the formality that "government takes the lead and paves the way for enterprises".

To some extent, China's active foreign energy policy guarantees its own energy safety, undertakes the responsibility of safeguarding global energy safety, and eases some geopolitical conflicts, all of which exert a positive influence. However, the more the Going Out Policy is implemented, the more risks China has to face. This can have a negative effect on diplomatic relations, tagging the "energy" label on the normal bilateral relationships and intensifying speculation about "resource plundering" by China. After twenty years of international energy cooperation, China has repositioned its foreign energy policy, and this reposition is based on China's facing up to its position and significance in the global energy order for the first time.

Considering the issues surrounding oil, gas, and national safety, China's foreign energy policy will continue its global energy policy based on the principle of emphasizing relations with Central Asia and Russia, increasing investment in the Middle East, strengthening cooperation in Africa, boosting South America and consolidating developments in the Asia-Pacific region.

目　录

第一章　绪论

第二章　"十二五"规划以前的能源体系和政策

第三章 "十二五"规划能源政策的影响

第四章　中国能源的发展与革命

第五章　中国对外能源政策历程

第六章 "一带一路"倡议下的能源合作

Contents

1. Introduction

2. The Energy System and Policies before the Twelfth Five-Year Plan

3. Effects of the Twelfth Five-Year Plan Energy Policy

4. China's Energy Evolution and Revolution

5. The Evolution of China's Foreign Energy Policy

6. Energy Cooperation under the Belt and Road Initiative

CHPATER 1

第一章

1

绪论

背景和动机

作为世界上最大的二氧化碳排放国（表1），中国做出了更大力度的单边减排承诺：到2020年碳排放强度将比2005年降低40%～45%。由于目标如此宏大，国际社会十分关注中国将如何实现这一目标。

表1　2011年世界及主要国家CO₂总排放量和人均排放量

世界及主要国家	CO₂排放量，千吨	人均排放量，吨/人
世界	33376327	4.9
中国	9700000	7.2
美国	5420000	17.3
印度	1970000	1.6
俄罗斯	1830000	12.8

来源：全球大气研究排放数据库EDGAR（2013）

"十一五"（2006—2010年）期间，针对能源强度降低20%的目标，中国主要通过直接监管和自上而下的行政法规降低了19.4%。尽管一些省份被迫在2010年底前关闭工业产能以完成其分配的节能指标，该目标仍未实现。由于中国正处于由计划经济转向市场经济的过程中，国家碳排放交易体系自然而然地就提上了议事日程。

排放交易体系（简称ETS，也称排放配额交易体系）是中国的政策工具之一，鼓励减排。与其他应税经济工具相比，排放交易体系允许政府在该体系引入前决定和设定一定时期内的总排放量。排放交易的初始概念见于克罗克（1966）提出的"大气污染许可证"。其背后的主要思想是通过拍卖或者免费的祖父制初步向企业分配排污许可。然后企业之间被允许交易排污许可，目的在于使得一个企业拥有一定数量的至少可以与其排放量相当的排污许可。因此，有富余排污许可的企业可以在市场上售卖，而需要额外许可的企业可以从市场购买。显然，企业需要考虑边际减排成本和减排许可市场价格的差价以此来确定减排选择。

根据美国 1990 年颁布的《清洁空气法》修正案，第一个大型的排放交易体系在美国电力行业实施，用来控制二氧化硫的排放。随后该体系又被美国用于控制氮氧化物的排放。在欧洲，1997 年所签订的《京都议定书》规定欧盟 15 个成员国可以分担将其总排放量在 1990 年基础上降低 8% 的目标。欧盟当前的减排目标是到 2020 年减排 20%。为此，欧盟采用了碳排放交易体系控制温室气体二氧化碳的排放。排放交易经历三个阶段：2005—2007 年，2008—2012 年和 2013—2020 年。欧盟现在提出了到 2030 年减少 40% 碳排放的目标。参与排放交易体系的所有国家都提出了各自的排放份额分配计划，决定给主要排放对象发放排污许可证，例如，发电厂将在本期发放之列。需要注意的是，其他温室气体对全球变暖的潜在影响，以二氧化碳来计算其排放量。

碳交易是"十二五"规划中重要的能源和环境政策之一。短期目标是 2013 年在北京、重庆、上海、深圳、天津、广东和湖北建立小型的跨区域碳排放交易体系，2015 年过渡到全国性的碳排放交易体系。当时的想法是用小型的碳排放交易体系解决排放份额分配体系设计上的一些重要问题，包括透明度、交易成本、对相关产业国际竞争力的影响，诸如最高价的价格稳定机制、缓冲排放量年波动的"储备"方案的价值，以及不同方式处理拍卖资金的效益含义。实际上，北京和河北在 2014 年底便率先开展了跨区域碳排放交易。

全国碳排放交易体系有望在 2017 年运行。

然而，在建立可靠的全国碳排放交易体系前，中国仍需靠直接监管和自上而下的行政法规来实现节能减排的目标。"十二五"期间，中国计划提高清洁能源使用比例，改变其能源结构，以同时实现能源保障和环境保护的双重目标。理论上来说，单纯改变能源结构并不能实现减排目标，但在全国碳排放交易体系启动前，这似乎是最适合的策略。

本书中，通过观察与讨论，我们总结了与能源结构相关的能源政策和环境政策，先谈"十一五"期间能源政策的实施效果，然后描述"十二五"时期的能源政策，同时分析这些政策带来的环境影响。由于改变能源结构使得中国对诸如石油和天然气一类的进口一次能源的依赖度更高，可能也会影响其他国家的能源保障。另外，能源领域的国际关系问题也是本书的一个重要部分。

引 言

"看得见的手"和"看不见的手"

理解中国的能源政策，我们需要回顾 1978 年经济改革后中国处于从计划经济转向社会主义市场经济的那段关键时期。邓小平，中国经济改革的设计师，在 1992 年南方视察时，坚定自信地说道：

"计划多一点还是市场多一点，不是社会主义与资本主义的本质区别。计划经济不等于社会主义，资本主义也有计划；市场经济不等于资本主义，社会主义也有市场。计划和市场都是经济手段。"[1]

> [1]《人民日报》，2012 年 2 月 3 日。

社会主义市场经济的核心是处理好政府"看得见的手"和市场"看不见的手"的关系，使二者和谐结合。因此，评价中国能源政策要根据政府和市场这"两只手"结合的比例关系，且随经济发展程度变化。对能源行业来说，其随着连续"五年计划"的发展阶段而改变。

能源保障，经济增长和环境保护

按照经济增长的趋势，能源政策旨在支持经济增长。而当能源行业不能自给自足时，能源保障便成问题。如果能源过度消耗，环境保护便成为能源政策中一个重要的因素。当然，能源保障，经济增长和环境保护这三者的权重依经济发展阶段而定。

中国的区域和行政区

"地区"是一个通用术语，用来指中国的地理行政单位，包括省、市、县和区。应该注意的是中国具体的行政区划包括省，自治区和直辖市。这些地区分为三大区域，如表2所示。

表2　31个行政区的分布

区域	行政区（即除香港、澳门、台湾外的省、自治区、直辖市）
东部	北京，天津，河北，辽宁，上海，江苏，浙江，福建，山东，广东，海南
中部	山西，吉林，黑龙江，安徽，江西，河南，湖北，湖南
西部	四川，重庆，贵州，云南，陕西，甘肃，青海，宁夏，新疆，广西，内蒙古，西藏

需要指出的是，文献中有几种不同的分类。例如，Chen 和 Fleisher（1996）为研究地区收入不均衡和全国经济增长，把中国分成沿海和内陆两个区域。Hu 和 Wang（2006）为分析中国不同区域的能源效率，采用了"七五"计划的"三个经济地带"的布局，即东部、中部和西部。Gelb 和 Chen（2004）为给中国政府实施的西部大开发战略提供一份进展报告，则用的是官方指定的西部地区。

为使结果与政策制定更相关，我们采用了 Hu 和 Wang（2006）的官方分类，即表 2 中有待调查研究的 31 个行政区。用"三个经济地带"的布局，必要时可简化讨论。

区域经济发展

中国各区域差异显著。"七五"计划期间（1986—1990 年），按照"三个经济地带"的布局，把全国划分为三大经济地带：东部、西部和中部。每个区域都包括不同的行政区（即省、自治区、直辖市）。三大经济地带特点如下：(1) 东部增长速度比中西部快，且拥有更多的直接外资；(2) 中部主要是农村和农业，是人口的主要聚居地；(3) 西部人口稀疏且经济相对落后。

行政管理

传统的中国体制结构比较灵活，能适应各地实际情况，用来协调自上而下的政策措施和当地、社会以及经济利益之间的冲突。中国能效和节能政策（EE&C）的目标为适应管理需要，已做出相应改动，将实现国家政治、社会目标的承诺和当地利益以及企业激励相结合。

能源效率

过去 20 年，中国数百家公司的技术一直在进步。能效发展投资的广泛利用和较低成本将对提高能源效率起决定性作用。中国企业提高效率的推动力来源于两方面的因素，即拥有国际水平竞争力的需要和遵守政府制定的能源强度标准的必要。

关键概念理解的差距

局外人对能源行业关键概念的理解有较大的差距，特别是西方人和中国人。基于特殊的文化视角、发展阶段、政治体系以及所有制，中国形成了独具中国特色的能源文化。弥补关键概念理解上的差距能够促进中国能源和环境问题被外界研究，形成对中国特色能源文化更准确的认识。本部分尝试以能源保障的概念为例，阐明中外对关键概念理解的误差。

能源保障和能源安全

① Asia Pacific Energy Research Centre, 'A Quest for Energy Security in the Twenty-First Century'. Paper presented by Institute of Energy Economics, Japan. Available at www.ieej.or.jp/aperc, accessed 27 August 2008.

亚太能源研究中心（以下简称 APERC，2007）①提到，能源保障的定义随时间而改变。20 世纪 70 年代石油危机之后，能源保障的定义与中东地区石油供应的风险相关。随着能源来源的多元化，石油保障演变成了能源保障，然而供应保障仍是头等大事。国际能源署（IEA）规定，"能源保障，广义上来定义，指的是以合理的价格获得充足可靠的能源供应"。很多西方人持与国际能源署（IEA）相同的观点。

亚太能源研究中心将与供应保障相关的要素分为：可用性（地质存在相关要素），可及性（地理政治要素），可购性（经济要素）以及可接受性（环境和社会要素）。Muñoz Delgado（2011）提出了一个相似的定义："能源保障可以分为能源输出国的能源需求保障和能源进口国的供应保障（SOS）。"

20 世纪 70 年代石油危机之后，当时大多数的发达国家通过拓展能源供应来源渠道、节能以及尽可能多地使用替代燃料，竭力降低自己国家对外能源的依赖度。随着自给自足率的提高，能源保障的关键已从供应保障变成能源保障、经济增长和环境保护（3Es）三者之间的平衡，即经济发展和能源保障的平衡，能源保障和环境保护的平衡以及环境问题和经济发展之间的平衡。以上三者构成了三角形关系。

福岛海啸灾难后，理解上的变革唤起了核能支持者对安全问题的认识。Yamashita（2011）2011 年从核能安全的角度指出，能源保障包括四个元素，能源利用，经济增长，环境保护和能源安全，即 3E+S。

在中国，能源保障的概念也在经历如上演化，从石油供应到 4As（可用性，可及性，可购性以及可接受性）的能源供应，从 3 E 到 3E+S。然而，当前对能源保障的理解更接近能源安全。中国政府官方用的是能源安全而非能源保障。"能源安全"涵盖能源保障的含义。中国致力于发展可再生能源以确保国家的能源安全。

中国能源产业经过半个多世纪的发展，能源保障新视野已成熟。2006年 7 月圣彼得堡八国峰会上，时任中国国家主席胡锦涛用以下话语推介了这个新视野：

中国能源战略的基本内容是：坚持节约优先、立足国内、多元发展、保护环境，加强国际互利合作，努力构筑稳定、经济、清洁的能源供应体系。中国是能源消费大国，更是能源生产大国。我们将在平等互惠、互利双赢的原则下加强同各能源生产国和消费国的合作，共同维护全球能源安全。

因此，中国的能源保障新视野包括以下三个要素：

- 能源保障：降低能源强度成为克服能源相关障碍的首要手段，且具有国家战略重要性。
- 环境保护：放慢能源利用增长，淘汰效率低和重污染的企业是中国解决环境问题的基础。
- 经济长期增长：摆脱资源密集型的增长模式，能源效率被看作是支撑经济长期持续增长所必需的。

如图 1 所示，"七五"到"十五"期间，能源政策导向由关注经济转变为关注能源本身以及环境保护。

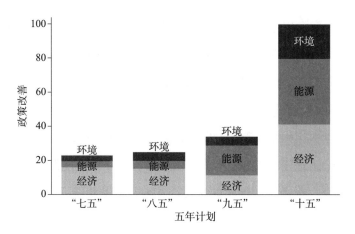

图 1　政策导向变化，"七五"到"十五"时期

能源政策和能源法

众所周知，能源政策是指国家政策中关于能源规划、生产、运输以及使用的相关规定。能源政策包括商业能源活动立法（交易，运输，存储等）和有关能源产品和服务的财税政策（税收，免税额，补贴；国有能源部门资产和组织的有关指示等）。

能源法管理再生能源以及不可再生能源的使用和税收，是所有关于能源的判例法、章程、规则、规章以及法令的主要法源。能源政策不等于能源法，但可以转变为法律。

尽管已有可再生能源法及节能法，能源法的草稿仍在修改和官方听证阶段。因而中国能源的发展是由能源政策导向而不是能源法。所以，政策经常是临时专设的。

与其他国家的区别不仅是政策和法律之间的区别，甚至于能源政策，本质或是能源行业的目标，中国也不同于外国，例如，不同于美国或欧盟。

能源政策的本质

2005 年，美国出台《能源政策法案》以法定形式建立了美国的能源政策。但各州之间可以采用最符合各州利益的不同政策，例如，加利福尼亚州的《2006年全球变暖解决方案法》。欧盟的能源政策基于2007年的里斯本条约，该条约调节能源供应平衡，在欧盟内部转化成能源政策。因而欧盟各国采用统一的区域能源政策。

相反，中国的能源政策是由可能永远不会转变为法律的一系列目标、目的和指示构成的。如有需要，将会修订法律以此来实现政策的效果。能源政策按照"五年计划"的指导方针发布，各省必须遵循和实现中央政府设定的能源政策目标。

能源政策的目标

美国能源政策的基础是以合理的价格获得安全可靠的能源确保国内未来就业（参见2005年美国的《能源政策法案》）。欧盟的能源政策旨在保护环境，尤其是防备气候变化和改善能源网的同时，建立一个安全、可持续、价格合理的能源体系（欧洲委员会2012年）。"十一五"时期，中国的能源政策是在考虑能源保障和环境保护的同时促进经济发展。

能源效率与节能（EE&C）

能源高效利用措施包括大规模地淘汰落后产能，以便为引进高效益的工厂"让路"。节能是在能源使用量上引入一个可以实际促进能源效率提升的上限。

节能指的是使用更少的能源服务降低能耗，不同于能源的高效使用。后者指的是持续使用更少能源。中国仍在使用整套的政策和举措来降低能耗。

"走出去"和国际合作

中国的"走出去"政策有双重含义。一方面，指的是中国的企业走出去，到其他国家直接投资；另一方面，也指吸引外资直接来华投资。对于中国寻求能源保障，国内外皆存在概念混淆和错误理解。

国内，针对投资海外油田来巩固能源保障的评论如下：中国的石油进口超过了中国的海外股本油生产；从海外运输石油并不划算；而且并无证据表明对处于供应危机中的中国客户来说，海外股本油更便宜或更易得。

国外，尚存在中国将会耗尽世界能源储备的不必要的担忧。然而，以下原因可以说明这只是个误解：

- 中国全部海外石油生产量比一个大型石油公司生产的还少；
- 由于中国企业更愿意去冒险和在不利的环境中生存，其海外投资将促进全球市场稳定；
- 中国石油公司大约75%的石油产量来自国内。中国国内石油生产量目前位居世界第四。

如果把"走出去"政策理解为一项国际能源或资源合作政策，或许国内将没有这么多的批评，国外也不存在不必要的担忧。

能源依赖度和石油依赖度

能源依赖是指一个国家的石油和能源依赖进口和其他外源。与能源自主不同，能源自给自足率是一个国家在既定年份一次能源（煤炭，石油，天然气，核能，水能以及可再生能源）产出与消耗的比率。这个比率适用于计算每种能源或者所有能源的自给自足率。比率超过100%（正如中国的电力）表明供大于求，生产过剩，净出口。

中国的能源依赖度不到11%，远远低于石油大约60%的依赖度。如果用石油依赖度来判断能源依赖度，那么国际上流行诸如"中国能源危机"的说法，不足为奇。对比图2和图3可知。

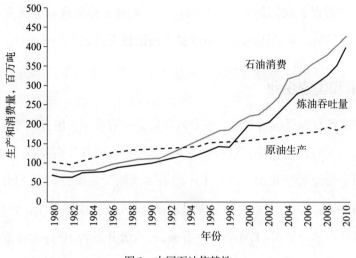

图 2　中国石油依赖性

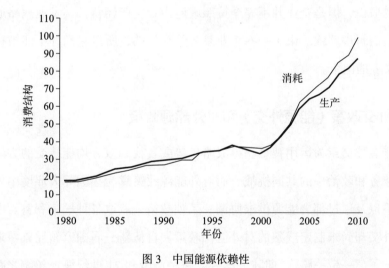

图 3　中国能源依赖性

能源自主和能源相互依赖

　　尽管几乎所有国家都寻求能源自主，并不存在绝对的能源自主。中国同美国一样，热衷于降低本国对进口化石燃料的依赖度，这两国与大多数（或许全部）国家有着共同的利益，即稳定的世界能源市场，可持续的环境和气候，繁荣昌盛的世界经济，以及睦邻友好的和平关系。总之，不论哪个国家想要

13

自主到多大程度，我们仍然相互依赖。因此必须正确处理自力更生和为创造稳定的全球经济、能源市场和环境所做出的治理安排之间的平衡。

国有企业和国家企业

中国的产权制度较为复杂，所有权有以下主要类型：国有/国家控股，集体所有制，合作社，合伙制，股份制，个人，合资企业以及外商独资。1998年后，中国的石油行业经过重组，成立了中国石油天然气集团公司（CNPC，中国石油，纵向一体化），中国石油化工集团公司（Sinopec，中国石化，纵向一体化）和中国海洋石油总公司（CNOOC，中海油，初次公开发售10%~20%股）。因此，这三大油气公司并不属于传统意义上的国有企业（SOE）。政府虽然掌握着大部分的股份，但是企业并不完全按照政府指令生产经营，其发展战略通常是协商后的折中路线。由于一些企业是公开交易的，所以它们并不能被称为严格意义上的国企。

能源外交政策（能源外交）和对外能源政策

能源外交意为运用智慧获得战略优势或者找到双方均能接受的方法解决能源业务和政治中的共同挑战。而对外能源政策意为在国际大环境中处理能源关系以及通过部署能源供求协调一系列政策来获取各种国家利益。中国有能源外交却尚未制定成熟的对外能源政策。自从新一届国家领导人习近平主席提出了"一带一路"，即陆上丝绸之路经济带和21世纪海上丝绸之路，中国似乎已准备好发挥其对外能源政策的潜力。

CHPATER 2

第二章

2

"十二五"规划以前的能源体系和政策

各行业能源发展

本节，我们按行业分类主要探讨亚太能源研究中心出版的《中国能源问题研究》（APERC 2008, 2009）中最具影响力的研究发现，必要处给出一些批注。

煤炭

获取和购买能力的问题

由于煤炭资源地域分布不均，对于中国煤炭供应的持续保障来说，煤炭运输是个主要问题。这是因为中国最大的煤炭存储地远居内陆，距离最紧需煤炭的沿海工业中心数百千米远。因此，每一吨煤炭都是用大约 18 升的柴油（Skeer 和 Yanjia，2007）通过轮船从山西省的大同运到广州。按照每升 6 元来算，从大同到广州仅仅是燃料的花费就高达 108 元 / 吨。除了高昂的原油和石油产品价格，煤炭运输的经济学将进一步限定有购买能力的用户地域范围。然而，图 4 表明，各省对外省区煤的依赖度不断上升，且这种趋势或将持续。简而言之，中国面临着大宗煤炭低效运输的难题。

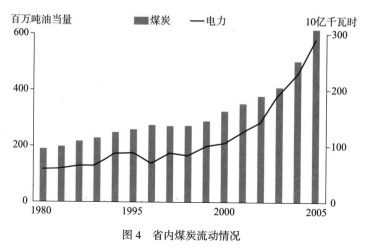

图 4　省内煤炭流动情况

来源：APERC，2008

政策：高效煤炭运输

未来煤炭供应的稳定性很大程度上依赖于负担得起的充足的煤炭运输。中国需要重大投资来更新和拓展其轨道交通基础设施。鉴于卡车运输煤炭是一种费钱费能的方法，解决轨道交通瓶颈也将减轻卡车运输煤炭的压力。鉴于石油价格上涨和运输能力不足，对于中国沿海省份的用户来说，煤炭运输的花费比矿坑价格增长得更快。

政策：修改煤电供应链

为满足煤炭运输需求，除了提高铁路运输能力，中国还可以采取措施降低运输需求，改善供应链。例如，运输电力或者煤炭密集型产品，而不是生煤。国家正在有序进行将电力从资源富饶的西部输送至东部沿海省份的工作。这些企业可以通过缩短提取和使用的距离简化煤炭供应链，将来也有望代替煤炭大宗运输。

当前限制矿井工业和电力发展的主要因素是煤炭富集区的水资源短缺和电力传输网超载。不过，主要电网公司正加大力度提高输电和配电能力，尤其注重改善"西电东送"工程中的远距离高压和超高压线路。井口洗煤也有降低运输需求的潜力，从而改善运输的煤炭产品的能源强度。但是这种方法并未在中国广泛实践，且在煤炭工业现代化中遇到了重重阻碍。

加入国际煤炭市场也有助于减轻国内煤炭运输压力。当前市场有利于中国从北部港口持续不断地向邻国出口煤，而沿海省份早已发现从东南亚和澳大利亚进口煤更经济实惠。"十一五"规划指导方针也强调提高国内输电和配电技术水平。而不断加强的对外合作可能进一步加快发展和部署的步伐。

电力行业

问题：煤炭运输基础设施瓶颈

煤炭基础设施和投资与中国电力基础设施和投资紧密相关。中国煤炭消耗的大约 45% 用于发电，79% 的发电来自于煤炭。因此电力供应保障依赖于煤炭供应保障，即及时的燃料供给。近年来，煤炭运输基础设施，特别是铁路运输瓶颈是造成电荒的主要原因。为解决这个问题，目前增加了煤炭轨道运输的投资。但是由于中国煤炭资源分布的地理位置和需求不对称，煤炭经常从中西部产煤区长距离地运往沿海发电厂，所以这方面压力还将持续。

2005 年运输的煤炭中，水运占 16.9%，公路运输占 24.2%，铁路运输占大部分，58.9%。自 2000 年以来，这几种运输方式所占份额每年都很稳定。事实上，2005 年煤炭运输占铁路货物总运输的 47.9%，该年煤炭运输总量达 12.9 亿吨。

据报道，自 2004 年以来，正常夏季高峰负荷条件下这三种主要煤炭运输路线往往出现运输能力不足问题，需要对铁路运输和乘客需求进行优先级排序以确保发电厂电煤的充足供应。铁路运输能力不足是 2005 年大型发电厂燃料短缺的主要原因。在 2008 年初，铁路线路的严重毁坏导致中西部广大发电厂的燃料库存耗尽以及大面积停电。

政策：铁路基础设施优先运输煤炭

在"十一五"规划的指导方针下，中央政府制定了以基础设施为基础的策略减轻煤炭运输的铁路瓶颈，包括新建货运线，现有线路改为双轨，货运和客运线分流，电气化，扩大河北、天津及周边七个港口装船运往南方省份的吞吐量。尽管当前情势急需改善这些方面，但这并不能直接解决长远的体制需求。也就是说，发达的东部沿海地区通过当地煤炭发电满足不了其日益增长的能源需求。随着中部地区煤炭资源耗尽，生产渐渐趋向广大西北煤盆地，随着能效和环境问题日益显露，将发电厂移到矿口向终端用户所在区输电而非固体燃料，或者更换当地发电燃料，将越发受到关注。如本书中其他处所述，意识到了这一点，中央政府自2013年将建设若干大型坑口火电站列为优先工作。

问题：输电基础设施投资不足

输电基础设施投资不足导致电力调度安排不稳定，为此这种传输脆性要靠发电机大范围地提高负载量来弥补。这不仅意味着发电机本身无法最大限度地运行发挥其热力学功效，也使它们不得不维持经济效率低下的燃料储备。发电计划的不确定性也造成在国家发展和改革委员会（以下简称"国家发改委"）制定的年度电力购买协议外管理直接电力销售更为困难。

电网投资在很大程度上仍然与市场信号隔绝。该投资通过自下而上的过程决定，即中央政府（通过国家发改委）汇集地方政府和其他部门的投资请求制定一个通用的投资指南在"五年计划"期间发行宣传。由于输电和配电关税不是竞争而定，甚至也没必要依据成本来定，因此两大国有电网公司几乎没有增加基础设施投资的直接动力。

政策：增加电网投资

在"十五"计划和"十一五"规划下，近期和当前的政策导向承认了这个投资缺口，计划大量增加电网投资。2004年国内电网投资较上一年增加了30.5%。在此基础上，2005年又增加了40.0%，达到了1586亿元（2005年实际投资额达193.6亿美元）。

"十一五"（2006—2010年）规划方针呼吁两大电网公司额外增加共12000亿元的投资，比"十五"计划期间总投资额增加90%。

中国对可靠高性能电网的强烈需求日益增长。区域间的总传输电量需求从2002年的8.976太瓦时增加到2006年的344.68太瓦时，占总发电量的12%。所以大部分的新电网投资将主要用于实现全国范围内的远程连接，例如"西电东送"和"南电北送"工程旨在更有效地分配整个经济体系中的电力资源。

2006年，220千伏及以上高压输电和配电线路长达281000千米，自2002年每年增长11%。然而，当前瞄准的目标更高，即在全国范围内构建与整合不同大小和不同层面的超高压输电能力。目前这种远距离输电在任何地方都无成功范例。第一个超高压电网示范项目，一个输送1000千伏交流电和800千伏直流电的电力传输网络，将绵延653.8千米，跨越黄河和汉江，将山西省的电经河南省输送至湖北省。但是，这个示范项目如今正面临着关于安全、经济、技术及可靠性的各种挑战。

石油市场

问题：进口依赖度高

随着需求增加，石油进口激增。中国自1993年成为石油净进口国，1996年成为原油净进口国。根据表3，在"十一五"前，2004年的石油进口依赖度是44.52%，意味着中国消费的44.52%的石油依赖于进口。目前的问题是石油进口依赖度持续上升，已于2009年超过50%。

表3　石油生产和需求，2004—2010年

项目	2004	2005	2006	2007	2008	2009	2010
生产，万吨	17587	18135	18477	18632	19044	18949	20301
需求，万吨	31700	32538	34876	36659	37303	38385	43245
净进口，万吨	14113	14402	16400	18027	18259	19436	22944
进口依赖度[①]，%	44.52	44.26	47.02	49.17	48.95	50.63	53.06

①进口依赖度＝净进口／需求×100%

政策：海外上游投资（"走出去"政策）

石油需求持续增长的前景迫使全球油气公司加紧海外油气上游投资。这种现象在国有石油企业中尤为显著，因为加强能源保障已成为广泛共享的政策议程。中国三大国有石油公司（中国石油，中国石化和中海油）由于在最近海外上游投资股份收购的热潮中较为活跃，且未来需要庞大的规模来满足中国石油需求，经常被看作是这方面的全球领导者。

为了弥合日益增长的石油需求和国内石油生产无法满足石油需求的差距，中国国有石油企业加紧收购海外油气股份。实际上，这些举措通常是由中央政府通过税收减免和低息收费支持的，由此也导致一些人认为此类行为威胁石油巨头和其他国家石油公司。例如，中海油2005年收购美国优尼科石油公司的失败加重了美国对中国的石油公司海外投资活动和影响的担忧。

确实，"十五"期间（2001—2005年），由于对进口能源的依赖与日俱增，中国已经强调海外上游投资的重要性。这个计划鼓励石油公司将主动参与国际石油开发运营作为"走出去"政策的一部分。无论是过去还是现在，这个策略都不仅仅为了收购上游股份，也为了促进中国的技术、设备、材料和劳动力在海外市场上得到更广泛的应用。

"十五"计划也规定为使企业自作决定和自承风险，将逐步取消很多上游项目需获得中央政府批准的制度。为促进"走出去"政策，中央政府支持石油公司以各种方式积极参与海外上游投资，确保海外上游股本油（海外份额油）生产安全。应该注意的是，石油安全不是海外上游投资的唯一目的。实际上，

石油公司并没有将原油供应给中国,而是在市场上售卖。

政策:战略石油储备

当 1993 年成为石油净进口国时(图 5),中国需要建立战略石油储备以确保石油安全。十年后,中国于 2003 年官方批准建立国家战略石油储备(SPR),计划到 2020 年总储备容量达到 5 亿桶(约 7000 万吨)。建立 SPR 需要 15 年左右的时间,现在正分三期进行:2008 年增加 1.032 亿桶的储备容量,2013 年 2.069 亿桶,2020 年 1.899 亿桶,依次递增。但 SPR 第二期的完成时间推迟到了 2015 年,晚于原定计划两年(表 4)。

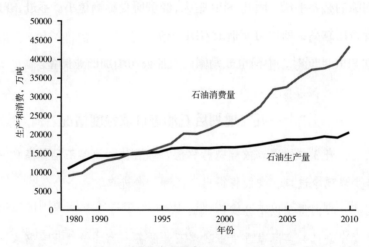

图 5 石油生产和需求,1980—2010 年

表4 中国战略石油储备

阶段	目标		完成		
	容量,百万桶	年份	容量,百万桶	累计量,百万桶	年份
第 I 阶段	103.2	2008	103.2	103.2	截至 2009
第 II 阶段	206.9	2013①	18.9	122.1	2011
			18.9	141	2011
第 III 阶段	189.9	2020			
SPR 总量	500				

①更新到 2015 年

假如中国有自己的战略石油储备，2005 年广州和深圳的石油危机就不会发生。该事件对经济发展和社会稳定造成了严重的负面影响。事实上，中国由此完成 SPR 第一期的时间也晚于原定时间。

1973 年全球石油危机后，一些工业国家成立了国际能源署（IEA），致力于维持相当于 90 天净进口的石油储备量。2010 年，中国每天净进口石油 450 万桶，SPR 容量是 1.032 亿桶，相当于 23 天净进口的石油量，远未达到国际能源署规定的达标线。

战略石油储备是降低石油短缺负面影响，抑制对经济体系冲击和提供缓解纠纷间隙的必要手段。因此，SPR 越大，经济所受影响越小。不过，SPR 越大，储存保管费用越高，所以可能造成 GDP 损失。

建立 SPR 的同时，中国也鼓励国内石油公司增加商业储备。

附注

"十一五"规划后石油进口依赖度情况

的确，表 3 中的进口依赖是标称值。如若诸如战略石油储备的一些政策能减少表观净进口，我们将得出"实际"净进口。

因此，我们得出以下公式：

表观净进口 = 实际净进口 + 战略石油储备 + 海外份额油 = 需求 − 生产

→ 实际净进口 = 需求 − 生产 − 战略石油储备 − 海外份额油

  $= D-P-SPR-OSO$

→ 实际进口依赖 = [实际净进口 / 需求] × 100%

  $= [(D-P-SPR-OSO)/D] \times 100\%$

  $= [1-(P+SPR+OSO)/D] \times 100\%$（RID）

从以上表达看，减少实际进口依赖，可以：

（1）增加国内石油产量（提高 P）；

（2）转移石油依赖（减少 D）；

（3）增加从政治稳定的海外国家获得的份额油（通过投资）（增加 OSO）；

（4）增加战略石油储备量（增加 SPR)。

有趣的是，在 SPR 和 OSO（海外份额油）的联合效应下，2010 年石油进口依赖有所改观。表 5 中，根据 SPR 和 OSO 的水平，分成了四种情形。表 6 是利用 RID 方程式计算出的不同情形的结果。结果表明，自从中国有了 SPR 和 OSO，石油进口依赖度从 53.05% 降到了 34.94%。如果考虑政治稳定性，依赖度为 45.43%。

表5　2010年石油供需情况

项目	数量
需求（D），百万桶	3089.00
生产（P），百万桶	1450.15
战略石油储备（SPR），百万桶	103.2
海外石油份额[①]（OSO），百万桶	132.31
OSO 的政治稳定性[②]，%	29%

①来源：IEA（2012），国有石油公司 2010 年（CNPC, Sinopec 和 CNOOC）的海外产量是 1.25 百万桶 / 每天（分别是 0.7 百万桶 / 天，0.35 百万桶 / 天，0.2 百万桶 / 天）

②来源：APERC（2008），原油进口来源的政治稳定性 =29%

表6　2010年石油进口依赖结果

无 OSO		有 OSO	29% 政治稳定性
		100% 政治稳定性	
无 SPR	53.05%	38.28%	48.77%
有 SPR	49.71%	34.84%	45.43%

天然气

2007 年中国成为天然气净进口国，但"十一五"期间并无保障天然气供应的特殊政策。不过，随着天然气需求的日益增加以及 2009 年出现天然气短缺后，2010年国家发改委（NDRC）和国家能源局（NEA）开始与天然气公司制定一些对策。

问题：自给自足能力降低

改善国内环境和应对气候变化的需求，全球性承诺和能源产业市场化的内部需求是将中国能源供应逐渐从煤炭变成天然气的主要驱动力。

2010年国家天然气产量为968亿立方米，相较于2000年的270亿立方米，年增长14%；而消耗量从2000年的245亿立方米增至2010年的1300亿立方米。2012年中国天然气的对外依存度达到了29%左右，2013年全国天然气消费量预计达到5000亿立方米（国际能源署，2012）。对比之下，2015年天然气进口总量是584亿立方米，消耗量是1930亿立方米（中华人民共和国国家统计局），对外依存度30%左右。

因此，与石油的发展趋势相似，天然气将来也可能过度依赖外国供应，这将不利于中国的能源保障。

政策：增加液化天然气和管道天然气的进口

国家能源局的数据表明，到2015年天然气消耗量预计达到2300亿立方米，甚至有可能突破3300亿立方米。尽管实际消耗量是1930亿立方米，国内1000亿～1500亿立方米的供应能力仍无法满足需求。所以很明显，有必要多渠道扩大进口量。液化天然气和管道天然气则是主要进口手段。

2011年，中国分别从澳大利亚、卡塔尔和印度尼西亚进口液化天然气50亿立方米、32亿立方米以及27亿立方米，总计109亿立方米。这是中国进口液化天然气的第一年。澳大利亚仍然是中国液化天然气的主要来源国。随着多渠道进口液化天然气的增加，中国已在福建、上海、大连和江苏等地建立了新的液化天然气接收站以承载日益增加的进口量。

中国也已开始与中亚国家（哈萨克斯坦、土库曼斯坦和乌兹别克斯坦）、缅甸以及俄罗斯展开合作，建设其东北和西南的国际天然气管道。2009年，中国—中亚管道开始输送天然气。2013 年 10 月，中国—缅甸管道（120 亿立方米 / 年）也开始投入使用。

政策：页岩气的勘探与开发

中国正努力结合供给和需求两方面的政策来减少对进口油气的依赖性。方法之一是开发碳采集、存储和利用（CCS/CCU）技术，使中国继续使用国内煤炭资源，同时限制二氧化碳的排放量；另一种倡议是开发国内页岩气，因其重要战略意义，得到了政府的强烈支持。但是，除非取得技术突破，否则这可能是个缓慢的过程。中国和美国已在讨论页岩气的合作（Robinson 和 Xu，2013）。中国石油已在四川万县勘探页岩气，目标是与壳牌公司合作，在 2015 年生产 10 亿立方米页岩气。但考虑到此项目不可能带来页岩气的大规模生产，2016 年 6 月底，壳牌公司撤回了其在四川页岩气勘探与开发的投资①。

① http://news.xinhuanet.com/fortune/2016-07/12/c_129138555.htm

问题：地缘政治风险

中国正面临的地缘政治风险包括三个层面：第一个是双边的，指的是长期天然气供给协议的可持续性；第二个是区域间的，有关正在开发的管道的安全性；第三个是全球性的，涉及中国与中亚、欧洲、俄罗斯及其他国家的能源关系。其中，跨境管道是最具风险性的，因其面临着由进口国天然气储备变化带来的诸多问题、金融和经济风险、能源基础设施损坏风险、各国内部冲突、恐怖主义袭击以及双边关系恶化等一系列问题。

▌附注

如何提高天然气发电？

众所周知，中国天然气发电大有前景。但如何提高天然气发电不得而知。主要有三个挑战：天然气供给，城市天然气基础设施，天然气相对于煤炭甚至石油的毫无竞争力的价格。

过去的"五年计划"和能源政策

第一阶段："六五"计划至"九五"计划（1981—2000 年）

第一阶段聚焦经济发展。因此，专门制定了能源发展和相应政策支持经济发展。

第六个"五年计划"（1981—1985 年）强调能源短缺是限制中国经济发展的一个重要问题。该"五年计划"目的在于每年工业增长 4% 的同时（看得见的手），仅增加 1.4% 的一次能源产量（看得见的手）。此外，节能政策强调支持经济发展。第七个"五年计划"（1986—1990 年）强调扩大供给满足由经济快速发展带来的需求的快速增长。第八个"五年计划"（1991—1995 年）制定了一次能源总供给每年增加 2.4% 和经济增长率每年达到 6% 的目标。为确保能源保障，1993 年开始进口石油。第九个"五年计划"（1996—2000 年）设定每年 8% 的经济增长率。1996 年中国开始进口原油。在这 2 0 年间，扩大能源供应主要由政府"看得见的手"调控，以实现经济增长的目的。

图 6 表明在此期间（1981—2000 年）GDP 增长率总是高于能源消耗增长。

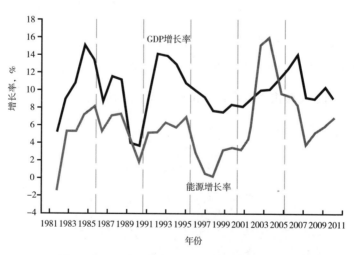

图 6　中国 GDP 和能源的增长率，1981—2011 年

第二阶段:"十五"计划（2001—2005 年）

遵循之前的实践,"十五"计划设定的年经济增长率和年能源强度(每 GDP 能源消耗量)的目标分别是 7% 和 4.5%。然而,图 7 显示 2001 年到 2005 年间能源强度回弹,图 6 显示 2003 年和 2004 年能源增长率高于 GDP 增长率。由于之前的举措并没发挥好作用,这已成为重要问题。

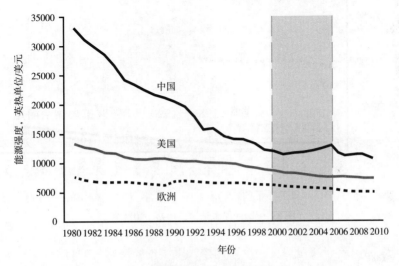

图 7　能源强度,1980—2010 年

2001 年 12 月 11 日中国加入世界贸易组织(WTO)。图 8 表明自 2001 年以来,各类能源消耗量快速增加,煤炭消耗量增加尤为明显。

图 9 显示了各行业能源消耗情况,表明自 2002 年以来相较于其他行业,制造业领域能源消耗增速较快。

图 10 进一步说明煤炭是制造业主要能源来源。表 7 证实了这一点,显示 2005 年制造业用煤占能源总消耗 77% 左右,制造业用煤占煤炭消耗总量的 63.8%。请注意,这些数据包括制造业发电所消耗的煤。因此,这些数据包括制造业直接消耗的煤和间接消耗的煤。如果从制造业看煤炭对 GDP 的贡献,根据表 8,2005 年煤的贡献率为 32.7%。也就是说,2005 年中国使用 63.8% 的煤创造了 32.7% 的 GDP。由图 11,我们可以对工业用油情况做出类似观察。

所以，在第十一个五年规划（2006—2010 年）之前，中国的 GDP 来源于非绿色能源。

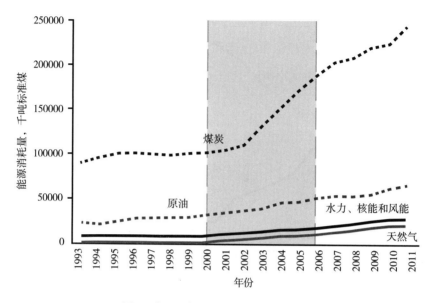

图 8　中国的能源结构，1993—2011 年

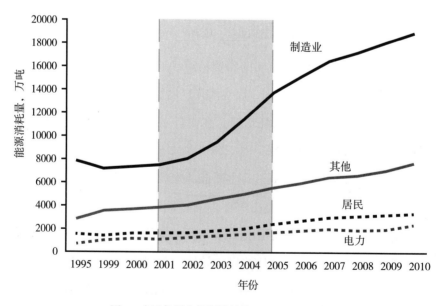

图 9　中国各行业能源消耗量，1995—2010 年

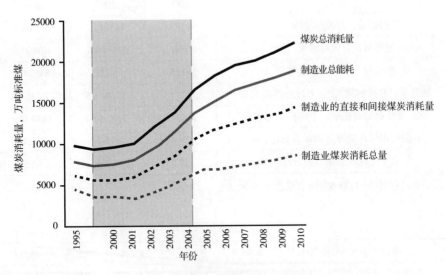

图 10　制造业中的煤炭消耗量，1995—2010 年

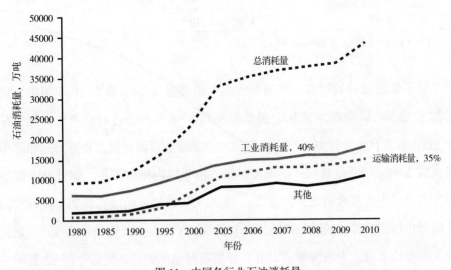

图 11　中国各行业石油消耗量

表7　制造业用煤

项目	2000	2005	2010
总消耗量，万吨标准煤当量	94287.6	165611.2	223030.5
发电量，万吨标准煤当量	40541.2	75920.6	107975.8
制造业，万吨标准煤当量	36127.8	65728.7	84874.2
制造业，直接和间接①，万吨标准煤当量	56384.1	105685.5	143761.4
制造业能源总消耗量，万吨标准煤当量	73824.3	137140.4	188497.9
制造业用煤占能源总消耗百分比，%	76.4	77.1	76.3
制造业用煤占总用煤百分比，%	59.8	63.8	64.5

① 制造业用煤 + 制造业用电百分比 × 煤炭发电

表8　制造业能源效率

项目	2004 年	2005 年	2006 年	2007 年	2008 年	2009 年
GDP，1 亿元	51748.5	60117.99	71212.89	87464.95	102539.5	110118.5
制造业在 GDP 中百分比	32.4	32.7	32.9	32.9	32.7	32.3
能源弹性值①		1.36	0.66	0.49	0.30	0.72
能源 /GDP	2.23	2.28	2.12	1.89	1.68	1.64
煤炭弹性		1.55	0.71	0.35	0.27	0.58
煤炭 /GDP	1.68	1.76	1.65	1.43	1.27	1.23

①（ Δ 能源 / 能源）/（ Δ GDP/GDP）

除了煤消耗量的增加，原油和天然气消耗量从 2001 年到 2005 年也分别增加了 42.5% 和 70.0%（表 9）。虽然原油自 1996 年开始进口，液化天然气在20 世纪 90 年代末才计划进口。由于油气需求增加得如此快，自那时起能源保障就成为中国能源政策的一个重要问题。由于国内供应不足，保证外来能源供应安全成为能源政策之一。为此，"走出去"战略鼓励国有能源企业投资国外能源市场和项目，从国际能源市场直接购买（石油和天然气）。但是，"走出去"的步伐太慢，无法缓解"十五"计划期间油气的强劲需求。图 12 表明中国自 2000 年起原油不再自给自足。另一方面，由于中国的高经济增长率目标，能源需求预计将因此激增。因此，2004年国家发改委发布了《节能中长期专项规划》解决需求侧问题。

表9　不同类型能源消耗的年增长率（2001—2005年）

年份	年增长率，%			
	煤炭	原油	天然气	水电，核电，风电
2001	2.0	1.5	12.7	21.1
2002	5.5	8.4	6.0	3.2
2003	18.3	9.6	20.1	2.6
2004	15.6	16.7	16.1	19.7
2005	12.6	2.8	15.0	12.2
2001—2005	62.6	42.5	70.0	42.3
2001—2011	131.7	97.4	382.0	146.8

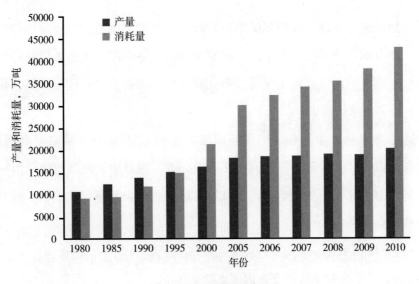

图12　原油产量和消耗量

简而言之，此阶段末期，中国面临非绿色GDP和油气供应安全问题。此外，对于能源供给安全来说，"走出去"的步伐太慢。尽管这个发展阶段主要由"看得见的手"调控，由于"走出去"政策，中国企业还要面对它们并不熟悉的国际能源市场的"看不见的手"。如上所述,能源政策不仅考虑经济发展,亦考虑能源保障。表10说明中国没能完成"十五"计划设定的能源强度目标(每年降低4.5%)。

表10 能源强度变化[1]

项目	2000 年	2005 年	2010 年
能源强度[2]	11986.4	12486	10842.2
变化百分比		4.1	−13.1
目标百分比		−20.6	

[1]来源:《BP世界能源统计评论》,2013年6月
[2]每年的英热单位(英、美等国采用的一种计算热量的单位)以2005年美元等值为准(购买力平价)

第三阶段:"十一五"规划(2006—2011 年)

中国已进入能源发展规划的第三阶段。此阶段不仅考虑经济发展和能源保障,亦考虑环境污染。由于煤炭和原油分别占据中国一次能源消耗的70%和20%,这里的污染问题不仅指二氧化碳排放,也指由二氧化硫,氮氧化物和煤矿开采带来的污染。

除了非绿色能源结构,中国还面临非绿色GDP和油气供应安全问题。因此,与以往"五年计划"不同,在"十一五"规划中,能源政策成为一个独立的政策。此外,规划也设定了减排目标解决污染问题。能源和环境政策的一些亮点如下:

- 经济增长率为每年7.5%;能源强度每年下降4.4%;
- 由出口主导型经济转变为内需支持型经济;
- 二氧化硫排放量减少3.2%;
- 能源结构策略包含可再生能源和天然气;
- 能源价格改革(在能源行业中首次应用"看不见的手")。

  "十一五"规划指导方针中的能源部分分为能源现状的回顾(包括能源发展面临的重要问题),总方向和目标,基础设施,节能与环境,科技以及其他总体政策。能源发展的总价值观与以往计划相似,解决能源供应和节能发展,但在强调能源消费多元化和能源供需结构最优化的同时,还注重节能(APERC,2009)。

  简言之,为支持经济发展,"十一五"规划指导方针中能源政策的目标是:(1)改善能源基础设施和体系;(2)提高能源效率和节能;(3)减少环境污染。这些目标解决"十五"计划后非绿色GDP和油气供应安全问题。

  尽管煤炭仍被视为中国能源的基础,规划方针的目标表明一次能源消耗的总体份额应有所下降。规划特别指出五年之内分别降低煤炭和石油份额3%、0.5%,分别提高天然气、水电、可再生能源和核电份额2.5%、0.6%、0.3%和0.1%。表11表明天然气份额增加了1.8%,低于2.5%的目标。水电,核电和风电的份额增加了1.8%,高于1%的总目标。

表11　能源结构总表(2005年和2010年)

	煤炭,%	原油,%	天然气,%	水电,核电和风电,%
2005 年	70.8	19.8	2.6	6.8
2010 年	68.0	19.0	4.4.	8.6
2010 年 –2005 年	–2.8	–0.8	+1.8	+1.8
目标	–3.0	–0.5	+2.5	+1.0

小结

  通过图13,图8和表11中的能源结构结果,可以看出2006—2010年能源结构并无明显变化。由此推断"十一五"规划并没有真正解决非绿色GDP和油气供应安全的问题。也就是说,"十二五"规划面临同样的问题,中国仍处于能源政策发展的第三阶段。

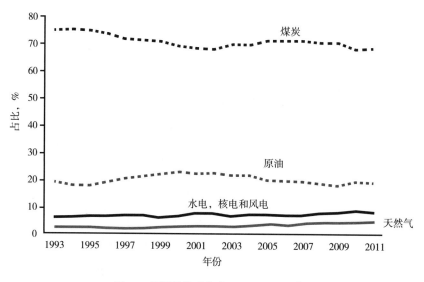

图 13 能源结构百分比，1993—2011 年

能源结构、能源强度和环境影响的变化

　　从改革开放到 20 世纪末，在能源强度降低一半（能源消耗 /GDP）的同时，中国经济发展实现了 GDP 翻两番。21 世纪之初，由于高耗能产业向重工业化加速并扩大，能源强度回弹。在 2003 年和 2004 年，能源强度分别增加了 4.8%、5.5%。2003 年到 2005 年，国家能源消耗的年平均增长率是 14%。在此期间，GDP 相较于 1990 年增加了 70%，能源消耗总量比 20 世纪末增加了 70%。连续三年增长意味着 2005 年的能源强度高于 1999 年。

　　因此，"十一五"（2006—2010 年）规划倡导逆转能源强度日益增加的趋势，实现能源强度降低 20% 的目标。此阶段的目标是主要污染物总量降低 10%。这个目标成功实现了。应该注意的是，能源强度降低 20% 的全国目标进一步分成了地区目标。中央政府采用了行政手段，法律手段和经济手段促进地方努力。各省通过这些手段和其他自发措施，制定了实施方案（APERC，2009）。

一般来说，中央政府力图通过施行最划算的措施平衡经济发展与环境保护。随着经济进一步增长，加大排放控制和环境保护的力度将更加实惠，也更有必要。

能源的使用以水污染、空气污染和引起全球变暖的二氧化碳排放的形式影响环境。本节主要探讨空气污染和二氧化碳排放方面的政策。

在中国，主要空气污染物是二氧化硫（S_O2），氮氧化物（N_Ox），悬浮微粒以及重金属。特别要说明的是，空气污染很大程度上是由于一次能源结构中煤的主导地位引起的，占 70% 左右（图 14）。

2006 年，煤炭消耗是绝大多数二氧化硫（约 90%）的来源，同时也是氮氧化物（67%）、悬浮微粒（70%）以及汞一类的重金属（38%）的重要来源。2001年到 2006 年间，煤炭消耗量年平均增长率为 11.8%，五年之内共增长 74.7%。与此同时，二氧化硫排放量也有所增长，虽然增幅较小，年均增长率约 5.1%，但五年内共增长了 28%（APERC，2008）。

在中国，空气污染主要来自于发电燃煤和交通燃油。因此，我们将依次讨论这两个行业。

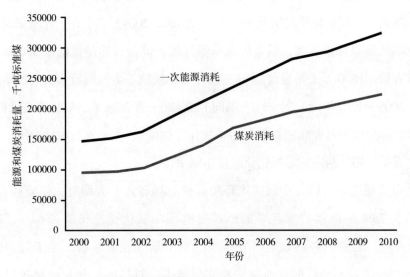

图 14　一次能源和煤炭消耗，2000—2010 年

火电

空气污染

"九五"期间，二氧化硫排放量有所减少，"十五"期间随着能源需求增加又稳步增长（APERC，2008）。中国并未实现其包括二氧化硫在内的主要空气污染物比 2000 年减少 10% 的目标。节能减排措施虽收效显著，却抵不上化石燃料消耗量的快速增长，表 12。

表12　火电的能源结构，2004—2010（百万吨标准煤）

能源	2004 年	2005 年	2006 年	2007 年	2008 年	2009 年	2010 年
煤炭	671.67	755.48	856.09	957.19	983	1015.39	1131.73
石油	21.76	19.23	13.74	9.71	7.17	4.77	4.4
天然气	18.12	24.25	42.52	61.61	67.48	81.63	122.83
其他能源	4.23	6.95	11.64	15.17	18.07	20.96	18.72
总计	715.78	805.91	923.99	1043.68	1075.72	1122.75	1277.68

为此，中央政府在"十一五"规划中加大力度控制二氧化硫排放，要求在现有及新建燃煤电厂安装烟气脱硫装置。随着电力行业的烟气脱硫技术趋于标准化，二氧化硫排放情况在改观（APERC，2009）。"十五"计划制定的二氧化硫减排目标很远大，制定的现行烟气脱硫设备目标却很低（1500 万千瓦装机容量，1600 万千瓦建设）。这些保守目标反映了烟气脱硫系统的预估高成本。2006—2010 年间（"十一五"期间），国家进一步加强了二氧化硫政策框架，要求大部分电力行业采用烟气脱硫系统作为标准。"十一五"规划沿用了过去的"五年计划"制定的二氧化硫减排 10% 的目标。

为实现这些目标，中国国家环境保护总局和六个大型电力供应商合作，承担了 75% 的减排目标，降低燃煤发电厂二氧化硫总排放量 61%，减到 500 万吨。为此，各燃煤电厂安装了 300 个烟气脱硫系统。至于能源强度目标，考虑到各地区的产业结构和支付能力，具体的二氧化硫减排目标因省份或地区而异。从 2006 年起，所有新建燃煤发电厂都必须安装烟气脱硫设备，现有燃煤电厂要在 2010 年前安装完烟气脱硫系统。此外，新的经济鼓励措施加大了对烟气脱硫的投资力度：投运烟气脱硫设施的发电厂的电价每千瓦时提高 0.015 元，以此抵消运营费用，同时享有电能馈入优先权。当然，这两个强有力的激励措施也面临着高额燃料费和监管电力定价的问题。由此，烟气脱硫容量增至 1.5 亿千瓦以上，占据 2006 年末总装机容量的 30%。这意味着中国实现其"十一五"规划增加 1.37 亿千瓦容量的目标毫无问题。

的确，中国见证了前所未有的烟气脱硫设施建设。到 2005 年底，煤电烟气脱硫装机比重仅为 14%。2010 年底，这个比重增加到 80%。由于烟气脱硫，整个经济范围内，二氧化硫排放量在"十五"期间比 2000 年增加了 28%，在"十一五"期间比 2005 年降低了 14%。表 13 显示的是各行业二氧化硫排放情况，右栏表示的是 2000 年、2005 年和 2010 年间排放量百分比的变化。

表13　2000，2005 和 2010年工业二氧化硫排放量（百万吨）

工业	2000 年	2005 年	2010 年	2000—2010 年变化，%
电力	7.07	11.67	9	27
矿产	2.33	1.78	1.69	－ 27
化工产品	0.82	1.17	1.04	27
钢铁	0.75	1.42	1.77	136
有色金属	0.71	0.71	0.8	13
石油 / 焦煤	0.38	0.71	0.64	68
其他产业	4.3	2.34	2.13	－50
非工业来源	3.58	5.69	4.8	34
总计	19.95	25.49	21.85	10

能源强度和二氧化碳排放

中国电力企业联合会（CEC）自 2002 年开始，发行了一系列电力行业节能和减少污染的政策法规（CEC，2012）。2006 年，国家发改委和能源办发布了《关于加快关停小火电机组的若干意见》，这是一项与"鼓励大型火电厂，淘汰小型低效率火电厂"相呼应的实施政策（国家发改委和能源办，2006）。2007 年，国务院批准了该政策。

下面是最近一项研究中国各地区火力发电排放量（Chung 和 Zhou，2013）的分析结果。中国的发电主要依赖于火电。图 15 显示的是 2004 年到 2010 年间火力发电占总发电量的比重。由于水力发电的引入，该比重由 2007 年的 83.38% 降至 2010 年的 80.51%。不过，煤炭仍然是火力发电的主要燃料。因此，火力发电是一个重污染的行业，自然而然成为节能和减少污染的关键领域。

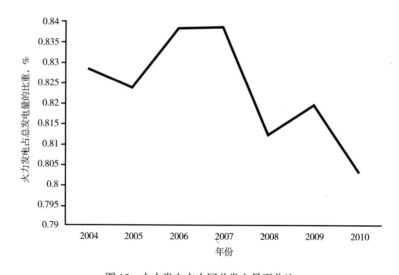

图 15　火力发电占中国总发电量百分比

如上所述，中国的发电主要依赖火力发电，煤炭依然是主要燃料。"十一五"（2006—2010 年）期间，能源强度降低 20% 的国家目标进一步分成了地区目标。因此，2004 年至 2010 年间地区电网的能源强度和二氧化碳减排量值得研究。表 14 总结了各省电网，地区电网和两个相应的电力公司间的关系。国家电网公司管辖华北电网公司、东北电网公司、华东电网公司、华中电网公司和西北电网公司，中国南方电网有限公司则管辖南方电网公司和海南电网公司。

表14 中国七个区域电网和省级电网

公司	区域/公司	省级电网
国家电网公司	华北	北京，天津，河北，山西，山东，内蒙古
	东北	辽宁，吉林，黑龙江
	华东	上海，江苏，浙江，安徽，福建
	华中	江西，河南，湖北，湖南，重庆，四川
	西北	陕西，甘肃，青海，宁夏，新疆
中国南方电网有限公司	南方	广东，广西，贵州，云南
	海南	海南

图16显示了所有地区电网的能源结构变化和电力输出，由此可以看出：

· 由于煤炭是火力发电的主要燃料，煤炭消耗增长几乎与火电产出一致；

· 天然气消耗增长快速，石油消耗量持续下降；

· 尽管2009年至2010年间其他能源消耗有所降低，仍保持快速增长。

地区能源强度和二氧化碳排放

图17是各地区电网的能源强度，此章附录中的表18和表19作了进一步详细说明。结果显示大部分地区电网的能源强度在2004年到2010年间有所改善，华中、华东和南方电网尤为显著。

采用LMDI分解方法（Ang, 2005），我们发现2005—2010年期间能源强度有所降低，这是实施鼓励大型火电厂，淘汰小型低效率火电厂政策以及推广有助于节省火力发电能源的大容量高参数机组的结果。能源结构变化持续促进2004年到2010年间二氧化碳排放量的减少。结果如表15所示。

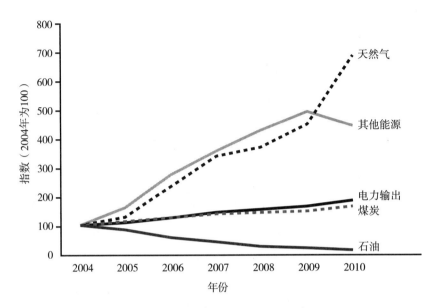

图 16　所有区域电网，2004—2010 年

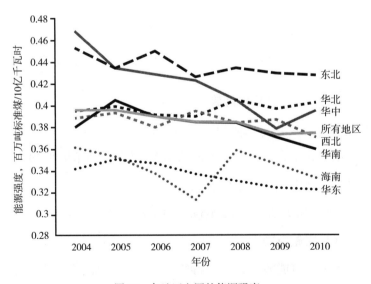

图 17　各地区电网的能源强度

表15 二氧化碳排放完全分解的变化（百万吨标准煤）（2004—2010年）

年份	ΔC_{act}	ΔC_{str}	ΔC_{int}	ΔC_{mix}	ΔC_{emi}	ΔC_{total}
2004—2005	219.57	2.17	0.27	−11.38	−3.94	206.69
2005—2006	318.42	9.48	−40.56	−32.16	−10.36	244.83
2006—2007	317.72	1.48	−33.01	−27.85	−8.33	250.00
2007—2008	73.79	−0.76	3.95	−13.76	−3.76	59.46
2008—2009	183.82	5.67	−79.83	−23.72	−3.27	82.66
2009—2010	354.08	−4.73	10.78	−25.81	115.98	450.30
2004—2010	1467.39	13.31	−138.40	−134.68	86.33	1293.94
碳浓度百分比	113.40	1.03	−10.70	−10.41	6.67	100.00

注：ΔC_x 等于二氧化碳排放，下标是相应的影响

"十一五"规划制定了到 2010 年火力发电效率达到 0.3550 百万吨标准煤/10 亿千瓦时的目标（APERC，2009）。为此，政府鼓励建设 6 亿瓦以上的大型燃煤发电机组，取代小型低效率的发电机组。

事实上，过去农村发展项目中所建的小型发电机组是造成中国发电行业效率低下的主要原因。表 16 显示 2006 年有 4804 发电机组的发电容量小于 1 亿瓦（占发电容量的 77%）。而超过 6 亿瓦的大型发电机组数量上仅占 2.1%，发电容量上占 18.4%。

表16 火力发电机组容量（2006年底）

机组容量，亿瓦	机组数量		发电容量	
	机组	占比，%	10 亿瓦	占比，%
>6	132	2.1	820	18.4
1~6	1307	20.9	2810	62.8
<1	4804	77	840	18.8

来源：CEPYEC（2007）

为进一步获得更高效率的电力供应，政策也在鼓励建设先进发电设施，如大容量的坑口电厂，废煤电厂，大型水电设施，大容量天然气联合循环电厂，

燃气轮机调峰电厂，节水发电厂以及核电站。在高压电网中限制容量小于等于 3 亿瓦的传统中小型发电机组的建设。

表 17 是 2007 年前 10 个月六个区域电网中关停的小型火电机组的容量。共计关停小型火电厂 103.9 亿瓦容量，远远超出全国每年 100 亿瓦的目标。

因而，火电厂平均燃料消耗从 2005 年的 0.3955 百万吨标准煤 / 亿千瓦时降到 2010 年 0.3790 百万吨标准煤 / 亿千瓦时。

表17　2007年1—10月关闭的小型火电站

区域	关闭容量	总容量	
	10 亿瓦	10 亿瓦	占比，%
中部	3.07	92.58	3.32
东北	1.15	41.38	2.78
南方	1.01	40.61	2.48
北方	3.00	164.8	1.82
东部	1.73	138.65	1.24
西北	0.43	35.62	1.2
总计	10.39	513.64	2.02

来源：CEPYEC（2007）

中国实施了加快关停数千个小型低效率的燃煤和燃油发电厂的政策（张中祥，2010）。面临关停的发电机组包括 5000 万瓦以下的；5000 万瓦以上 1 亿瓦以下，运营 20 年以上的；1 亿瓦以上 2 亿瓦以下，已达到设计寿命的；高于省平均煤炭消耗 10% 或者高于全国平均水平 15% 的；以及环境标准不达标的。2006 年至 2010 年期间，需关停的火电机组容量共达 50 亿瓦。

以下几种电厂将面临关闭：发电量低于 5000 万千瓦时的发电厂；发电量低于 1 亿千瓦时且使用时间超过 20 年的发电厂；发电量低于 2 亿千瓦时且已经达到使用年限的发电厂；煤消耗量高于省平均水平 10% 或高于全国平均水平 15% 的发电厂；以及不符合环境保护标准的发电厂。计划 2006 年到 2010 年间，需要关闭的电厂总发电量将会达到 5000 千瓦。

如图 18 所示，从能源强度的影响来看，关闭小型热电厂似乎只对中部电网十分有效,而对北方电网效果则不是很大。从表 11 中可以看到,中部地区需要在 2007 年关闭更多的发电厂。

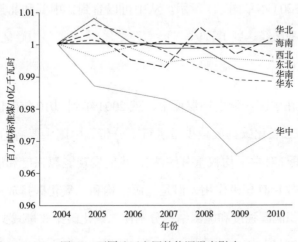

图 18　不同地区电网的能源强度影响

从图 18 我们还可以看到,在中部和北部电网中,强度影响具有曲棍球棒效应。原因可能是到 2009 年上半年末,关闭的小型和老旧发电厂总发电量已经达到 5400 万千瓦,提前一年半完成了 2010 年关闭的发电厂总发电量达到 5000 万千瓦这一目标(张中祥,2010)。关闭小型老旧发电机组这一政策实施的结果如图 19 所示。

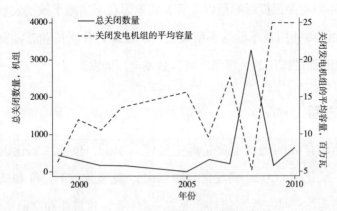

图 19　1999—2010 年关闭的小型热电机组

来源:马春波,赵晓丽 .2015. 电力市场重组和技术要求:1997 到 2010 年间中国改变电厂运营效率的证据,《能源经济学》,第 47 卷,7~237 页

出现曲棍球棒效应还有一个可能的原因，那就是提前一年完成了计划2010 年达到的能源强度（单位 GDP 能耗）的区域目标。能源强度较 2005 年减少百分比如表 20（本章附录）所示。从中可以看到，中部和北部地区在 2009年的时候就几乎已经达到了目标。

总结

我们已经在中国区域电网层面上，就 2004 年到 2010 年间区域性热发电的能源效率和二氧化碳排放减少量进行了分析。中国主要有七大区域电网。利用 LMDI 分析（对数平均权重分解法），我们发现能源强度和能源结构对减少二氧化碳排放具有积极作用，但是能源结构和二氧化碳排放因素的影响却微乎其微。累积能源强度和能源结构分别使二氧化碳排放量减少了 10.70% 和10.41%。这可能得益于实施了相关政策，如鼓励发展大型发电厂、关闭能源利用效率低的小型发电厂，以及促进大容量、高参数发电厂的发展，这些发电厂在热发电中对节约用电有促进作用。然而区域结果显示，北部电网绩效较差，中部和北部电网的能源强度影响都存在曲棍球棒效应。因此，我们建议建立区域性移动平均指标。杜立民等人（2009）认为没有证据表明，从 1995年到 2004 年间，和电力改革相关的燃料投入效率有所提高。他们认为 2005年到 2010 年间能源强度影响得以改善，其原因在于实施了鼓励发展大型发电厂、不鼓励能源利用效率低的小型发电厂的政策，并支持和鼓励在热发电中对节约用电有促进作用的大容量、高参数发电厂的发展。

交通运输方面

交通运输排放的尾气主要是温室气体（GHG），包括二氧化碳，有毒污染气体如一氧化碳（CO）、碳氢化合物（HC）、氮氧化物（N_{OX}）和微小颗粒物（PM）。交通运输业是三大高能耗产业之一（工业、建筑业和交通运输业），在保护资源和环境保护方面面临重重挑战。中国是发展中国家，人口众多，资源短缺。因此平衡好交通运输业发展、保护资源、环境保护三者之间的关系，

同时和交通运输业通力合作从而实现环境的可持续发展，对中国政府来说至
关重要。

环境政策

亚太能源研究中心（APERC，2008）给出了如下背景：

虽然交通运输燃料仅占中国能源使用量的一小部分，但交通运输产生的
污染对中国众多大城市产生了重要影响，再加上有车族的壮大，这种影响正
在日益加剧。在北京，机动车排放了全市 40% 的 PM10、68% 的二氧化氮和
77% 的一氧化碳。近来，PM2.5 被认为是有害性最严重的污染物，可以通过
呼吸进入人肺部，有些甚至可以进入血管，加剧心脏和肺部疾病。因此，减
少空气中 PM2.5 的含量已经成为全社会共同关注的问题。北京市环境保护局
的一项研究显示，北京的机动车排放了全市 31.1% 的 PM2.5。为了解决交通
运输尾气排放问题，中国已经对机动车制定了更高的尾气排放标准。

虽然中国的机动车尾气排放标准相对严格，但在标准的实施上还存在一
些挑战，那就是需要更高质量的燃油供应。如果燃油质量达不到机动车引擎
要求，那尾气排放也就达不到标准。低质量的燃油还会加剧先进引擎的磨损、
缩短机动车使用寿命、增加机动车维修费用等。

一般来讲，中国的发动机燃油质量比发达国家普遍偏低，其结果就是机
动车排放了更多的污染物。但是中国的燃油质量标准已经逐渐取得了巨大进
步。中国经常是先在一些主要城市实施更高的燃油质量标准，然后向其他地
区慢慢扩展。比如，1997 年先是在全国八个城市禁止使用含铅汽油，到 2000
年含铅汽油在全国范围内停止使用，北京市总是第一个采取更高的燃油质量
和尾气排放标准的城市，实行和欧盟国家相同的标准。

类似的还有逐步地采取措施减少汽油和柴油中硫黄的含量。虽然做出了
种种努力，但是自 2007 年起，每次要在全国范围内实行新的汽车尾气排放标
准（相当于欧Ⅲ标准），国家发改委就会延迟标准的实行，因为中国的炼油厂
容量不足，生产不出足够的低硫黄燃油。2008 年北京和上海开始实行相当于

欧Ⅳ的汽车尾气排放标准，炼油厂再次竭尽全力，提供所需的高质量燃油。

国家发改委决定暂缓在全国范围内实行新的汽车尾气排放标准，也有可能是因为受到了小型机动车生产厂商的影响，他们必须努力才能达到更高的技术规格。这就表明，不同产业之间的协调配合（机动车生产厂商和燃油生产厂商）对清洁结束的成功落实至关重要。而且这个例子还强调了促进国内技术发展对发展中国家实施环境规章制度的必要性。

问题的复杂性还在于中国不同的交通运输方式由不同的组织机构管理。道路和水路运输由交通部管理，铁路运输由铁道部管理，航空运输受中国民用航空总局监管，而管道运输则由中国石油天然气集团公司（中国石油）、中国石油化工集团公司（中国石化）和中国海洋石油总公司（中海油）共同管理。虽然困难重重，但是在第十个和第十一个"五年计划"中（2001—2010年），中央政府针对环境保护的能源节约方面制定了一系列相关政策。以下会对这些政策进行概述。

2004年，交通部印发了乘用车燃料消耗量限值规定。根据整车整备质量，限值分为十六个等级，分两个阶段付诸实施（执行日期分别为2007年7月1日和2009年1月1日），第一阶段目标是到2008年，百公里耗油量（升）减少10%，第二阶段要求机动车耗油量在第一阶段的基础上再减10%。该限值适用于所有整车整备质量低于3500千克、核载少于9人、最高设计速度低于50千米/小时的汽油和柴油客车。

2005年印发了《关于鼓励发展节能环保型小排量汽车的意见》,意见鼓励：

• 低油耗、低排放、小排量、小型化、高动力性汽车的生产和投资；
• 实施营运汽车的燃料消耗量限值国家标准；
• 控制高油耗汽车生产；
• 以及提高节能、环保、小排量汽车的生产技术标准。

2006年修订了消费税，增加了大型机动车和能源利用效率低的机动车的税收负担。

同年，交通部印发了《建设节约型交通指导意见》和《关于交通行业全面贯彻落实〈国务院关于加强节能工作的决定〉的指导意见》。2007年，交通部又印发了《交通部关于进一步加强交通行业节能减排工作的意见》和《关于在交通行业开展节能示范活动的通知》。同年，中国政府修订了节约能源法，使"十一五"规划中的节能措施和在交通运输方面促进提高能源利用效率的政府权威有了更清晰的法律基础。同年，交通部还印发了《关于港口节能减排工作的指导意见》。2008年，交通部颁布了《公路、水路交通实施〈中华人民共和国节约能源法〉办法》。

对不同种类的汽车分别实施不同的政策。如2007年，中国出台了轻型商用车的燃料消耗量限值，该限值适用于总重在3500千克以下的汽车和核载9至12人的轻型商用车，包括轻型货车和公共汽车（2008年2月1日施行）。2008年印发了运营客车的燃料消耗量限值和实施办法、运营货车的燃料消耗量限值。这些规定、办法也适用于柴油和汽油汽车、总重在3500千克以上的客车和货车、总重在3500到31000千克之间的运营货车、自动倾卸货车以及最大总重49000千克的半挂汽车。

与美国、加拿大和澳大利亚相比，这些节能标准更加严格，但没有欧洲和日本的标准严格。

自2007年起，中国开始采用欧洲的排放标准。但实际上，政府实施的是国标Ⅲ（相当于欧Ⅲ）的机动车排放标准。

2008年，交通部印发《公路水路交通节能中长期规划纲要》，把公路交通、水路交通和港口作为重点节能领域。交通部还对2015年到2020年的工作提出了全面目标和主要任务。2009年，政府发布《关于开展节能与替代能源汽车示范推广试点工作的通知》，还启动了"十城千辆"汽车示范运行计划，计划3年内在全国挑选至少10个城市，利用政府补助金在每个城市至少引进1000辆可替代能源汽车。目前已经选出25个试点城市并开始行动，这一数目很有可能还会继续增加，因为截至本书撰稿时，该计划还处于试行阶段。

2009 年，政府下发《关于开展"节能产品惠民工程"的通知》，旨在促进发展节能产品，包括通过政府补助金和其他资金生产节能汽车等。

中国也在推进铁路的电气化，减少燃油火车的使用量。电气化火车占全国火车总量的份额已经从 2005 年的 31.2% 增加到 2010 年的 46.2%，中国电气化铁路运营里程 2011 年居世界第二位（国家统计局，2011）。2013 年电气化火车占比达 52.4%，电气化铁路里程也跃居世界第一位（凤凰财经网）。

为考察以上这些政策的实施效果，我们先来看一下交通行业的整体能源利用效率，然后再看一下区域性能源利用效率。

交通行业能源面面观（2003—2009年）

交通行业的能源利用效率可以定义为周转量能源消费，周转量可以是乘客千米数（PKM）和吨千米数（TKM），能源消费、PKM、TKM 和能源结构的变化如图 20 和图 21 所示。从图 20 可以得出以下结论：

- TKM增长速度高于PKM。
- 2003年至2004年间的能源消费增量和PKM持平。然而，在2004年到2005年间能源消费有一个突然的上升。2005年到2009年，能源消费增量和TKM不相上下，比PKM增长速度快。

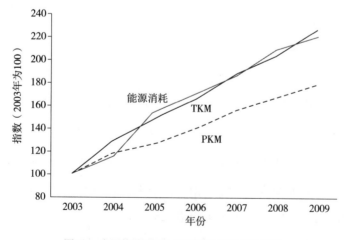

图 20　中国能源消费、PKM 和 TKM 指数变化

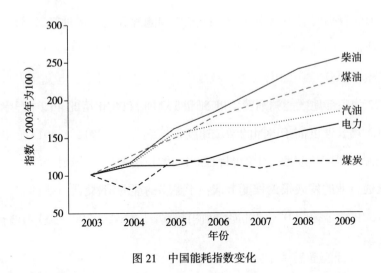

图 21　中国能耗指数变化

注意：因其无关紧要，本图不包括"其他能源"。

从图 21 可以看出：

· 整体能耗的增长主要来源于柴油和煤油消耗量的增长。

· 如果柴油是货运的主要燃料，那么柴油的高增长率可归因为TKM的高增长率。

· 因为煤油主要用于航空运输，因此可以推断航空运输行业发展迅猛。

· 自2006年以来，汽油的消耗量增长率一直是最低的，原因可能是自2004年和2006年起实施了多项有关公路交通运输的政策。

· 自2006年耗电量一直在增加。

· 2003年到2004年煤的使用量显著减少。然而，2004年到2005年间耗煤量突然增长。因此耗煤量基本保持不变。

区域性结果

虽然中国政府针对不同地区提出了不同的能源强度目标，但并非所有的能耗行业和对应的能源测量都能本地化。交通行业就是如此，政府出台了针对交通行业的能源利用效率全国性目标。比如，政府提高了国产新汽车的省油标准，从 2002 年的每升 12.3 千米调整到 2009 年的每升 15.3 千米（APERC，

2009）。因此有必要对中国交通行业的能耗和能源利用效率进行区域水平上的调查。

A. 东部地区

图 22 为东部地区能源消费、PKM 和 TKM 指数变化情况。图中显示：

- TKM 增长速度高于 PKM 的增长速度；
- 能源消费增长速度高于 PKM 和 TKM 的增长速度；
- 交通行业的发展很大程度上依赖于更多的能源消费；
- TKM 的增长和 2003—2007 年间的能耗增长一致，2007 年 TKM 增长突然减缓。

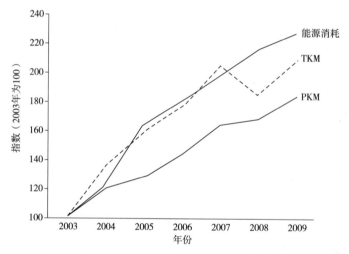

图 22　东部地区能源消费、PKM 和 TKM 指数变化

图 23 为东部地区能耗指数变化情况。图中显示：

- 煤油和柴油消费的增长是能耗整体增长的主要原因；
- 因为煤油主要用于航空运输，因此可以推测航空运输发展迅速；
- 假设柴油是货运的主要燃料，那么柴油消费的高增长率可归因于 TKM 的高增长率；
- 2004 年到 2005 年间发生了明显变化。自 2005 年起柴油和汽油的增长率就达到最低，原因可能是 2004 年实施了若干有关公路运输的政策。

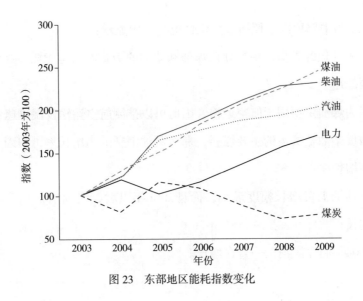

图 23　东部地区能耗指数变化

B. 中部地区

图 24 为中部地区能源消费、PKM 和 TKM 指数变化情况。图中显示：

• 2003—2007年间TKM和PKM的增长幅度相同，2007年后TKM的增长速度就超过了PKM的增长速度；

• 2003—2007年间能源消费增长幅度和PKM、TKM相同，有意思的是，2007年后TKM的增长速度大大超过了能源消费的增长速度。

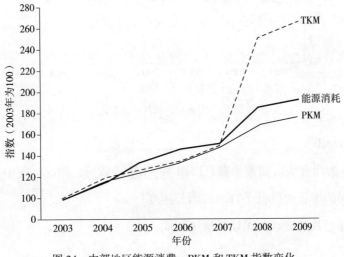

图 24　中部地区能源消费、PKM 和 TKM 指数变化

图 25 为中部地区能耗指数变化情况。图中显示：

- 和东部地区类似，中部地区煤油和柴油的消费增长是能耗整体增长的主要原因；

- 因为煤油主要用于航空运输，因此可以推测航空运输发展迅速；

- 假设柴油是货运的主要燃料，那么柴油消费的高增长率可归因于TKM的高增长率；

- 汽油的消费增长幅度最小，而且2006年以后，汽油消费几乎就没有再增长；

- 2004年起煤炭消费一直在增长。

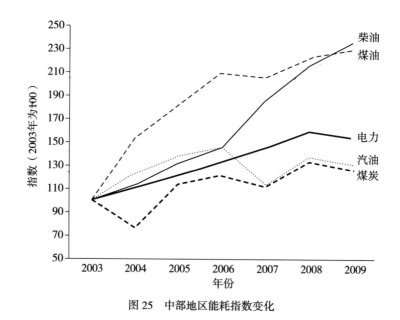

图 25　中部地区能耗指数变化

C. 西部地区

图 26 为西部地区能源消费、PKM 和 TKM 指数变化情况。图中显示：

- PKM的增长速度低于TKM的增长速度；

- 能耗增长速度和TKM增长速度相同。

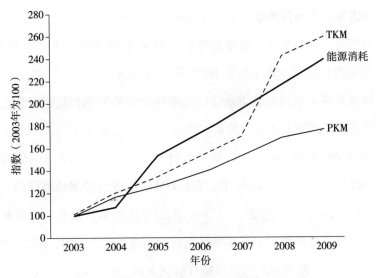

图 26　西部地区能源消费、PKM 和 TKM 指数变化

图 27 为西部地区能耗指数变化情况。图中显示：

· 柴油消费的增长是能耗整体增长的主要原因；

· 假设柴油是货运的主要燃料，那么柴油消费的高增长率可归因于TKM的
高增长率。2004年柴油消费有明显变化，从那以后柴油消费增长率变快。

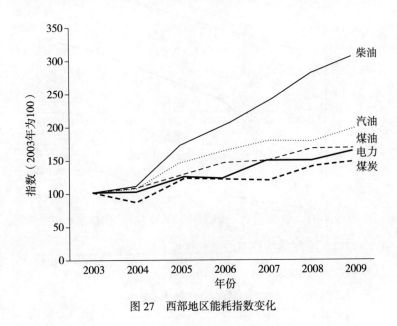

图 27　西部地区能耗指数变化

交通运输能源利用效率

如前所述，把能源利用效率定义为每 TKM 的能源消费量，要计算能源利用总效率，就必须把计算单位从 PKM 转换成 TKM，因为我们已有了 PKM 和 TKM。根据政府采用的换算方法，客运和货运的换算周转量等于客运周转量除以换算系数，再加上货运周转量。

图 28 和图 29 显示的是地区能源消费和周转量。东部地区的能源消费是中部和西部地区的两倍。原因可能是东部地区能源消费增长率更高，且外商投资比中部和西部地区更直接。然而，东部地区的周转量也比中部和西部地区增长得更快。2003 年以来东部地区周转量一直呈上升趋势，但 2008 年因为金融危机的影响，东部地区的周转量有所减少。

中部地区人口众多，农业在社会生产中占主要地位，西部地区人口密度相对较低，是中国最不发达的地区。虽然中西部差别显著，但中部地区和西部地区在能源消费和周转量特点方面却有着相似之处。不过，自 2005 年起西部地区交通行业的能源消费就超过了中部地区。

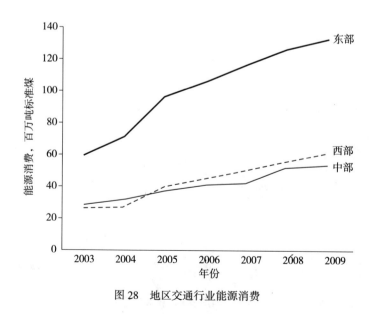

图 28　地区交通行业能源消费

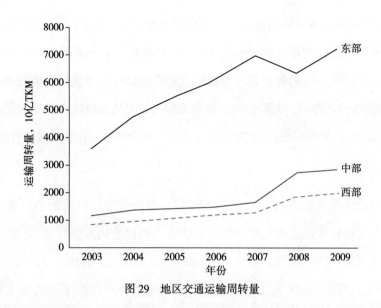

图 29   地区交通运输周转量

图 30 显示的是所有地区的能源利用效率总体结果。东部地区一直在提高其能源利用效率，是全国能源利用总体效率提高的主要促进因素。中部地区的能源利用效率从 2008 年之后有了明显降低。

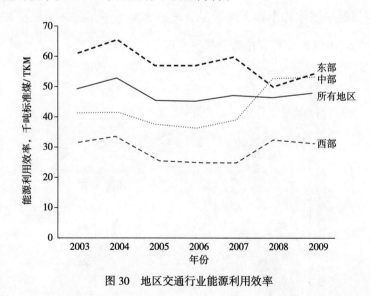

图 30   地区交通行业能源利用效率

用 LMDI 方法（Ang，2005）来分析地区层面上能源变化的多重影响，我们可以发现能源强度影响和能源结构影响，如图 31 和图 32 所示。

图 31 表明，2005 年后整体能源强度就有所提升，这和"十一五"（2006—2010）期间实施的政策引导是一致的。交通行业实施了一系列新政策，试图转变能源强度增强这一趋势。这些政策的实施在中部和西部地区效果更明显。

从图 32 可以看出，能源结构的影响无关宏旨。从二氧化碳排放的分解分析中也可以得出相似的结果。因此就没有必要进行多余的二氧化碳排放的分解分析。

总结

虽然近年来能耗和污染物排放的增长率有所减慢，但总的绝对量仍在增长。提高交通行业的能源利用效率、减少污染物排放仍需继续做出更大努力。

上文分析所得结果和"十一五"（2006—2010）期间的政策导向是一致的，这一期间在交通行业实施了一系列新政策。单从环境保护绩效指数来看，东部和中部地区要优于西部地区。但从复合环境保护绩效指数来看，除 2003 年和 2005 年之外，东部地区都不如中部和西部地区绩效好，且中部地区优于西部地区。近些年来，中部地区总体的环境保护工作有所好转，但东部和西部地区的环境保护工作却不如人意。尽管政府下发了一系列环境保护政策，但交通行业的环境保护还有着很大的提升空间。

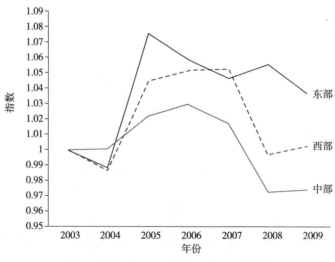

图 31　交通行业——不同地区的能源强度影响

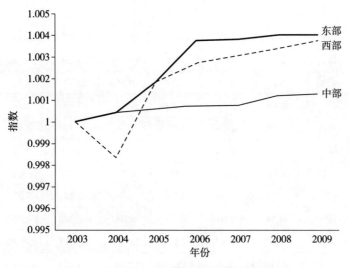

图 32　交通行业——不同地区的能源结构影响

本章附表

表18　地区热发电能耗总结（百万吨标准煤）

地区	能源	2004 年	2005 年	2006 年	2007 年	2008 年	2009 年	2010 年
北部	煤炭	199.63	235.27	264.41	299.81	320.03	326.92	367.23
	石油	0.30	0.25	0.31	0.25	0.11	0.53	0.79
	天然气	5.70	7.59	11.53	18.92	24.19	28.56	45.33
	其他	2.03	2.67	4.80	7.18	7.68	9.17	4.15
东北部	煤炭	72.08	74.99	83.96	86.44	91.57	90.45	97.39
	石油	0.30	0.25	0.22	0.18	0.22	0.11	0.16
	天然气	4.80	2.13	4.25	5.72	5.36	6.76	7.81
	其他	0.32	0.16	1.13	0.71	0.92	1.44	1.11
东部	煤炭	139.41	162.62	184.24	204.79	213.32	222.97	242.34
	石油	6.06	4.98	2.57	1.75	1.23	0.83	1.17
	天然气	4.65	9.31	17.34	18.44	17.64	20.67	31.17
	其他	0.30	0.63	0.56	1.47	1.96	3.12	4.58

续表

地区	能源	2004 年	2005 年	2006 年	2007 年	2008 年	2009 年	2010 年
中部	煤炭	125.12	129.99	146.18	163.39	154.86	156.72	175.30
	石油	0.34	0.28	0.23	0.26	0.32	0.24	0.69
	天然气	0.68	1.41	4.49	7.14	7.33	10.67	22.17
	其他	0.55	0.40	1.35	1.76	2.34	2.42	4.15
西北部	煤炭	49.58	52.54	60.27	70.73	77.28	81.46	98.42
	石油	0.06	0.06	0.06	0.07	0.06	0.04	0.04
	天然气	1.32	1.60	1.45	2.79	2.84	3.07	3.74
	其他	0.24	0.10	0.49	1.04	1.30	1.23	0.21
南部	煤炭	84.50	98.43	115.20	129.61	123.17	133.98	147.68
	石油	14.69	13.39	10.32	7.19	5.23	3.01	1.54
	天然气	0.27	1.34	2.46	7.87	9.30	11.08	11.60
	其他	0.79	2.99	3.31	3.01	3.63	3.38	4.29
海南	煤炭	1.35	1.64	1.83	2.42	2.77	2.89	3.37
	石油	0.01	0.02	0.03	0.01	0.00	0.01	0.01
	天然气	0.70	0.87	1.00	0.73	0.82	0.82	1.01
	其他	0.00	0.00	0.00	0.00	0.24	0.20	0.23
总结	总	715.78	805.91	923.99	1043.68	1075.72	1122.75	1277.68
	其他（%）	0.59	0.86	1.26	1.45	1.68	1.87	1.47

表19　地区电力能源强度（百万吨标准煤/10亿千瓦时）

电网	行政区	2004 年	2005 年	2006 年	2007 年	2008 年	2009 年	2010 年
北部	北京	0.4245	0.3775	0.3762	0.3491	0.3269	0.3128	0.3121
	天津	0.2987	0.3362	0.3374	0.3292	0.3428	0.3484	0.3504
	河北	0.3853	0.3925	0.3856	0.3866	0.4220	0.4127	0.4305
	山西	0.3985	0.3823	0.3877	0.3980	0.4086	0.4066	0.3857
	山东	0.3860	0.4061	0.3736	0.3676	0.3626	0.3538	0.3842
	内蒙古	0.4525	0.4432	0.4442	0.4323	0.4695	0.4467	0.4353
东北部	辽宁	0.4448	0.4074	0.4209	0.4049	0.4023	0.4076	0.4265
	吉林	0.5163	0.5212	0.5018	0.4875	0.5224	0.4877	0.4420
	黑龙江	0.4252	0.4197	0.4594	0.4184	0.4222	0.4243	0.4169

续表

电网	行政区	2004 年	2005 年	2006 年	2007 年	2008 年	2009 年	2010 年
东部	上海	0.3626	0.3735	0.3714	0.3782	0.3627	0.3669	0.3549
	江苏	0.3401	0.3471	0.3485	0.3295	0.3301	0.3222	0.3133
	浙江	0.3390	0.3456	0.3359	0.3280	0.3180	0.3130	0.3093
	安徽	0.3467	0.3771	0.3688	0.3622	0.3298	0.3279	0.3493
	福建	0.3159	0.3119	0.3059	0.3114	0.3218	0.3071	0.3152
中部	江西	0.4512	0.4382	0.4305	0.4282	0.4224	0.3991	0.4173
	河南	0.4721	0.4286	0.3972	0.3976	0.3861	0.3705	0.3851
	湖北	0.4229	0.4143	0.4175	0.4219	0.3937	0.3392	0.4302
	湖南	0.4317	0.3315	0.3889	0.3942	0.3603	0.3289	0.3865
	重庆	0.4396	0.4040	0.4176	0.4197	0.4337	0.4257	0.3895
	四川	0.5763	0.5982	0.5908	0.5517	0.5299	0.4664	0.3747
西北部	陕西	0.3971	0.4245	0.3968	0.4512	0.4065	0.4020	0.3886
	甘肃	0.3526	0.3395	0.3410	0.3403	0.3461	0.3444	0.3430
	青海	0.3784	0.4778	0.4333	0.3739	0.3763	0.3610	0.3476
	宁夏	0.3795	0.3758	0.3631	0.3679	0.3934	0.3893	0.3771
	新疆	0.4340	0.4111	0.4025	0.4020	0.3750	0.4032	0.3631
南部	广东	0.3513	0.3606	0.3500	0.3451	0.3405	0.3319	0.3140
	广西	0.4628	0.5172	0.5181	0.4473	0.4340	0.3856	0.3817
	贵州	0.3798	0.3935	0.3652	0.3781	0.3874	0.3662	0.3799
	云南	0.5154	0.6080	0.5310	0.5319	0.5562	0.5107	0.5115
海南	海南	0.3610	0.3530	0.3367	0.3127	0.3581	0.3445	0.3328
所有地区		0.3954	0.3955	0.3892	0.3836	0.3838	0.3728	0.3740

表20　各地区能源强度较2005年减少百分比[①]

地区	行政区	2006 年	2007 年	2008 年	2009 年	2010 年	2010 目标[②]
中部	重庆	12.6	15.3	21.5	25.5	29.2	20
	湖北	4.7	10.4	17.0	22.9	28.9	20
	湖南	6.4	11.5	18.6	22.5	27.4	20
	江西	7.4	12.5	17.8	19.7	24.7	20
	四川	4.4	8.8	14.5	17.3	22.9	20
	河南	3.7	8.1	12.9	16.6	20.9	20

续表

地区	行政区	2006 年	2007 年	2008 年	2009 年	2010 年	2010 目标[②]
东部	安徽	3.3	7.4	12.1	18.1	25.0	20
	江苏	5.1	9.0	14.5	18.4	23.4	20
	浙江	5.1	8.9	13.1	17.7	23.2	20
	福建	2.9	6.9	9.5	15.1	20.0	16
	上海	5.4	10.1	10.8	15.7	17.6	20
海南	海南	2.7	2.2	6.3	8.1	14.9	12
北部	内蒙古	7.2	14.9	24.9	28.9	32.9	22
	北京	8.5	17.8	22.9	28.0	32.8	20
	山西	3.3	9.4	19.6	20.9	29.7	22
	天津	7.3	9.9	19.4	21.9	23.5	20
	山东	5.4	8.5	15.9	18.6	22.1	22
	河北	1.6	6.1	12.6	15.7	20.5	20
东北部	吉林	4.6	10.2	14.5	19.5	24.4	22
	辽宁	4.1	7.2	14.7	17.6	23.3	20
	黑龙江	1.9	2.9	6.8	5.2	12.4	20
西北部	宁夏	5.0	14.0	25.3	29.7	36.4	20
	陕西	13.5	17.2	24.1	25.9	31.3	20
	甘肃	6.6	10.5	13.6	16.1	22.4	20
	青海	3.0	7.4	13.2	13.5	20.2	17
	新疆	4.8	5.7	7.7	3.2	12.5	n.a.
南部	贵州	5.8	10.5	18.7	22	26.4	20
	广西	3.7	7.3	10.2	13.5	19.1	15
	广东	4.6	7.9	11.3	15.2	18.1	16
	云南	2.5	7.1	13.3	14.1	17.8	17

①区域 GDP 单位为 2005 年定值美元；区域能源强度为单位 GDP 能耗

②来源：APERC（2009）

CHPATER 3

第三章

3

"十二五"规划能源
政策的影响

"十二五"规划能源政策的背景

中国政府为中国的能源发展制定了总体目标，可以大致分为以下几个阶段：2030 年以前主要发展化石能源，其次是新能源和可再生能源；从 2030 年到 2050 年，新能源、可再生能源和化石能源同等重要，可以并行发展；2050年以后，新能源和可再生能源将代替化石能源成为中国的主要能源，化石能源退居其次。

要达到这一宏伟目标，施行优化能源结构、提高能源利用效率、使用清洁能源等策略是关键所在。如果"十二五"（2011—2015）规划中的能源政策成功落实，那么预计中国的能源市场和能源体系也会继续稳定长足发展。这一章将对能源政策的提出背景、实施困难、指导方针和注重点一一做出阐释。

提出背景

2013 年"十二五"规划正式出台，在此之前，中国的能源产业一直发展良好，特别是"十一五"规划的实施奠定了坚实的基础，有助于政府做出进一步努力。但中国的能源产业也同时面临着发展的有利条件和不利条件。

有利条件

能源自给率提高了。一次能源生产量从 2005 年的 21.6 亿吨标准煤提高到 2010 年的 29.7 亿吨标准煤，年增长率 6.6%。2010 年中国的国家石油储备量已经提高到了 1640 万立方米。

能源结构得到优化。新能源和可再生能源在能源结构中的占比从 2005 年的 7.4% 增加到 2010 年的 9.4%，非化石燃料占比从 6.8% 增加到 8.6%，天然气占比从 2.6% 提高到 4.4%。单位 GDP 能源强度已经减少了 19.1%，二氧化硫和二氧化碳排放量分别减少了 14.29% 和 12.45%。增加的新发电量超过 4.3 亿千瓦，总发电量达到 9.5 亿千瓦，拥有包括新疆和海南在内的世界上最大规模电网。海外权益油增加到了 9 亿吨，并购、收购总共达 350 亿美元。

不利条件

煤炭是中国的主要能源。经过多年的发展，中国的煤炭开采量从世界第 13 位增长到现在的世界第 1 位。一方面，这有助于国民经济的发展，但从另一方面来说，也给中国的环境污染和煤矿事故问题带来很大压力。

中国的核能产业发展迅速。政府新批准了 13 个核电站，总发电量 3702 万千瓦，共 34 个发电机组，分别建在红沿河（辽宁）、宁德和福清（福建）、阳江（广东）、方家山和三门（浙江）、海阳（山东）、台山（广东）、昌江（海南）和防城港（广西）。现在在建的共有 28 个发电机组，总发电量 3097 万千瓦，占世界核能总发电量的 40%。福岛核泄漏事件引发了公众对核能安全性能的担忧，随之公众在核电站建设区域举行了一些抗议活动。

2006 年到 2010 年，水电厂及其发电机组建设量迅速增加，中国水力发电机组超过了 2 亿千瓦，新增加的发电机组数量几乎相当于过去 95 年内建设的机组。但同时建设的很多小型水电厂导致了很多生态破坏，比如云南省连续四年遭遇的干旱。

风能产业同样发展迅速。全国累计风力提升能力达到 3100 万千瓦，但电网的垄断所有权一直阻碍着用于公共电网的风力发电。因此一些所有者放弃了其在内蒙古、河北、吉林及其他地区的电厂，造成了大约 20%~30% 的风力发电缩减率，经济损失达 100 亿元人民币。

太阳能一直在持续发展。建立了一套相对完整的光伏电池产业链，年产量达 800 万千瓦。然而，中国的太阳能消费占世界总体太阳能消费的比例不到 1%，使中国不得不在很大程度上依赖海外市场，这就导致了很多贸易冲突的发生。

阻碍因素

中国的能源发展还有诸多阻碍因素存在。

能源增长和资源短缺之间的矛盾

中国正在成为世界上最大的能源消费国。但是，中国的人均能源储备非常低，尤其是人均石油和天然气储备，仅占世界平均水平的 6%。"十一五"期间国民经济的年平均增长率为 11.2%，而这一成果的取得依靠的是 6.6% 的能源消费平均增长率。尽管这一期间能源弹性指数从 1.04 下降到了 0.59，但是能源需求还会随着国家现代化的进程大幅增加。能源供应短缺的问题对能源安全也提出了很大挑战。

以煤为主的能源结构和低碳发展之间的矛盾

2014 年，煤炭消费量超过 30 亿吨，占世界煤炭总量的 47%，比世界一次能源消费水平高出 40%。

在电力行业，热力发电占主导地位。中国政府制定了建立资源节约型和环境友好型社会的发展策略，但这无论对现行的资源密集型发展模式还是对高污染的煤炭行业来说，都是一个巨大的挑战。以煤为主的能源结构和低碳发展之间的矛盾将会长期存在。

化石能源集约型消费和提出更高生态要求之间的矛盾

石油行业是国民经济的支柱。石油产品广泛应用于工业生产的方方面面、日常生活、国家安全科技等，对工业的进步和经济的发展有至关重要的影响。然而，长期以来化石能源的发展对国家的生态环境造成了严重影响，且已经成为建设环境友好型社会的主要限制因素。

国内能源和国内供需之间的矛盾

中国西部地区能源供应充足，而东部地区资源匮乏，然而中国的能源需求模式恰恰相反。未来中国能源的发展会更注重西部地区，但能源需求仍然集中在东部和中部地区。因此，跨越大范围多个地区，将能源从西部长距离输送到东部，将更加成为工作的重中之重。

技术发展和人才不足之间的矛盾

技术创新已经成为能源发展的重要推动力。在中国，用于能源发展的技术一直处于管理不善的状态；高级人才不足、自主创新薄弱，很多关键的创新型技术受到其他现有技术条件的制约；行业发展高度依赖国外技术。基于以上这些原因，中国很难达到成为技术先进型世界能源大国的目标，并引领世界能源的发展。

指导方针

为了克服这些困难和阻碍因素，"十二五"规划为能源发展提出了明确计划。

优化化石能源

A. 煤

一方面，计划的目的是通过加快新煤炭基地的建设，如陕北、黄陇、神东、蒙东、宁东等煤炭基地，来促进传统的煤炭生产，改善以前的煤炭基地，如晋北、晋中、晋东、云贵煤炭基地，并在新疆建立煤炭基地。

另一方面，通过对煤炭的非传统利用，如通过煤炭转化成天然气、液体燃料、煤炭联合生产的研发，来促进工业化的稳定发展。此外还将通过利用高效、大容量的煤燃料装置，以及在大中城市和工业园区内建设热电联产机组，实现煤炭的清洁高效利用。将优先建设发展综合发电厂，如大型燃煤发电厂。

B. 石油和天然气

计划在发展和利用非传统型燃料如煤层气和页岩气的基础上增加油气产量。计划将塔里木盆地、准噶尔盆地、松辽盆地、鄂尔多斯盆地、渤海湾盆地和四川盆地合并为大规模生产地区。还计划加快海上油气田的勘探和研发工作，并进一步发展对煤矿中煤层气的开采和利用。

C. 管道

国内干线管道网络竣工。将在西北、东北、西南和海上地区建立进口油气战略管道系统，包括天然气进口管道、液体天然气接收站、跨地区天然气干线管道网和输配管道网。将建立一个天然气、煤层气和煤制气协调运作的天然气供应格局。中国—哈萨克斯坦原油管道第二阶段的建设、中国—缅甸油气管道部分建设、中亚天然气管道第二阶段的建设、西气东输工程第三、第四阶段的建设都将开工。加上气仓储建设，计划油气管道总长度达15万千米。另外，节能设备如石油储备系统、天然气应急储备和煤炭储备也在计划之中。

大规模发展非化石能源

A. 太阳能

"十一五"期间光伏市场在中国兴起，地方政府针对太阳能电池和光伏建设出台了很多金融刺激方案，促进光伏产业和光伏市场的共同发展。同时，2009年之后出台的一系列政策，如财政补贴集成光电的建设、金太阳示范工程等，打开了通过联合私人光电企业和国家能源企业促进光电厂和集成项目建设的新纪元。这一趋势在"十二五"规划中得到了延续。光伏产品是出口导向型产品，很大程度上依赖于国际市场，而中国主要依赖进口硅原材料和硅锭来制造光伏产品。这两个问题制约着中国光伏产业的发展。因此，保持光伏技术的远见属性、建立行业准入标准，已经成为未来政策制定的重点。一些省份如西藏、内蒙古、甘肃、宁夏、新疆和云南等已经成为光伏产业发展的焦点，并已制定了超过 500 万千瓦的太阳能发电计划。

B. 风能

2005 年《国家发展改革委关于风电建设和管理要求的通知》一文发布，文中规定国内风力发电设备率应达到 70% 以上。2010 年 1 月，中央政府又取消了这一规定。国内风力发电市场的开放和外资风力发电设备制造商不会受到国内政策的限制。国外制造商也能够直接参与市场竞争。国内的风力发电设备制造商则面临着合并和竞争日益激烈两大问题。同时，由于中国的风能资源分布不平衡，因此计划走建设大型基地、连接大型电网、注重电网与二级分布式发电相连接的发展模式。至于技术层面，大型涡轮机制造和风能电网连接是研发工作的重点，要着力改善风力发电设备和电网连接的控制工作。比如，计划"十二五"期间建设六个陆地风力发电厂和两个海上风力发电厂，总发电量超过 7000 万千瓦。

C. 核产业

政府计划在沿海和内陆省份加强核能的发展，目标核能发电量 4000 万千瓦。

D. 水电

计划在主要流域如金沙江、雅砻江和大渡河地区建设一批大型水电厂，发电量 1.2 亿千瓦。

E. 生物质能

面对原材料成本日益增长和原材料有限的问题，根本的解决办法就是大规模生产木质纤维生物质燃料乙醇。计划从一些地方特产农作物出发，如广西和海南的木薯，山东、黑龙江、内蒙古和新疆的甜高粱，还有四川和云贵地区的麻风树等，来促进各地区的产业发展。而且，项目和计划的可应用性，如应用于生物质能发电的绿色能源计划和非粮食生物质能交通运输燃料的应用计划，都会成为促进生物质能发展的重要指标。

注重点

"十二五"规划的重点就是对能源结构进行深度系统的改革，改革工作主要在以下四个方面展开。

能源价格体系

中国的能源价格体系已经有了很大改善，市场在其中发挥了越来越大的作用。以煤炭价格为例，作为中国最主要的能源，煤炭的价格在 1993 年和 1994 年首次实现了自由定价，但仍有一大部分的能源用户在使用由政府定价的合同电煤。2009 年，合同电煤价格也得以取消，煤炭价格由此实现了完全市场化。同时，石油价格逐渐实现国际化，基准价格与布伦特、迪拜和辛塔原油价格挂钩，再加上运输关税、其他税和成本等。天然气价格已经调整为根据不同情况由政府引导或直接由政府定价。然而，如今中国的能源价格体系还存在三大问题。第一，能源市场中无论是上游产业还是下游产业都没有形成真正的竞争，煤炭除外。第二，能源价格无法真实反映成本，包括资源的浪费和对环境的污染。第三，没有明确的能源分类标准。

A. 能源国企

能源国企的去行政化对中国国务院来说一直是个严峻的挑战。对能源国企的改革面临诸多挑战，如何利用这些企业的优势条件，如工作的高效率、对国家能源的安全保障、对中央政府策略需要的快速反应，同时与市场中的中小能源企业相互协调，改变国企垄断能源市场的局面，这些就成为"十二五"规划改革的重点。

B. 政府角色

我们在绪论部分讨论了看得见的手和看不见的手的问题。无论是中央政府还是地方政府，都属于看得见的手。保持中央政府和地方政府、政府和企业、政府和社会之间的平衡，这是一件很困难的事。经过长期的计划经济和30年改革开放政策的实施，时下中国政府应该区分开哪些事需要政府监管、哪些不需要政府监管。政府角色应当最大程度上从一个管理者转变为一个服务者。

C. 再城市化

以习近平总书记为领导的新一代中央领导集体执政以来，"再城市化"就作为一个行业术语被反复提到，新任领导人希望把农民从农村解放出来，解决土地所有制的问题，从而扩大内需，最大限度地利用农村大量的低价劳动力。毋庸置疑这也增加了对能源的需求。如何有效地转变能源消耗和能源生产方式，使之与城市发展相适应，是再城市化之外的另一个严峻挑战。

D. "走出去"政策

既然中国无法达到能源供需平衡，那么利用海外资源来补偿国内需求的短缺问题就成为"十二五"规划能源发展的另一个注重点。中国提出从"能源大国"转变成"能源强国"的目标。计划实行以下措施：

- 加快"走出去"：扩大外资额，提升开发海外资源的能力，增加能源工程服务和能源设备的出口；

- 提高能源贸易水平：优化中国的对外能源贸易结构，稳定提高油气进口，在控制煤炭、铀、电力出口的同时积极促进进口；

- 改善进口能源技术现状：引导外商投资国内新能源产业，通过将"引进来"技术与中国管理和人才相结合，鼓励高新技术发明创造。

能源结构、能源强度和环境影响

引言

能源发展"十二五"规划于 2013 年 1 月 1 日正式发布，为增强能源安全，为能源产业设定了主要的发展目标，主要强调清洁能源和能源利用效率两个方面。"十二五"规划的主要发展目标如下：

- 能源强度（单位国内生产总值能耗）：能源强度比2010年减少16%；
- 能源消费总量：2015年能源消费总量40亿吨标准煤，其中国内生产36.6亿吨标准煤；
- 总耗电量：2015年用电量6.15万亿千瓦时；
- 能源综合效率：2015年提高到38%；
- 优化能源结构：计划到2015年非化石能源消费占一次能源消费比重提高到11.4%，天然气比重提高到7.5%；
- 国内能源基地建设：加快建设山西、鄂尔多斯盆地、内蒙古东部地区、西南地区、新疆五大国家综合能源基地。到2015年，五大基地一次能源生产能力达到26.6亿吨标准煤，占全国70%以上。

除以上这些总体目标之外，针对众多不同的行业还有一些具体的政策，在下一节会提到。

煤炭政策

煤炭供应和煤炭安全

如前所述，中国的西部和东部之间存在极大的供需不平衡问题，这就使得长距离输送煤炭的成本很昂贵，也给铁路运输能力提出了更高要求，并加重了公路交通拥堵问题。因此，"十二五"规划明确指出未来的煤炭发展方向是存储。中国计划在沿海地区和内陆港、中部和西北地区建立国家煤炭应急储备，建立并改善操作和管理系统，以确保充足的煤炭储备。

另一项政策是关闭效率低的小型煤矿，同时：

• 在陕西、内蒙古、宁夏、山西、云南和广州等省建立大型煤炭生产基地；

• 在新疆维吾尔自治区西部新建煤炭生产中心，补充生产能力；

• 新建14个煤炭基地，年生产量28亿吨煤；

• 利用煤层瓦斯抽采更好地利用资源；

• 实行煤炭和环境保护。

生产预算

"十二五"规划中煤炭年生产量预算为40亿吨。此外，中国还利用法规控制限制环境恶化、偷税漏税、煤矿事故等问题的发生。目标是将煤炭企业从11000个左右减少到4000个。估计2015年全国煤炭生产总量中，有近60%来自于近10个大型煤炭企业。

使用清洁煤炭能源

洗煤比例预计会增长。新建煤矿建设过程中同时安装洗煤设备，增加洗煤的使用量。现有煤矿要加快自身建设和革新。计划到2017年筛选原煤的比重超过70%。禁止进口低品质高烟煤和高硫煤。推行保证煤炭品质的新举措新方法。限制进口高硫石油焦炭。大力鼓励在中国北方的农村建立清洁煤发放中心，推广使用清洁煤。

促进全面改善，减少多重污染物排放

要改善烧煤锅炉。要加快中央热力供应、煤气、煤电等工程项目的建设。到2017年，要在所有地级市及以上城市内，去除每小时蒸发量在10吨及以下的烧煤锅炉，必须使用的除外。已经禁止新建任何每小时蒸发量在20吨以

下的烧煤锅炉。在其他地区，不允许建造任何每小时蒸发量在 10 吨以下的烧煤锅炉。在管道运输热力和天然气无法到达的地方，要充分利用电力、新能源和清洁煤，推进高效率、能源节约型锅炉的使用。在化工、造纸、印刷、制革、制药等行业密集的地区，逐渐将私人烧煤锅炉替换为天然气发动子系统。

重点行业脱硫、脱硝、除尘

脱硫设备安装用于燃煤发电厂和钢铁企业里的烧结机器和制粒设备、炼油厂里的催化裂化和有色金属厂，还用于每小时蒸发量在 20 吨以上的烧煤锅炉。除循环流化床锅炉外，所有的烧煤机组都要安装脱硫设备。在新型干法水泥窑中也用到了低氮燃烧和脱硫。要对现有的烧煤锅炉和工业窑炉中的除尘设备进行升级和创新。

煤炭市场效率

中国允许电力生产商和批发终端用户如工业客户之间进行直接谈判。要进一步改革煤炭市场，包括发展煤炭交易市场和期货市场。

石油政策

石油供应和石油安全

"十二五"规划中没有明确的关于石油供应安全的政策。但是中国一直在努力提高石油供应的安全性，鼓励中国企业参与国外的上游投资活动，与国际或当地企业进行合作，并加快大型战略石油储备的发展，将石油探明储量提高到 65 亿吨以上。

中国不允许国外石油公司在中国运营，以此来保护本国的石油公司。但是，国际石油公司可以通过签订共同生产的协议接触到海上石油的勘探，如渤海湾地区的海上石油勘探。如今中国共有五大石油生产中心，分别位于塔里木盆地、准噶尔盆地、松辽盆地、鄂尔多斯盆地、渤海盆地和四川盆地。鼓励海上和深水油田的开发和利用。2015 年开工建设长途石油输送管道（将原油管道总长度增加 8400 千米，成品油管道总长度增加 21000 千米）。

市场效率

2013 年 3 月宣布石油产品价格每十个工作日调整一次，以便更好地反映全球石油市场的变化。

天然气政策

天然气供应和天然气安全

天然气由于其自身的高热值、低成本、少污染等特性，在中国主要用作民用燃料和工业燃料。天然气还作为化工业的一种原材料，用来生产一些化学产品如合成氨和甲醇。近来，制造业、电力行业和交通行业的天然气消费量迅速增长。中国的天然气供应主要来自国内生产、管道进口和液化天然气供应。"十二五"规划的目标就是将液化天然气终端的输入容量提高 5000 万吨以上。截至 2015 年底，已经提高至 4980 万吨，这一目标基本达成。2012 年，天然气的出口量和进口量分别为 1077 亿立方米和 425 亿立方米[①]。

① http://www.cs.com.cn/sylm/jsbd/201301/t20130128_3839899.html

2010 年，天然气占一次能源消费的比重为 4.6%，能源发展"十二五"规划计划到 2015 年将这一比重提高至 7.5%。2015 年，天然气占一次能源消费比重为 5.9%。规划还打算到 2015 年页岩气生产量达到 65 亿立方米，相当于 2015 年全国天然气生产的 2%~3%。

长距离输气管道的建设也在计划之中，包括西气东输工程的第三、第四阶段，总长度将于 2015 年达到 15 万千米。然而到了 2016 年建设项目还未开工。大型战略天然气储备的建立也被提上日程，来确保天然气供应的安全。

2010 年批准启动了西气东输管道工程，将西气东输、陕西至北京第二输气管道、忠县—武汉天然气管道、涩北—西宁—兰州输气管道连接起来，从而实现了天然气资源的多样性和北部、东部、中部和西北部供电的可靠性。

2012 年，国家发改委下发了《国家发展改革委关于印发天然气发展"十二五年"规划的通知》。通知旨在扩大天然气的使用范围，促进天然气行业的发展。国家发改委和相关部门一起研究制定了天然气"十二五"规划。规划侧重天然气基础设施的建设，认为上游资源的勘探和发展同下游市场的利用同等重要。规划同时涵盖了煤层气、页岩气和煤气的发展，为引导中国天然气行业的健康发展打下了重要基础。

2012 年国家正式发布《页岩气发展规划（2011—2015 年）》。规划明确了"十二五"期间的主要任务，就是攻克天然气开采和发展的关键技术壁垒，为"十三五"期间页岩气的大规模发展奠定基础。需要指出的是，中国地理条件很复杂，对页岩气的发展来说，技术和投资条件都是极大的挑战。

环境保护

要加快清洁能源的利用和替代，就需要增加天然气、煤制天然气和煤层沼气的供应量。计划到 2015 年，建成额外输送量在 1500 亿立方米以上、覆盖京津冀、长江三角洲和珠江三角洲地区的天然气管道网。目前，已经完成了输送总量达 770 亿立方米三个阶段的工程。为了优化天然气的使用，要优先把烧煤民用供热替换为天然气民用供热。鼓励效率高的利用项目如天然气分布式能源，限制天然气化学项目的发展。计划系统地发展天然气调峰装置，不再新建天然气发电厂。

计划扩大城市高污染燃料限制区，并逐渐向郊区扩展。通过补偿措施、实行峰谷电价、季节电价、阶梯式电价和峰荷电价等手段，中国在进行城中村、城乡接合部和棚户区改造的过程中，会逐步加强天然气的使用和替代煤的使用。

电力政策

2013 年 3 月份中国简化了与能源相关的规章条例。"十二五"规划中呼吁应该把电力主要管理者国家电力监管委员会与国家能源局合并，从而减少能源改革过程中出现的责任重叠现象，减少投资和项目审批。

电力供应和电力安全

2009 年中国非化石燃料发电占比为 8%，"十二五"规划中计划到 2015 年将这一比重提高至 11.4%，到 2020 年提高至 15%。也就是说，到 2015 年底，中国计划——并成功实现——非化石燃料总发电量达到 4.64 亿千瓦，占全国总发电量的 30%。

"十二五"期间，计划可再生能源新发电装置的发电容量达到 1.75 亿千瓦，包括：

- 水力发电：6200 万千瓦

- 抽水蓄能发电：1200 万千瓦

- 风力发电：7000 万千瓦

- 太阳能发电：2000 万千瓦

- 生物质能发电：1100 万千瓦

目标是可再生能源发电量到 2015 年达到总发电量的 20% 以上。

2010 年中国总发电量 9.7 亿千瓦，预计 2015 年将达到 14.9 亿千瓦。到 2015 年不再使用化石燃料能源和可替代能源的发电量预计如下：

- 烧煤火力发电：9.6 亿千瓦

- 天然气火力发电：4000 万千瓦

- 核能发电：4000 万千瓦

- 水力发电：2.6 亿千瓦

- 抽水蓄能发电：3000 万千瓦

- 风立发电：1 亿千瓦

- 太阳能发电：2100万千瓦

- 生物质能发电：1300万千瓦

- 其他：1000万千瓦

表21总结了2010年和2015年发电的能源结构。

表21　发电能源结构总结

能源类型	2010年[①]	2015年	"十二五"期间			2010年	
			新增	增长百分比	能源占比	能源占比	预计发电量占比
天然气，万千瓦	2642	5600	2958	112%	3.76%	2.72%	
煤炭，万千瓦	64660	96000	31340	48%	64.43%	66.66%	
核能，万千瓦	1082	4000	2918	270%	2.68%	1.12%	
水能，万千瓦	19821	26000	6179	31%	17.45%	20.43%	0.837/13.6%
抽水蓄能，万千瓦	1784	3000	1216	68%	2.01%	1.84%	
风能，万千瓦	2957	10000	7043	238%	6.71%	3.05%	0.19/3.1%
太阳能，万千瓦	86	2100	2014	2342%	1.41%	0.09%	
生物质能，万千瓦	170	1300	1130	665%	0.87%	0.18%	
其他，万千瓦	3692	1000	0	0	0.67%	3.81%	
总计，万千瓦	97000	149000	52000	53.60%	100%	100%	
耗电量	4.2	6.15	1.95	46			

①来源：中国电力企业联合会，国家电网能源研究所

A. 关闭效率低的发电厂

"十一五"期间关闭效率低的发电厂和工业设备，对实现减小能源强度的目标有促进作用。据报道强制关闭的老旧火力发电厂总发电量达7210万千瓦，因此计划"十二五"期间剩下的老旧和效率低下的发电厂都会强制关闭。

B. 气产电（2642万—4000万千瓦）

和煤炭发电相比，天然气发电启动快速，调峰便捷，并能减少温室气体的排放。但是中国的天然气资源有限，供应量不足，并且天然气的价格受石油市场价格的影响严重。因此，天然气发电应主要在中国东部地区发展，满足最大用电量，发展热电联产机组。2010年燃气发电装机容量仅为2642万千

瓦，要求到 2015 年达到 4000 万千瓦的目标。

C. 煤产电（6.466 亿千瓦—9.6 亿千瓦）

按照"十二五"规划的要求，中国着重对电力部门进行去碳化，建立新型燃煤发电厂，效率更高，产生相同电量的情况下比老旧燃煤电厂消耗的煤炭量更少。

D. 水力发电（6200 万千瓦—2.6 亿千瓦）

到 2010 年，中国水力发电厂共计 48500 个。水力资源最丰富、最适合水力发电的省份（四川、云南、贵州、湖北、湖南、广西）都位于中国西部，而如前所述，用电大省（河南、河北、山东、江苏、浙江、广东）都位于中国东部。

E. 太阳能发电（100 万千瓦—2100 万千瓦）

中国决定减少国家电网内的能源供给成本，给太阳能开发提供更高成本预算。还计划将太阳能发电的装机容量扩大四倍，实现到 2011 年太阳能发电量超过 200 万千瓦。但是因其低成本生产，中国的太阳能光伏市场 95% 是出口型的。然而中国国内的光伏市场缺乏生产聚硅原材料的技术，光伏设备生产商也严重不足。中国要计划发展国内的光伏市场，特别需要在这两个方面做出更大努力，进行研发工作[1]。

① http://newenergy.giec.cas.cn/tyn/gfdt/201108/t20110808_220911.html

F. 风力发电（3000 万千瓦—1 亿千瓦）

到 2015 年，中国连接到电网的风力发电装机容量会达到 1 亿千瓦。中国已经建立了八个风力发电厂，其中六个陆地风力发电厂，两个海上风力发电厂。到 2015 年年发电量可以达到 1900 亿千瓦时。

G. 生物质能发电（到 1300 万千瓦）

"十二五"规划计划将生物质能发电量提高至 1300 万千瓦，其中 300 万千瓦产自城市有机垃圾。

电网基础设施

中国证券报公布的数据显示，从 2012 年 4 月起，国家发改委已经批准了超高压电力输送线路和配套配电网络的建设项目，投入动态投资共计 76.61 亿元。相比传统电线，超高压电线可以跨越更长的距离，输送更多的电力，输电能力约为 100 万伏，而传统输电线的输电能力只有 50 万伏左右。预计从北部和西部边远地区的燃煤发电枢纽和可再生能源发电枢纽，到集中在东部和南部省份的人口密集、用电需求中心等地，超高压输电线网络都可以覆盖。根据提出的方案，从西部地区输送的 20% 的电力都将由新输电线输送。

除此之外，预计建设长达 20 多万千米、33 万伏的电网。另外，在执行电力发展战略计划的同时，给电动汽车充电用的智能电网、智能电表和相关基础设施也会得到相应的发展。

可再生能源电价补偿

2011 年，国家发改委同国家电力监管委员会共同下发了《2010 年 1—9 月可再生能源电价补偿和配额交易方案的通知》，通知明确了电价补贴项目和金额，明确了配额交易和电费结算等问题。

能源利用效率

2011 年，工业和信息化部发布了《关于做好工业领域电力需求侧管理工作的指导意见》，详细说明了有序改进工业区电力需求侧的管理，优化了电力使用的产业结构，调整了电力使用的方式方法，提高了工业的能源利用效率，促进了工业和国民经济的可持续发展。

市场效率

2012 年 7 月中国开始实行阶梯电价制度。

2011 年，国家发改委下发了《关于完善太阳能光伏发电上网电价政策的通知》。通知指出，2011 年 7 月 1 日前，批准的光伏发电项目电价分别为每千瓦时 1.15 元。通知下发后，光伏发电电价调整为每千瓦时 1 元。这标志着国内光伏产业市场开始真正形成。

到 2013 年，国家发改委又下发了《国家发展改革委办公厅关于进一步降低农产品生产流通环节电价有关问题的通知》。

终端使用效率政策

"十二五"规划还包括 2015 年的总能耗和电耗预算。规划还提出了强制性指标，要将经济能源强度在 2005 年的基础上下降 16%，包括为最大的工业用户制定了 2015 年节约能源指标的前 10000 个项目。对能源集约型行业，如水泥生产、炼油业、化工业等提出的能源利用效率标准，要求他们将能源利用效率提高至少 10 个百分点。

交通行业

A. 基础设施

"十二五"期间中国交通行业基础设施投资约为 62000 亿元，资金主要用于高速公路的建设。因此，高速公路网络规模有望扩大，预计高速公路网络总长度可达 450 万千米，高速双车道公路总长度预计可达到 108000 千米。计划这一高速公路网将连接 90% 以上的人口超过 20 万人的城市和城镇。

B. 减少私家车的使用

为了减缓私家车使用率的增长，中国在城市公共轨道交通系统和高速铁路方面进行了投资。汽车所有权将根据城市发展与规划进行适当管理。在一些特大城市如北京、上海和广州，对城市机动车数量设置了严格限制。

C. 提高机动车效率

2011 年 3 月中国提出了燃油消费测评和管理机制，并根据这一机制，出台了一份符合 2011 年燃油消费标准的机动车模型名单。规定到 2020 年客车平均燃油消费标准为每 100 千米 4.5 升，达到欧洲同类标准。

D. 提高燃油质量

加快炼油厂的改造升级。争取到 2013 年底，达到国四标准的汽油在全国范围内得以供应；到 2014 年底，达到国四标准的柴油可以在全国范围内得以使用；到 2015 年底，达到国五标准的汽油和柴油可以在主要城市和地区，如京津冀、长江三角洲和珠江三角洲等地区大范围使用，争取到 2017 年底在全国范围内供应使用。政府要对油品质量加强监督和检查，严厉打击生产和售卖不达标机动车燃油的非法行为。

E. 淘汰黄标车和老旧车

中央政府设立了禁区并给予财政补贴，逐步淘汰掉黄标车和老旧车。黄标车指不符合国家排放标准的汽油车。预计到 2015 年，所有 2005 年底之前注册的黄标车都要停止上路，包括京津冀、长三角地区和珠三角地区的 500 万辆黄标车。到 2017 年，争取淘汰掉所有的黄标车。

F. 增强环境保护

环境保护、工业和信息化、质量监管、工商等相关部门要通力协作，对汽车生产进行环境保护监督。任何生产和售卖不符合环境保护标准的机动车的违法行为都要受到检举和惩罚。每年车检中，未达到环境保护要求的机动车不能颁发行驶证，也不允许机动车所有者继续驾驶机动车。要加快柴油车尿素添加剂供应的建设。其他政策如缩短老旧公共汽车和出租车强制报废的时间限制、鼓励每年更换高效率排气净化装置、对轮船和其他不使用公路的机器进行污染控制等也应该考虑在内。

G. 加快低速机动车升级

中国还应该对低速机动车（包括三轮车和低速货车）设定更高的环境保护要求，减少污染物排放，加快相关产业和生产技术的替换升级。从 2017 年开始，新低速机动车和轻型货车将实行相同的能源节约和排放标准。

H. 促进可替代能源汽车发展

公共交通、环境卫生和政府组织要以身作则，首先使用可替代能源汽车。

在《节能与新能源汽车产业发展规划（2012—2020）》中提到，重点是要发展电动汽车和插电式混合动力汽车，增强国内汽车行业的竞争力，减少碳排放。对购买新能源汽车的个人给予免费车辆牌照和财政补贴等优惠政策。另外，计划通过政府购买项目对电力汽车进行强制推广，主要面向公共汽车和出租车：给每个试点城市的 1000 辆电力公共汽车 45 万元的财政补贴，给电力出租车 5.5 万元的财政补贴。

国内最大的几家国有企业联合起来建立了企业联盟，加快电动汽车的发展，投资额有望达到 1000 亿元。预计到 2015 年，电动汽车和插电式混合动力汽车的生产和销量总共可达 50 万辆，到 2020 年可达到 500 万辆以上。为电动汽车和插电式混合动力汽车提供补贴和免税福利。预计到 2015 年将建成 2000 多家充电站，配备 40 万台快速充电机供电动汽车使用。在北京、上海、广州等城市，每年新增加或升级的公共汽车中，新能源或清洁燃料公共汽车将占到 60% 以上。需要特别指出的是，"十二五"规划提出目标，新车的耗油量和碳排放要减少 30%。

建筑

政府为民用建筑和公共建筑建立了高能效设计标准，还有一套高能效建设工程的验收检查程序。比如 2012 年，财政部同住房和城乡建设部下发了《关于完善可再生能源建筑应用政策和调整资金分配管理方式的通知》。通知要求积极促进家用和公共建筑使用太阳能和其他新能源产品，进一步扩大可再生能源建筑应用政策的影响力，提高可再生能源建筑应用的安全性能，促进正常化，提高财政资金的使用效率。

另外，2013 年，住房和城乡建设部下发了《绿色建筑行动方案》，深入贯彻落实科学发展观，有力改变城乡建设和建筑发展模式，提高资源利用效率，达到能源节约和减排双重目标，积极应对全球气候变化，建立资源节约型和环境友好型社会，提高生态文明水平，人民生活质量得到改善。

终端产品

2011 年 10 月底，中国制定了一份能效标识计划，涉及 25 个产品品类。为强化这一项目的执行力度，2012 年财政部同住房和城乡建设部下发了《关于完善可再生能源建筑应用政策和调整资金分配管理方式的通知》。这一举措意在积极促进家用和公共建筑太阳能和其他新能源产品的发展，进一步扩大可再生能源建筑应用政策的影响，提高其安全性能，促进正常化，提高财政资金的使用效率。

工业

2012 年，工业和信息化部办公厅下发了《关于发布 2011 年度钢铁等行业重点用能产品（工序）能效标杆指标及企业的通知》，贯彻落实国务院"十二五"规划节能减排全面工作计划精神。通知给 2011 年划分的 16 类重点用能产品，如钢铁、有色金属、建筑材料、轻工业、纺织业和其他行业以及相关企业制定了能效基准指标。

环境保护

"十二五"规划包括了碳定价计划，另外宣布了即将在城市和省级试点进行碳排放交易的计划。

关于碳排放，中国制定了国家目标，即到 2020 年将碳浓度降低 40% 到 45%。"十二五"规划包含了一个指令性指标，即将碳浓度在 2005 年的基础上下降 17%，其他污染物如 COD、二氧化硫等的排放量减少 10%。

2013 年，中国开启了又一个"五年计划"，使严重污染的环境得到改善。这份环境改善计划的目标如下：

- 全国空气质量提高，空气质量严重污染天数减少；
- 京津冀（北京、天津、河北省）、长三角（长江三角洲）、珠三角（珠江三角洲）等地区空气质量明显提高；

- 用五年或更长的时间消除严重污染导致的恶劣天气，全国空气质量显著提高。

到 2017 年具体目标为：

- 到2017年，地级市及以上城市的PM10浓度和2012年相比至少降低10%，空气质量良好的天数增加；
- 京津冀、长三角和珠三角地区PM10浓度分别降低25%、20%和15%；
- 北京年平均PM2.5浓度控制在60微克/立方米以内。

CHPATER 4

第四章

4

中国能源的发展与革命

电气行业改革的艰辛之路

2015 年 4 月，中国政府发布了三项公告：一，下调非居民用城市天然气最高门站价格（15%）[1]；二，下调全国电价（约 4%）[2]；三，批准建立国家大型燃煤发电项目（500 亿元，±1100 千伏高压输电工程，线路长度约 3500 千米，额定输送容量 660 亿千瓦）[3]。

中国会继续对电力和天然气市场实行统一规划吗？中国是否会延续 1978 年以来的电气改革？根据 2015 年 5 月以前收录的相关信息，本章将回顾中国的能源改革历程。

背景简要

中国的能源价格改革发生在快速工业化和更广泛的经济体制转型（即计划经济转向市场经济）这一背景下，着实加大了改革推进的难度（APERC，2008）。中国能源体系的某些特征对能源的基础价格产生了持续影响，即：

[1] 国家发改委宣布自 2015 年 4 月 1 日起调整中国非居民用天然气城市最高门站价格。这一举措包括增量气最高门站价格每立方米降低 0.44 元（15%），存量气最高门站价格每立方米提高 0.04 元（1%）。

[2] 电价下调自 2015 年 4 月 20 日生效。国家发改委（NDRC）官网表示，因煤炭价格下跌，并受煤电价格联动机制影响，全国燃煤发电上网电价平均每千瓦时降低约 2 分钱（约 4%），工商业用电价格平均每千瓦时降低约 1.8 分钱（约 2.5%），以降低企业成本，促进经济增长。

[3] 作为"新疆电力走出去"的重要一环，准东煤电项目得以开建。项目包括一个 500 亿元投资支持的燃煤电厂和一条新疆准东至中国东部的 ±1100 千伏高压输电线路，总长约 3500 千米，预计额定输送容量 660 亿千瓦，消耗 3300 万吨煤炭，实现总产值 30 亿元。

- 能源蕴藏情况不同，地理位置分布多样；

- 区域发展类型不同，能源产业差异明显；

- 不同时期政府政策存在变化。

例如，中国使用天然气的发展历程表明了不同地区的能源蕴藏量对其影响。

中国中央政府的能源价格政策力图反映大范围内经济、社会和政治目标的实施情况。与此同时，地方政府通常尽可能地促进地方经济发展。行业协会致力于联合政府，实现行业利益，个体企业试图提高市场份额和利润，以确保财务活力。

然而，当前能源价格的失调反映了定价系统的不全面性。例如煤炭定价传统意义上不包括外部成本（如环保费用），以及其他隐形开支（如折旧和出于安全考虑的费用），但现在却将这些费用包含在内。

发电行业的定价政策

在过去的 20 年，电力行业的定价改革持续推进，延续到今。

1985 年之前，中国政府对发电项目和电价实行统一建立、统一管理的模式，这一政府主导的价格体系设定了末端用户的用电价格，却没有涉及上网用电事项。中国经济飞速增长的同时，电力工业却发展缓慢，造成严重缺电的现象。

因此，中国在 1985 年通过设置多级电价来集资建立发电厂，该政策用以促进发电行业的多方投资：

一，根据集资建厂的贷款和利息调节电价；

二，电价与燃料、交通运输价格挂钩，以反映成本变化；

三，2 分钱 / 千瓦时的费用用于投资建立当地发电项目。

虽然该政策的实行极大地促进了电力行业的发展，但却引发了无序的电价系统，新电厂新电价，老电厂旧电价，不同电厂和发电机组间的电价也有不同。久而久之，电价也随之增长，进一步提高了建厂成本，阻碍了电厂的建设和发展。

从 1997 年开始，中国采用经营期电价的测算方法，从原来的还本付息转向基于"社会发展水平"平均成本的电价政策。同时规范发电项目的投资回报率。

2002 年，发电企业从原有电力网络中分离出来。在这一改革下，独立的发电厂设定了电力网络的上网电价，该网络规定了末端用户的用电价格。除上网电价由政府和新能源发电项目控制以外，同一地区的发电厂采用统一的上网电价基准，并逐步延伸至现有电价体系下的其他发电企业。

2008 年，电力输送和配置上没有相应的定价机制，而是通过政府制定的上网电价和用电价格间的价差来反映。

然而，不同地区上网电价和用电价格间的价差具有显著差异。末端用户用电价格分阶而定，中国政府根据不同用电类型制定了不同价格，包括：住宅用电，非居民照明用电，商业用电，工业用电，大工业用电，农业生产用电，贫困地区农业排灌用电。农业和住宅用电受相关政策保护；例如提高住宅用电价格必须经过听证会的同意。

过去为刺激经济发展，高能耗的大工业用电户可以享受政府的优惠电价，近些年为实行差别电价取消了该项优惠政策。

燃煤发电定价事项

现今能源定价体系的完善取得了较大进展，越来越趋于市场导向。例如，煤炭作为中国主要的能源，在 1993 年和 1994 年第一次实现了自由定价，但对能耗大户而言，则采用政府引导的热能煤合同价。中国对煤炭价格的控制有所放宽，但电价仍调控严格，这使得煤电价格联动机制无法顺利实施。2005 年 5 月，在第一次启用煤电价格联动机制后，中国的电价上涨了 2.52 分钱/千瓦时；2006 年 5 月，第二次根据联动机制调整电价，电价上浮较小，但用于燃煤发电的煤炭合同价却超出了调控范围；第三次电价调整因高通货膨胀而延期。而后，为影响电力的供求需要，煤炭价格和电价之间的关系日益得到突显。

2009 年取消了热能煤合同价，煤炭价格完全市场化。

深化能源体制改革是"十二五"规划的重点，主要围绕以下四个领域（Xu and Chung, 2014）：能源定价系统，国有能源企业和政府职能，再城市化，及"走出去"政策。

但仍存在三大问题：一，除煤炭外，能源市场价格在上游和下游行业都未出现实质的竞争现象；二，能源价格无法反映资源浪费和环境污染在内的成本；三，没有输配电的定价机制，不利于电力经济网络的发展和结构优化。

现有的末端用户电价机制效率较低，不同用电类型价格不同，扭曲了成本结构，因此电价不能准确反映和调节发电行业的供求平衡。

市场效率

2012 年 7 月，中国实行阶梯电价制度。

2011 年，国家发改委出台《关于完善太阳能光伏发电上网电价政策的通知》，7 月前后，已通过审批的光伏发电项目电价分别为 1.15 元 / 千瓦时和 1 元 / 千瓦时，这标志着光伏发电产业在国内市场的一个真正开端。

之后，2013 年国家发改委办公厅出台了《国家发展改革委办公厅关于进一步降低农产品生产流通环节电价有关问题的通知》。

然而，这些政策都不能缓解电网企业不参与太阳能和风能电力产业的问题，自 2002 年以来，这些电网企业在末端用户零售方面已占据市场垄断地位。因此，电力行业需要一次结构转型。

2015年3月15日出台的电改九号文

2015 年 3 月 15 日出台的这份文件《中共中央国务院关于进一步深化电力体制改革的若干意见》推动了电力市场的改革进程。该意见由中共中央和国务院共同签署，视为上一部关于电力体制改革的国务院 5 号令（2002 年出台）

的配套文件,进一步提高了改革的重要性。在燃煤占近50%的火力发电行业中,该文件的出台铺垫了电力行业的改革深化之路。

该文件指出,改革应关注减少排放,提倡利用可再生能源,提高能效,同时保证电力安全指标紧跟电力服务快速增长的需求。

同时,该文件列出电力行业政策应遵循的五项基本要求:

· 保证电力安全的需要;

· 积极利用市场机制;

· 稳定非工业部门的用电费用,如住宅和农业用电;

· 注意节能减排,提高可再生能源和分布式发电的利用;

· 实施更好的管理、规定和规划,加强监管机构和机制的职能。

除上述要求外,中国政府计划将批发业务引入电力市场,放开发电厂和高耗电用户间的商业来往,最好也能畅通微电网和分布式能源的商业模式渠道。因此,以下几项政策值得重视:

A. 电网运营商改革

通过设定基于合理的利润和成本的输配电价格来改变中国电网运营商的收益模式,该模式的改革在深圳(2014 年 10 月 23 日出台的《深圳市输配电价改革试点方案》)和内蒙古西部都已实现。继 2002 年电力改革后,电网运营商不再为末端用户制定用电价格。基于政策实施细则,电网运营商将被纳入收入上限监管制度,同时致力于能效提高,为分布式可再生能源发电企业取得更多的发展机会。新政将深圳市电网企业试点的监管方法推广至全国范围。值得注意的是,深圳电网企业试点方案于 2014 年 10 月 23 日出台,第一次测评期从 2015 年 1 月 1 日持续到 2017 年底。因此,九号文的颁布不是深圳方案测评的结果,而应视为中央政府为加速电改进程,覆盖更多区域而出台的政策。

B. 多方电力零售商

政府意将多方电力零售商纳入工业园、高新技术产业园、社会资本投资运营公司、分布式发电末端用户（及能源服务企业，这利于可再生能源企业的发展）、水和煤气工程及发电厂等销售市场。

C.零售业竞争

该政策允许用电大户绕过电网企业，直接和发电厂协商电价。文件要求供求双方接受政府审查，并且此项目只适用于能效较高、符合环保规定的用电企业。

D.高电耗用户市场

根据各方在节能减排方面的表现，政府公布了一份包括高电耗用户、电力零售商和发电商在内的名单，名单内的任何单位均可加入电力市场并参与议价。不符合节能减排条件或处于淘汰行业的单位不享受此待遇。

E.无特定末端用户市场

政策不适用：住宅用电、农业用电及社会重要服务行业用电。

针对上述政策的综合评价

2002年，改革第一步是实现电网运营商和发电商间的脱钩。十多年后，中国通过九号文将批发业务引入电力市场，很明显这一文件勾勒了未来几年电力市场去管制化的设想。但该文件仅适用一些普遍条款。中国政府希望在未来几年里出台和深化更多关于监管方面的细则。充实细则和付诸实践方面需要政府下更多的工夫。关于这些问题的解决，笔者从自身观察提出了以下建议：

电力市场去监管化还需一段时间。在九号文中，住宅用电、农业用电和社会重要服务行业用电价格统一由中央政府制定，但就上述用户如何及何时加入电力市场的问题没有给出答复。

节能减排表现达标的标准由何部门如何制定？

如企业未达该标准，后续应采取什么措施？文件中指出未达标准的企业不得参与市场活动及议价，那么这些企业会选择继续依靠老旧技术制造更多的非绿色 GDP 吗？

新工业用户和新市场机制下发电商的电力供求不包含在九号文 D-13 条款下的中央统一规划中。那么，何部门可决定新发电厂的动力燃料类型呢？这项决定同时也将影响能源结构和减排情况。

在完善省内及跨区域电力交易体制的同时，文件中未提及的地方政府也会成为电力市场的参与者吗？如果是的话，地方政府又如何运用这一预设标准呢？

电力规划应充分考虑环境承载力。文件强调了发电行业规划中的环保责任，但仅凭预设标准就可缓解环境承载力问题吗？

外资进入的机会：国家发改委经济体制综合改革司高级官员王强告诉中国日报记者，是否允许外资进入中国的电力分销市场取决于国家考量的"负面名单"。负面名单将明确外资受限的具体领域。其他领域外资可随意进入，不用经过政府审批[①]。现今，中国政府通过外资投资行业的指导目录来完成相关工作。政策制定者表示，政府将积极探索负面名单的管理模式。根据国家发改委改革计划的预计，中国将进一步优化能源结构，提高发电行业中可再生能源的使用比例。2014 年，我国发电装机总容量（中国发电量）已达到 13.6 亿千瓦。

① http://usa.chinadaily.com.cn/business/2015-03/26/content_19912857.htm

天然气行业的定价政策

APERC (2008) 显示，天然气行业实行平行定价体系：1995 年前后建成的项目分别适用旧价和新价。1997 年的改革指的是"新线路新价格"，利用成本加成法计算末端用户价格。

开采地至用户的天然气运输包括：

- 勘探；
- 气田开采与净化；

- 长途管道的气体运输；

- 城镇用气的汽化和配送。

天然气价格由以下三个部分构成：

- 气田开采与净化费用（项目费用，多种税费，包括资源税，增值税，城市建设及教育成本在内的附加税，所得税和整体利润）；

- 长途管道运输公司的管道运输费（由消费地区，管道内径，运输距离，税费和利润决定，其中税费包括营业税，海关税和所得税）；

- 当地政府的配送费。

目前，这三个部分很大程度上由当地政府和为政府提供咨询服务的企业管理（尤其是国家发改委）。国家发改委确定天然气出厂价（开采和净化费用），管道运输价由当地物价局经国家发改委审批后报出。通过成本加成的方法，省及直辖市的物价局直接制定配送费。

开采费分为三类：配额价（天然气销售配额内）；配额外价格；制造商和消费者自由协商的控制价。

2005 年，国家发改委出台《发展改革委关于改革天然气出厂价格形成机制及近期适当提高天然气出厂价格的通知》。这一政策将使用天然气管道运输网络用气的住宅用户、商业用户和小工业用户联系起来。气价分类简化为化肥制造，工业用气和城镇用气三类。同时，天然气出厂价根据出厂产品的状况和末端用户的价格承受力决定。第一类天然气指油气田开采的计划价格或临近计划价格下的已有天然气产品，以及其他计划内的天然气产品，这些产品包括四川油气田，长庆油田，青海油田和新疆油田（除西气东输管道项目的天然气外）；现有计划内天然气分布在大港油田，辽河油田和中原油田。第二类油田指所有其他类型的天然气。

简而言之，天然气价格受政府引导，同时政府会根据气井品质的不同进行定价。随着中国天然气供给的进口比例不断增加（2014 年达 32%），国家发改委意图将天然气价格与其替代品的市场价格联系起来，因此市场价格的反映极为重要。现有价格和增量价格的转换会生成一个公平的操作环境。天然气改革的最终目标是实现市场机制下原料价格的自由化；这意味着天然气城市门站价为反映替代品的价格变动要不断地调整价格，并且政府会继续监管天然气的配送费。

中国的能源革命

　　坚持节约优先、立足国内、多元发展、保护环境，加强国际互利合作，调整优化能源结构，建立安全、稳定、经济、清洁的现代能源产业体系。全国人民代表大会"十二五"（2011—2015）规划第十一章关于"推动能源生产和利用方式变革"中如是写道。中国国家主席习近平多次在公开场合谈到"十三五"（2016—2020）规划，明确指出：为保障国家能源的长期安全，需要寻求能源生产和消费的新方式。考虑到中国能源最新的发展情况，以及之前计划的线路和实际结果，这节试图预测并评价未来计划中会遇到的因素，以及中国的能源政策是否会经历一场革命。

中国长期能源结构的发展

　　中国庞大的人口规模需要经济高速增长的刺激，但能源消耗密集型产业的较低水平难以转变，确保能源安全的压力不断增加，面对严重的环境污染，减排前景不容乐观，尤其在经历过 2013 年重度雾霾之后。国际社会努力控制气候变化，不断向中国施压，要求减少碳排放。面对全球能源资源竞争加剧的现状，中国必须加快调整能源生产和消费结构。中国能源长期发展的调节因素必将影响国际能源市场、政治、经济的形势，尤其在亚太地区。

　　为确保中国能源安全，总体规划应：

- 向"非清洁能源"的使用逐步施压，如煤炭的使用；

- 快速发展清洁能源和新能源，特别是气态资源，主要包括常规天然气、非常规煤层气、可燃冰、页岩气、非生物成因气、加工过的甲烷、煤气、液化石油气、人工气、氢气等；
- 及时开发核能项目；
- 大力开发国外能源。

我们总结了不同研究机构关于中国能源前景的研究结果，如表 22 所示。

表22 中国社会科学院中国能源组，中国工程院和国务院发展研究中心的研究结果总结

能源		2014 年	中国社会科学院中国能源组（2035）	中国工程院（2050）	国务院发展研究中心（2020）
化石燃料	煤炭	66%~67%	48%	35%~40%	25 亿 ~33 亿吨
	石油	22%	14%		
	天然气	5%	14%		
非化石燃料	核能	7%	7%	>15%	
	水电	1%	9%		
	生物能源	~1%	3%		
	其他		5%		

国务院发展研究中心

国务院发展研究中心《中国能源综合发展战略与政策研究》报告分析了能源需求和发展的三种方案。基于精准的能源战略和相关政策，报告指出2020 年之前，主要能源为 25 亿吨至 33 亿吨的标准煤，平均值为 29 亿吨标准煤。这之后，能源结构需求将发生重大变化。总能源消费中，交通部门和建筑的能源利用率从 2000 年的 35% 以下上升到 2020 年的 57%~75 %。

中国科学院能源战略研究组

中国科学院能源战略研究组完成了《中国能源 2050 年中长期战略技术发展研究报告》，给出了从 2010 年到 2050 年的战略路线图。报告指出，战略发展的目标应该更具前瞻性，以确保从化石能源到可持续能源的平稳过渡。基于 2005 年的数据，化石能源消费的增长不应超过 50%，能源消费作为国内生产总值的单位应等于中等发达国家，非水电可再生能源应占总能源的 25% 以上。

中国工程院

2008 年中国工程院开展了中国中长期（2030 年，2050 年）能源战略发展研究课题。研究指出，中国能源的可持续发展战略是"科学、绿色、低碳"：合理的煤炭安全生产量应控制在 35 亿吨标准煤内。2050 年前的煤炭消费比重应降低到 40%，甚至应低于能源消费总量的 35%，核能和可再生能源的总消费量应占能源消费总量的 15% 以上。

中国社会科学院中国能源组

中国社会科学院中国能源组预测的 2035 年前中国能源结构中各能源消费比重占总消费的情况如下：煤炭、石油、天然气分别为 48%；14%；14%；核能 7%；水电 9%；生物能源 5%；其他能源 3%。

如上所述，中国能源结构的中长期调整将对国际能源市场和政治经济发展产生巨大影响。

习近平提出中国能源革命的五点要求

金融和经济事务部于 2014 年 6 月 13 日召开了领导小组第六次会议，中国国家主席习近平领导学习了关于中国国家能源安全战略的研究，并发出号召推广"中国的能源革命"。

习主席的讲话指出，中国在能源发展上取得了很大成绩，但仍然面临着许多挑战，如能源需求的巨大压力，能源供应的诸多限制，能源生产和消费对生态环境造成的严重损害，能源技术普遍落后的水平等。我们将从国家发展和安全的战略角度，调整形势，抓住机遇，探索符合能源大势的道路。

讲话明确描述了中国能源革命的大背景，定义了能源安全的三个 E（3E），即能源、经济和环境。在平衡能源、经济和环境的前提下，为了国家能源安全，中国开始实施能源革命，并希望解决低碳发展中遇到的各项问题，如经济发展的能源瓶颈问题；同时改善能源产业技术落后、能源发展与自然环境低相容性的境况。

习近平就推动中国能源生产和消费革命提出了五点要求：

第一，关注能耗，坚持节约能源的首要地位。推动能源消费革命，抑制不合理能源消费。坚决控制能源消费总量，有效落实节能优先方针，把节能贯穿于经济社会发展全过程和各领域，坚定调整产业结构，高度重视城镇化节能，树立勤俭节约的消费观，加快形成能源节约型社会。

第二，关注能源供给。坚持推进中国的环境保护和多元化发展。推动能源供给革命，建立多元供应体系。立足国内多元供应保安全，大力推进煤炭清洁高效利用，着力发展非煤能源，形成煤、油、气、核、新能源、可再生能源多轮驱动的能源供应体系，同步加强能源输配网络和储备设施建设。

第三，推动能源技术革命，带动产业升级。立足我国国情，紧跟国际能源技术革命新趋势，以绿色低碳为方向，分类推动技术创新、产业创新、商业模式创新，并同其他领域高新技术紧密结合，把能源技术及其关联产业培育成带动我国产业升级的新增长点。

第四，逐步利用市场规律实现能源体制革命。即推动能源体制革命，打通能源发展快车道。坚定不移推进改革，还原能源商品属性，构建有效竞争的市场结构和市场体系，形成主要由市场决定能源价格的机制，转变政府对能源的监管方式，建立健全能源法治体系。

第五，关注能源安全。全方位加强国际合作，实现开放条件下的能源安全。在主要立足国内的前提条件下，在能源生产和消费革命所涉及的各个方面加强国际合作，有效利用国际资源。

评价能源需求、能源结构与市场化方面的中国能源革命

能源需求

习近平指出，能源革命是为了确保满足中国的能源需求，这一点完全可以理解。自 2011 年以来中国以 1017.81 百万亿英热单位的惊人能源消费量成为世界上主要的能源消费国，这一数字在过去的几十年里稳步增长，同时也将继续随着中国国内生产总值的不断增加而增加。事实上，一些经济学家提出了 GDP 增长与能源消费之间的因果关系——高水平经济增长引发高能源需求，反之亦然。而且，当分析中国庞大人口数量的数据时，我们发现，根据 2011 年的数据，中国的人均能耗为 1.69 吨油当量，略微低于世界平均水平的 1.79 吨油当量，是经济合作与发展组织（OECD）成员国 4.27 吨油当量的 40%。因此有预测称，中国已经是能源消费大国，并将继续在未来几年实现从发展中国家向发达国家的转变，这一过程伴随着能源消费量的不断增加。考虑于此，能源结构的保持和优化不仅是经常性的需求，也必将是未来规划的一部分。

能源结构

为了满足这一巨大且不断增长的能源需求，中国的能源结构仍主要是化石燃料。最新数据显示，煤炭仍是主要的能源来源，占中国能源总耗的 66%。因中国相较于进口产品而言，更多使用国内能源产品，所以煤炭一直倍受青睐。煤取自当地且产量丰富，目前估计中国拥有世界第三大探明煤炭储量，达 1145 亿吨。煤炭用作中国工业化的燃料，中国的煤炭消费量已升至每年 4 亿吨，等于 2014 年其他国家和地区的总产量[1]。这带来了中国巨大的环境成本，据估计目前煤占中国二氧化碳排放量的 70%，二氧化硫排放量的 90%，粉尘排放的 70% 以及氮氧化物排放量的 70%。中国的电力生产高度依赖不

[1] EIA,. (2015). *International Energy Statistics*. Eia.gov. Retrieved 24 July 2015, from http://www.eia.gov/beta/international/data/browser/#/?pa=8&tl_id=1--A&c=ruvvvvvfvtvvvv1vvvvvvfvvvvvvvfvvvsu20evvvvvvvvvvvvvvvvuvg&ct=0&f=A&cy=2013&sta rt=1980&end=2013

可再生的化石燃料，其消耗留下了很深的生态足迹。然而，煤炭产自当地的好处在于其可继续作为电力的主要来源，但仅适用于特定条件下。

最新规划要求优化煤炭的使用，为实现这一目标相关部门做出了大量努力。中国的煤炭通常采自西部，运到东部进行加工，目前的趋势是在西部建立更多的工厂和基础设施，将燃料运至电力生产和消费中心。此外，关停和取代规模较小、效率不高且不符合环保标准的煤厂。2014 年关停总产量 330 万千瓦的煤厂，替换为用中国西部气化煤作动力的天然气发电厂。此外，技术方面，碳足迹减少技术取得进展。尤其是在煤炭脱硫技术和碳捕捉技术上成果显著，前者有助于减少煤燃烧污染物排放量，后者可储存二氧化碳，使其不进入大气。可以看出，许多激励机制正在得到发展，以优化燃煤发电的效率并减少对环境的影响。鉴于中国能源结构中煤炭长期的显著地位，最新规划实施的煤炭优化政策应延续到未来"五年计划"中去。

其他化石燃料，包括石油和其他液体以及天然气分别构成了中国能源结构的 22% 和 5%。这些燃煤不具有煤炭产自本地的特点。事实上，中国曾经是一个石油净出口国，但生产多年来都没有跟上，中国现在成为石油净进口国，是当今世界上最大的石油进口国，2014 年每天平均进口 610 万桶。此外，中国就增加天然气进口与土库曼斯坦签订协议。中国当前主要的天然气供应商是土库曼斯坦（2013 年中国天然气进口量的 88% 来自土库曼斯坦）、缅甸和俄罗斯。

当前形势下，中国石油对外依存度 64%，天然气对外依存度 32%。中国是这两类能源净进口国，共同占中国能源对外依存度的 11%。然而，由于这些资源在中国目前产量不足，政府希望与进口国签订协议以保障中国第十二个"五年计划"的能源安全，这些协议应延续到下一个"五年计划"中去。

国际合作除可获得石油和天然气外，也可以促进中国能源技术和能源产量的提高。2011—2015 年的计划高度重视海洋石油开采，海洋石油产量已升至中国总产量的 20%。同时，有消息称中国和美国的页岩油气储量相当。但提取页岩油气需要广泛的技术知识，中国此刻还不具备。尽管如此，中国国有企业一直在澳大利亚、加拿大和美国进行投资，以获取页岩油气开采方面的技术知识。

例如，中海油（CNOOC）收购了加拿大企业尼克森，后者主要参与页岩油气相关项目，2013年参与交易量高达151亿美元（包含尼克森28亿美元净负债）。以前的"五年计划"只是简要地提及了页岩油气，却没有给出明确的目标。考虑到中国已有的能源资源和获得的相关技术，海洋石油的开采肯定会在将来成为"五年计划"的一部分，并极有可能在未来占据更大的比重。

能源多元化似乎是解决化石燃料诸多不便的方案之一。上文还未提及的能源，也有助于小规模内调节总体能源结构。水电、核电和可再生能源（如太阳能和风能），分别占能耗总量的近8%、1%和1%。某些能源领域上的投资较为丰硕。2013年初在增加了十个容量大于1000万千瓦的反应堆后，中国核电产量大幅增长，2015年4月中国的核电装机容量已超过2300万千瓦。此外，截至2015年4月，中国企业还在建设一个2300万千瓦的发电项目，这将超过全球1/3的核电产能。同时水电产量也在不断增加。随着2012年三峡大坝的建成，中国已经成为世界上最大的水电生产国，发电量达8.94亿千瓦。2020年有望提高水电装机容量，从2.8亿千瓦上升至3.5亿千瓦。尽管水电的排放量低，大坝施工还是会对环境造成大规模破坏，同时会引起周边民众的不安。风能和太阳能方面的大规模投资也在顺利进行中。2020年，中国希望将风能和太阳能的产量从2013年的9600万千瓦和1500万千瓦提高至2亿千瓦和1亿千瓦。2014年，中国以890亿美元的投资额成为可再生能源的第一大投资国。这项巨额投资合乎逻辑，因为这些可再生能源产于中国，留下极少的碳足迹。同时，多元化和清洁技术的使用也在最新规划中予以重视。中国也将继续多样化发展，以减少能源碳足迹，这一点也将延续到下一步计划中。

市场化

之前的"五年计划"涵盖了前文提到的大多数因素，市场定价却还是一个新课题。习近平已经在各级政府层面上提及，未来的中国要实行产业革新。过去，许多低效、重工业依赖能源补贴维持生产。然而，国内外对重工业品内部需求正不断下降，中国正进入利用经济有效的手段平衡生产和消费的阶段。为了停止给处于通货膨胀的能源密集型产业提供燃料补贴，政府可以实施能源部门的自由化。因此可以确定，习近平将推动"分阶段监管定价系统"到"以市场为基础的能源定价系统"的进程。如果这一变动出现在下一计划中，将会成为中国能源革命的重要部分。例如，2014年上海建立了石油产业的未来市场。天然气管道行业和电网公司已分离于现有的垂直一体化能源系统，拥有独立的所有权和经营权。

结论

正如上文所析，习近平倡导的能源革命包含了往届领导人已经落实的许多因素。事实上，大多数想法已经出现在过去的"五年计划"里，并将在今后的计划中得以考虑和重视。然而，创新因素的比重将会增加，如开始页岩气的开发和实现能源部门的自由化。页岩气曾是北美能源革命的发端，能源自由化又会对中国能源公司的经营方式带来巨大变化。尽管前后几年的计划较为相似，但在下一个"五年计划"里，中国的能源革命将会得以实现。因此，为了满足中国能源的长期可持续需求，需要各方认真仔细地落实这些政策。

CHPATER 5

第五章

5

中国对外能源政策历程

国家能源安全和对外能源政策的影响

本部分重点论述自 1987 年改革开放以来，能源政策随安全重点转变的变化。从中国能源工业的发展历程中，我们可以看出，中国的能源安全实现了从能源自给到能源依赖的过渡，政策重点从传统能源转向可再生能源，从而改变了中国的国际能源合作模式。

改革开放前，鉴于大庆油田产量高，国内能源需求小，国际贸易额低的缘故，我国能源产业长期以来一直处于自给自足的状态。然而，随着需求量的增加，这一状况有所改变，1996 年第八个"五年计划"里，中国成为石油净进口国，从而开始了中国能源政策的调整。从那时起，中国的能源安全逐渐与能源安全的经典释义相一致——可承受价格下稳定的能源供应。

鉴于国内供应不足，确保国外能源供应成为中国能源安全的重要部分。通过两种方式实现：一是通过海外项目合作获得股权石油，二是直接从国际石油市场进行购买。这两项措施构成了"走出去"战略，并成为中国对外能源政策的核心。早在 1993 年 12 月，时任中央财经事务领导小组主席的江泽民就提出了利用海外石油和天然气来补充国内的能源供应，成为中国能源企业进军海外的发端。因此，能源安全由传统的能源自给自足变为以供应为核心，这些进一步提高了中国能源的对外依存度。

"走出去"的过程中，中国的三大能源公司中国石油、中国石化和中海油积极参与越来越多个分布在不同地区的海外能源项目。因为直接交易石油进口量的缘故,中国的石油对外依存度急剧上升,如图 33 所示。

1993—2013 年间,股权石油方面,中国石油的合作伙伴数量从两个增加到 100 多个,海外项目超过了 70 个,主要分布在北非、中东,中亚和加拿大。这些合作项目包括石油天然气勘探、石油炼制和运输业务以及销售。中国石油已通过"走出去"政策成为上游、中游和下游的综合性能源公司。中国石化的海外业务主要集中在中东和中亚地区。2003—2007 年签订的新合约经营价值由 18 亿元增长至 193 亿元,增长率达 81%。自 20 世纪 80 年代,在中央政府的允许下,中海油作为中国第三大能源公司,与多个世界顶级跨国公司如壳牌、康菲石油跨国集团、美国国际集团等从事海上油气勘探合作项目,垄断了海上国际能源合作业务。

中国能源安全形势的变化也影响了对外能源政策的形成和实施。我们把这个过程分为两个阶段。

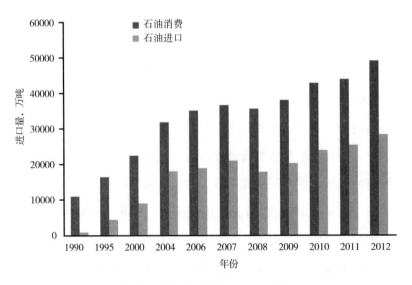

图 33 石油进口状况,1990—2012

石油为中心的能源供应安全

与丰富的煤炭储量相比，中国的石油和天然气较为稀缺，尤其是在人均数量上，政府对此表示担忧。勘探世界各地的石油和天然气是三大公司走出去的重要目标。例如，1997—2007 年间，中国石油在非洲、中亚、俄罗斯、南非、中东、亚太地区和苏丹的穆格莱德盆地设立了五个石油和天然气战略投资区，同时收购了哈萨克斯阿克纠宾公司，开发卡拉科莱斯油田和委内瑞拉的英特甘博油田。截至 2007 年底，中国石油在超过 29 个国家开展了海外业务，石油产量达 8939.2 万吨，天然气产量为 170.6 亿立方米，输送管道超过 6100 米。中国广泛勘探世界各地的石油和天然气，这扰乱了西方能源公司现有的工业分布。外界指责中国进行新殖民主义，抵制中国"威胁"世界能源的行为。

国内石油短缺的压力越来越大，来自国外抵制的压力不断增加，中国已经意识到加强国际交流和增加能源供应来源的重要性。近几年中国的能源安全政策已经做出了一些调整，通过改善市场条件、促进技术交流、与发达国家和发展中国家分享经验来寻求平衡各种能源的渐进式发展道路，并重视可再生能源的利用。2006 年 7 月 17 日，时任中国国家主席胡锦涛在八国集团首脑会议上阐述了中国的新能源安全愿景，包括节约能源，能源使用多元化，保护环境，与其他国家互利合作，为世界构筑稳定、经济、清洁的能源供应体系。这种新的能源安全愿景对中国对外能源政策和实践产生了巨大影响。

注重环境保护的能源安全

1998 年，中国建立了节能自愿协议制度。环境保护成为第十个"五年计划"最重要的目标之一。然而，由于经济的快速增长刺激了能源的需求，这一制度没有产生任何的具体措施来加强环保力度。直到"十一五"规划，能源安全和环境保护的关系才再次得以重视。2004 年出台了《节能中长期专项规划》，提出了有关节能的十项措施，包括优先节能，制定行业法规，税收，定价和投资政策等，来提高社会环保意识，增加可再生能源发电的比重等。2005 年通过的《中华人民共和国可再生能源法》为民营企业进入可再生能源市场提供了一系列的指导。之后，2008 年通过修订法律来提高建筑和运输行业的节能贡献。为发展可再生能源，国家于 2007 年出台《中华人民共和国可再生能源中长期规划》，其中包括能源的国家建设计划和核电的中长期计划（2005—2020）。"十二五"规划明确了 2015 年前非化石燃料占能源总消费量 11.4% 的发展目标，结果实际消费比例为 12%，超出了原定计划。

评价

总而言之，中国能源安全的转型主要表现在两个方面，即开放性和多样化。开放意味着中国能源产业的经济取向由自给自足转向积极参与国际能源贸易和能源勘探。多元化意味着以石油为中心的能源安全已经取代了发展各项能源的政策。同时，能源需求安全重于能源供应安全。

对外能源政策的转变

中国的对外能源政策最初指获取能源利益的一系列外交活动，也可称为能源外交，"走出去"政策是其核心。中国与中东、中亚、俄罗斯和非洲的利益相关方的官方会谈奠定了中国国际能源合作的基础。但随后主要参与者和政策措施逐渐从单纯的能源外交转向对外的能源政策。

能源外交方面，以中沙关系为例，建交以来高层互访频繁。中国多名高层官员出访沙特阿拉伯，其中包括外交部部长钱其琛（1990）、国务院总理李鹏（1991）、国务院副总理李岚清（1993）、国务委员罗干（1995）、国防部部长池浩田（1996）、国家主席江泽民（1999），国务委员吴仪（2002）和国家主席胡锦涛（2006）。此外，沙特阿拉伯高级官员及各行代表也已访问中国，覆盖外交、金融、商业、能源、法律、农业、电信、教育和卫生等行业。两国合作成果颇丰，其中包括王储阿卜杜拉2006年第一次到访中国时签署的《石油天然气矿产合作协议》及其他四份文件。

中国与邻国俄罗斯和中亚国家在能源勘探和管道建设方面进行了合作。根据中国石油和哈萨克斯坦佩特罗公司签署的阿拉山口输油管道建设的基本原则，2003年6月和2004年5月，中哈分别签署了《关于共同开展中国—哈萨克斯坦石油管道分阶段建设投资论证研究的协议》和《关于在油气领域开展全面合作的框架协议》。2006年4月，中国与土库曼斯坦签订《中华人民共和国政府和土库曼斯坦政府关于实施天然气管道项目和土库曼斯坦向中国出售天然气的总协议》，2007年7月在北京又签署共享契约。中俄能源合作源远流长；早在1996中国和俄罗斯就签署了《中华人民共和国政府和俄罗斯联邦政府关于共同开展能源领域合作的协议》。随后，江泽民主席于2001年7月访问俄罗斯，签署了《关于开展铺设俄罗斯至中国原油管道项目可行性研究主要原则协议》。同年，朱镕基总理和俄罗斯总理卡西亚诺夫正式签署了《中俄关于共同开展铺设俄罗斯至中国原油管道项目可行性研究工作的总协议》。此外，胡锦涛主席2007年访问苏丹，中国政府非洲事务特别代表刘贵也频繁到访苏丹，与当地政府共同应对达尔富尔危机。

随着"走出去"政策的发展，中国的对外能源政策已经演变成国际合作的两种模式。

从政府导向型到企业导向型

中国的合作方式逐渐脱离以往的政府导向型，能源安全也愈加趋向多元化。早在20世纪70年代和80年代，政府间合作仍是交流的主要方式，中国与欧洲、美国就可再生能源及相关技术进行过沟通。然而，这种交流的方式还远远不够，中国需要向发达国家学习先进的技术和管理模式。清洁发展机制（CDM）是京都议定书下三个灵活的实现机制之一，是推进可再生能源的最佳方法之一。在这种机制下，项目级合作由发达国家出资并在发展中国家实施。项目产生的核证减排量（CERs）用来帮助发达国家履行京都议定书下承诺的限排或减排义务，同时协助发展中国家可持续发展。

审批过程中，一个项目最初由发展中国家的相关部门批准；中国的审批部门是国家发改委，然后再提交联合国清洁发展机制执行委员会等待进一步批准。关于清洁发展机制的实施，政府是唯一的审批者，由各能源企业负责具体实施。表23列出了2010年9月至2012年1月开始实施的几个大型项目（不属于122个清洁发展机制项目）。

表23　部分中国清洁发展机制项目

项目名称	减排类型	项目所有者	国外合作方	年减排近似值（吨二氧化碳当量）
新疆温泉135兆瓦水电站项目	新能源和可再生能源	国电新疆水电开发有限公司	Eco资产管理公司	632614
吉林省风电场二期工程	新能源和可再生能源	镇赉风电有限公司	联合碳资产有限公司	101774
风电场二期工程	新能源和可再生能源	中广核风电有限公司	碳资产管理公司	110737
河北福宽生物油脂项目	新能源和可再生能源	河北福宽生物油脂有限公司	国际清洁基金	212224
佳木斯风电项目	新能源和可再生能源	国电风电开发有限公司	瑞士维多石油集团	117789
27兆瓦余热回收项目	节能和提高能效	东方希望重庆水泥有限公司	梅斯菲尔德碳资源公司	154178
江苏大丰风电项目	新能源和可再生能源	中电大丰风力发电有限公司	日本节能投资公司	314050
通辽市建华2号300兆瓦风电场项目	新能源和可再生能源	东协和新能源有限公司	俄罗斯天然气工业营销与贸易有限公司	633268
四川华电木里河立州水电站	新能源和可再生能源	四川华电木里河水电发展有限公司	英国瑞碳有限公司	1110980

来源：http://www.cdmpipeline.org/cdm-projects-region.htm

2006年7月3日，第一批清洁发展机制减排项目获得联合国清洁发展机制执行委员会审批（表24）。截至2013年1月，中国已经获得了2980个项目，占全球清洁发展机制项目的 52.1%（图 34），中国的项目增长率排名世界第一。

表 24　清洁发展机制委员会批准项目

减排类型	年减排近似值（吨二氧化碳当量）	总减排比例	项目数量	总项目比例
新能源和可再生能源	10410193.4	10.91	86	72.88
HFC-23 分解	58813446	61.66	10	8.47
节能和提高能效	5673085	5.95	8	6.78
甲烷回收	4307347	4.52	8	6.78
氧化亚氮分解	14726343	15.44	3	2.54
代用燃料	1300233	1.36	2	1.69
垃圾焚烧	150158	0.16	1	0.85
造林和再造林	0	0	0	0
其他	0	0	0	0
减排总量	95380805.4	100	118	100

数据：2006 年 7 月 3 日至 2009 年 6 月 12 日

来源：http://cdm.ccchina.gov.cn/web/item_data.asp?ColumnId=63

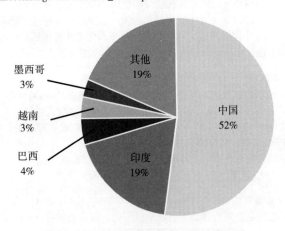

**图 34　联合国清洁发展机制执行委员会
在不同国家批准的清洁发展机制减排项目（2013 年 6 月）**

来源：www.chinawe.org/news/news_933.shtml, January 8, 2013

从双边到多边

如上所述，政府主导的合作突显了现世能源观，特别强调了地缘政治的影响。近年来，特别是 2006 年八国集团首脑会议上胡锦涛提出了中国的新能源安全观后，中国注重可再生能源发展和多边合作的多边能源合作想法受到了世界的广泛关注。毕竟，通过积极参与国际组织来共享信息，中国可以更好地维护世界能源共同安全保障体系下的能源安全。从几个主要的全球和区域性组织中，我们可以看到 21 世纪的中国正积极参与国际能源机构的合作（表 25）。

表25　中国参与的多边能源组织

亚太经合组织

自 1989 年亚太经合组织成立以来，能源一直是部长级会议的重点问题。1993 年后，中国一直积极参与能源部长级会议、能源工作组和亚太能源研究中心的工作。2004 年 11 月，中国国家主席胡锦涛建议应加强能源讨论，以提高能源效率，处理贫困和发展可再生能源问题。2010 年第九届能源部长会议通过了福井宣言，开展低碳示范城镇项目，并将于家堡金融区提名为天津市滨海新区的先行示范区。2014 年的 APEC 中国年，中国与其他 APEC 国家寻求更大的合作空间。

东南亚国家联盟（东盟）

多边能源合作因共同区域的能源安全而变得更加重要。2004 年 6 月 9 日第二十二届东盟能源部长会议和第一届东盟与中日韩能源部长会议建议应加强能源供应和合作，为中国与东盟的能源合作提供新渠道。2010 年 1 月 1 日启动的中国—东盟自由贸易区无疑将扩大地区间的能源合作。2010 年 9 月，中国—东盟研讨会在成都召开，会议就新能源和可再生能源技术进行讨论，专家们认为两地区在新能源和可再生能源领域合作潜力巨大。

海湾合作委员会（GCC）

GCC 成员包括阿拉伯联合酋长国、阿曼、巴林、卡塔尔、科威特和沙特阿拉伯，构成了主要的石油出口基地。虽然中国与 GCC 的每个成员国都有频繁的双边接触，但尚未与该组织进行多边合作。自 2004 年 7 月推出 FTA 谈判以来，中国与 GCC 成员国在许多领域已达成共识。2009 年 2 月，中国国家主席胡锦涛会见了 GCC 秘书长阿蒂亚，他指出自贸协定会为两地区带来长期利益，应尽快签署该协定及其他相关文件。

国际能源署（IEA）

中国尽管不是国际能源署成员，但 1996 年就开始与该组织进行接触，当时国际能源署执行主任访问中国，同意签署能源合作谅解备忘录。因此，双方经常进行沟通交流，允许年度报告加入有关中国的章节。中国参与国际能源署的部长级会议、研讨会等。中国—国际能源署展开了普遍性合作。直到 2009 年 10 月 15 日，中国才加入国际能源署，参与机构内部政策协调。

评价

随着越来越多的中国国企和私企成为能源行业的参与主体，寻求发挥更大的作用，中国现在更倾向于加入多边合作的能源机构，不仅体现在可再生能源领域合作，也体现在传统能源合作形式，如与海湾合作委员会的合作。

中国对外能源政策实施的 20 年回顾

自 1993 以来，中国成为成品油净进口国，1996 年以来，成为原油净进口国。在 20 世纪 90 年代初，为了贯彻中央政府的政策"充分利用双方的资源和国内国外市场"，中国开始实施"走出去"战略，积极开展国际能源合作。如果视 1993 年为中国国际能源合作的第一年，那么 2012 年就是中国对外能源政策实施的第 20 年，紧接着是 2013 年中国共产党第十八次全国代表大会的召开。因此，2013 年是中国能源国际合作的过渡年。本部分回顾中国过去的 20 年里的国际能源合作历程，讨论分析合作成果、影响的政策因素及国际合作的双面影响。

成果

经过 20 多年的探索和发展，中国的国际能源合作取得了显著成效，进入了快速发展阶段，成果如下。

一是能源外交取得显著成效。通过高水平的政府访问和各种峰会，中国已与世界多个国家签署政府间能源合作协议，与几个国家级机构签订能源合作框架协议，这为中国开展双边和多边国际能源合作奠定了坚实的基础。

中国已经在全球 33 个国家开展了超过 100 个国际油气合作项目。确定了五大国际油气合作区：拥有苏丹项目的非洲地区；拥有阿曼和叙利亚项目的中东地区；拥有哈萨克斯坦项目的中亚和俄罗斯地区；拥有委内瑞拉和厄瓜多尔项目的美洲地区；拥有印度尼西亚项目的亚太地区。因此，中国一直在全球范围内开展油气资源的国际合作。2012 年，中国油气公司的海外油气利息超过了 1.0015 亿吨石油当量。

中国已经建立了一个对外能源交易系统。能源进出口贸易体系最初建立

① CIEESS report, 2013

The China International Energy Cooperation Report 2012/2013, Center for International Energy and Environment Strategy Studies of Renmin University (CIEESS), Energy Outlook

Magazine and the China Council for the Promotion of International Trade (CCPIT)

在石油、液化天然气、天然气、煤和铀领域上，主要靠油轮进行运输，用管道和铁路进行补给，并通过多种形式进行交易，如库存、石油期货和国际市场的长期采购协议①。中国能源企业的国际竞争力大大提高。经过 20 年的发展，中国的能源企业不仅掌握了国际能源合作项目的运作模式，同时也积累了丰富的资本运作、合同谈判等经验，不断提高海外投资的效率，日益增长自身的实力和国际影响力。2012 年，中国石油和中海油进入加拿大市场就是中国企业实力的写照。

中国的国际能源合作在渠道、内容、机制和合作伙伴方面经历了很大变化。总体而言，这些变化主要有以下三个特征。

能源类型

能源合作类型继续多样化。中国的国际能源合作主要始于石油和天然气，逐渐扩展到各个领域，包括天然铀、煤炭、电力、风能、生物燃料、节能、能源技术与设备等。

国际能源合作参与者

国家级和非国家级组织均参与了国际能源合作，如国际政府和非政府组织。中国已与近 40 个国家建立了双边能源合作机制，如中美能源政策对话、中美石油天然气论坛、中俄能源谈判机制、中哈能源小组委员会、中日能源部长对话、中印能源论坛等。合作国家已经从最初的周边国家和中东地区，逐渐扩展至中亚、非洲、美洲、大洋洲的大部分地区，覆盖世界主要能源生产国、消费国和途径国。

合作方式

中国正在探索更多的创新合作方式。一方面，这种创新表现为"金融要素的不断介入"，即中国利用外汇储备实现能源和金融上的国际能源合作，如近年来的各种石油贷款协议。另一方面，它代表了"合作参与者不断增加下，民营企业的参与"，就是形成多层次、多国家、多所有制的合作体，该体制主要基于国有企业，资源生产国和投资国的非国有企业从中参与。

政策背景

中国能源领域国际合作迅速发展的主要原因在于中国能源安全观的根本性转变。换言之，中国对外能源政策的基础已经发生了根本变化，从现实主义转到自由主义。这种转变不仅体现在政府对能源安全和能源企业经济活动的官方政策上，而且表现在允许中国参与国际能源合作的转变上。能源安全观念的变化引发了一系列能源多边合作的趋势，促使能源企业逐步进入市场，从而打破"政府先为企业铺好道路"的能源合作固有模式。

1959 年大庆油田的发现是石油工业在中国能源发展史上的一个转折点，一时间实现了石油的自给自足，并少量出口。然而，随着 20 世纪 90 年代经济的持续发展，中国的石油需求开始回升。1993 年，中国成为石油净进口国，由此，石油对外依存度逐年增加。中国的石油工业已经与国际石油市场有着千丝万缕的联系。同时，中国以煤炭为主的能源消费结构增加了碳排放，在巨大的国际压力下，中国正在积极开展各项减排措施。在发展的过程中，中国的能源安全观从最初的能源独立变为现在的能源相互依存，从关注能源供应安全变为注重能源需求安全。这表明，中国参与国际能源合作的方式也相应发生了变化，从现实主义转向自由主义的能源安全观。

自改革开放以来，中国能源安全观的演变可以分为两个阶段。第一阶段是改革开放初期（始于 1978 年），从能源自给向国际能源合作发展。第二阶段是"十一五"（2005—2010）期间，从关注石油和天然气为主的能源供应安全转向多能源平衡发展的能源安全观。2006 年，胡锦涛在圣彼得堡八国峰会上提出了新的能源安全观。到目前为止，中国能源安全观已经从孤立的国家能源自给安全逐渐转向 3E+S 能源安全观：关注能源、经济、环境和社会保障，重视多种能源共同发展的能源安全观。期间还经历了 4A 能源安全观，4A 指符合四项要求：供应充足，价格适中，方便运输和环境容许。党的十八大后，能源安全观又与整个社会的生态文明联系越来越密切，并着眼于可持续发展。

随着能源安全观的不断变化，21 世纪初，中国开始积极参与国际多边能源合作。与此同时，随着中国进一步扩大对外开放和世界能源形势发生深刻的变化，中国参与的多边和双边合作呈现快速增长的趋势。到目前为止，中国已经与世界上主要的能源生产国、消费国和国际能源署（IEA）建立了交流与合作关系。目前，中国是国际能源论坛（IEF）、世界能源理事会（WEC）、亚太经合组织能源工作组（APEC）、中亚区域合作能源协调委员会和其他多边能源合作机制的正式成员。此外，中国是能源宪章的观察员，与国际能源署密切合作。中国还与海湾合作委员会、石油输出国组织、欧盟和其他区域组织建立了日常合作机制。

国际影响

自 20 世纪 90 年代初以来，中国经历了 20 多年的国际能源合作。绝大多数带来了积极影响，但也存在一些问题。

积极影响

中国的国际能源合作和发展有助于建立中国负责任的大国形象。20 年来，中国已经实现了从最初的交流与对话到举办了一系列会议、发起多项倡议的转变，从交流信息缺乏到与全球主要的组织建立能源数据信息的畅通渠道，从国际能源系统的追随者到成员国，并能够参与和影响国际规则的制定。中国的国际能源合作不局限于走出去的中国企业在油气行业上中下游的企业并购，也包含了中国在能源发展理念创新上日益增长的影响、协商机制的整合以及国际能源问题的解决，等等。例如，中国提出和实现了关于各类区域性多边合作机制的一系列新举措，并对世界产生了广泛的积极影响。中国企业实施"走出去"政策时，也积极帮助能源紧缺国家建设各种能源配套设施。例如，在乍得建立炼油厂，以改善当地人民的生活，这也反映了中国企业的社会责任感。

此外，中国的国际能源合作和发展在一定程度上改变了地缘政治生态。以能源关系为例，中国国际能源合作加强了主要国家和地区的政府间和民间组织的交流，促进了双方相互理解，缓解甚至消除潜在的地缘政治危机。以亚太经合组织为例，2012年，亚太地区的形势最为紧张，而中国的多边和双边能源合作弱化了地区冲突，为未来合作的光明前景奠定了基础。

2012年是中国的选举年，标志着一个新的政治周期的开始。大国关系上，美国等西方发达国家在地位和影响力上的传统势力不断受到新兴国家的挑战。没有任何国家或组织能够单级领导国际秩序，因此参与多边外交和国际机制的行为越来越可取。中国的崛起和对美"再平衡"战略日益凸显了亚太地区在全球政治中的重要地位。国际制度结构变化的背景下，中国面临周边冲突升级的问题。亚太地区是中国与周边国家在磨合期内建立正常国家关系机制，控制冲突的最重要试验场。亚太地区多边能源合作的顺利开展，不仅为所有地区提供了有利的局势，也为构建和谐、繁荣的亚太新秩序提供了坚实的物质基础。

最后，中国的国际能源合作与发展重塑了国际关系。国际能源合作依赖于能源产品，能源的第一属性是商品，这一点已经满足了共同的商业利益。因此，着重于特殊商品属性的能源合作，不太可能受到意识形态和冷战后思维的干扰和影响。在这种情况下，建立在国际能源合作基础上的国际关系将超越各国之间文化、政治制度和经济发展的差异。能源净出口国、能源消费国和能源途径国将全面发展这种国际关系。经过20多年的实践，取得的最大成果是，由于中国在能源勘探、生产、运输和消费上的贡献，国际关系的世界秩序变得更加稳定。

负面影响

发展过程中也存在一些问题，而如何解决这些问题将是中国对外能源战略的重点。最关键的是中国企业"走出去"政策后的潜在政治风险,因为"走出去"势必会受到全球、地区间以及地缘政治经济的影响。"走出去"的步幅越大，意味着相互依存的程度越高，也意味着中国的前景面临越来越大的风险。在这种情况下，中国的国际能源合作可能对中国对外关系产生负面影响,正常的双边关系也会被贴上"能源"的标签，增加了伙伴国家对中国"资源掠夺"的怀疑。缅甸、哈萨克斯坦、俄罗斯、拉丁美洲和其他资源丰富的国家，从私企到政府，反对中国企业的声音不绝于耳。此外，在经历最初的蜜月期后，中国庞大的经济、人口和能源需求使得世界上的其他国家更难主动接受中国。

政策建议与展望

在过去 20 年成功的基础上，实现负面影响到积极影响的转变需要更高层次的系统规划。具体来说，我们提供以下三项建议。

增强正确理解中国能源安全政策的互信

面对中国巨大且不断增加的能源需求，许多国家都显示出了担忧和焦虑。作为世界上最大的能源消费国，中国使用常规能源外交来满足能源需求的行为常常受到外界的批评，这不利于发挥中国在全球和国际区域中的能源合作作用。因此,中国需要对外做出更多的努力，解释并承诺坚持互惠互利的原则，保证外部能源稳定政策的有效实施。

谨慎细微地协调各国之间关系

能源的特性使得世界上主要的能源出口国、消费国和途径国对能源安全问题十分敏感，为了保证自身的能源安全，激烈的竞争也时有发生。此外，中国与周边国家存在领土争端，保证领土完整的核心利益和油气资源的战略特质使问题变得更加敏感。在某种程度上，这种复杂而敏感的国际关系制约了中国在全球和区域的能源合作作用。

鼓励工商企业和非政府组织参与全球和区域性双边及多边能源合作

工商企业和非政府力量的参与在一定程度上削弱了合作的政治敏感度。企业也是大多数能源合作计划或倡议的最终实践者，区域合作机制和政府层面的合作协议也必须依靠企业和机构实施。因此，鼓励企业甚至是民间力量的参与是中国顺利开展能源国际合作的重要措施。

结论

2013 年后，中国的国际能源合作面临着更大的机遇和挑战。机遇方面，随着全球日益关注气候变化问题，一场新的工业革命已经发生，它将彻底改变世界经济和人们的生活方式。新工业革命的基础是能源革命。这种能源革命标志着人类生产和能源使用类别的改变，如 2009 年开始使用页岩气的转变，从传统油气发展到非常规油气资源的使用。这种能源革命也改变了人类生产和使用能源的方式，如使用分配能源。能源革命也将大大拓宽国际合作的领域。

挑战方面：能源安全观从老需求到新需求，从纯能源到更高层次 3E+S 能源安全（福岛事件后，将经济、环境和社会安全结合起来）的转变，中国对外能源政策不仅承担着保障中国传统能源安全的重担，也从满足传统能源安全延伸至符合其他国家的安全规范。中国对外能源政策实施过程中还存在一些问题。行政审批程序繁重，合作协调机制有待完善，国际能源合作资金需要国家财政政策更强力度的支持。中国需要建立合作风险保护和应急机制；需要建立和完善外部能源交易系统以避免能源价格波动的影响（表 26）。

表26 中国"走出去"政策面临的主要挑战

国家政策	如何看待国有企业在"走出去"战略中的作用：凭借政府背景，国有企业在进行海外投资时可以获得强大的政治和财政支持，但是，他们也会在一些资源储备国遭受歧视性待遇。在实施"走出去"战略中，如何减少国有企业因背景而招致的困难是一个值得关注的课题。
	如何协调"走出去"的过程中企业间的利益冲突：中国在资源进口方面仍然实行严厉的限制措施，这意味着民营企业与国有企业相比将面临更多的困难。同时，在"走出去"战略的实施过程中，中国能源企业在海外市场间的竞争给中国带来了一定程度上的负面影响和损失。对于未来的发展，协调和避免各类企业的利益冲突是"走出去"战略的过程中的一项紧迫任务。
	如何评价技术整合和创新问题：中国企业走出去的一个重要目标是获取高端资源开发利用技术。在实施"走出去"战略的过程中，这一目标能否得到有效实现？在获取技术方面还存在哪些困难？中国企业在资源开发领域的技术优势和劣势是什么？
"走出去"政策的连续性和安全性	如何协调持续的海外扩张和稳健经营间的关系：近年来，中国企业的海外扩张发展迅猛，一些中国企业已迅速成为国际能源市场的主要参与者。与此同时，企业的负担在不断增加，尤其体现在负债问题上。根据中国三大石油公司的股票价格表现，盈利水平有待商榷。在此背景下，大型海外并购和扩张是发展的长久之计吗？如何保证和促进企业持续的盈利水平？针对这些问题，中国企业已经考虑并制定相应的经营计划了吗？
	如何解决海外扩张所引起的文化多样性问题：中国海外扩张的目标国家已从经济不发达，政治局势不稳定的第三世界转移到发达国家。不同国家的企业管理风格和制度与中国相比大有不同，如加拿大和美国。中国企业已逐步接受国际财团的发展模式，协调不同文化下的不同企业不可避免。中国企业实施"走出去"战略时，如何保持自己的风格，如维持目标国家中国员工的较高比例。中国企业有制定相应措施来应对文化多样性现象吗？
	如何应对海外扩张地区政府和人民的问题：中国企业在"走出去"过程中面临的社会关系问题越来越多。由于能源资源与国家经济安全关系密切，地方政府和人民对国外企业利用当地能源的现象十分敏感。在这个过程中，中国企业不仅要考虑项目的经济成本，还要考虑当地的政治和社会成本。中国企业在应对这些问题上有一定的经验和措施吗？
国际能源治理	参与全球能源治理和改进国内能源结构：作为主要的能源消费者，中国在决定国际能源问题结果上发挥着越来越重要的作用，要求中国参与全球能源治理的呼声也愈加强烈。在参与全球能源治理时，中国需要调节自身的能源战略要求。因此，完善国家能源使用结构对中国参与能源治理的效果具有显著影响，同时也可以引导中国企业未来实施"走出去"战略的走向。中国政府改善能源结构的目标和措施是什么？在非常规天然气和新能源利用技术不断完善的背景下，如何才能实现这些目标和措施？
	如何解决能源定价问题：中国工业界一直谴责高价购买石油的行为。作为未来世界最大的石油和天然气进口国，中国要求拥有能源定价权合情合理，但面临两大困难。首先，中国国内没有可以在相关领域自由流通的石油种类；其次，中国作为油气主要进口国，很难实现为国际市场制定基准的愿望，日本就是一个典型的例子。在这样的背景下，中国政府是否有详细的计划来解决国际能源价格问题，使其能够更准确地反映世界的供求关系，更好地符合中国的利益？

双边能源关系	美国能源独立的影响：在美国，非常规油气资源的有效开发使该国的能源独立成为可能。全球工业和学术界高度重视可能引发全球能源革命的所有事件。中国人民大学国际能源战略研究中心就这一主题举行了国际学术会议，讨论了以下议题：中国如何看待美国的能源独立？美国的能源独立将对中国造成怎样的影响？
	关于中俄能源合作：近年来，中俄能源合作进展显著。石油领域取得重大突破，中俄原油管道建设具有重大的战略和经济意义。然而，为促进天然气的发展和合作，中国企业在获取俄罗斯上游产业资源上仍存在巨大困难。如何理解中俄能源合作的历程和现状？影响中俄能源合作的因素有哪些？中俄能源合作的未来是什么？

中国的区域对外能源政策

正如之前所言，中国尚未完全建立起其对外能源政策体系。不过，由于中国经济是投资导向型的并正处于快速增长当中，能源是保证经济可持续发展的必要条件。1959 年，中国在黑龙江省大庆发现了第一个大油田。直到 1993 年，中国才开始感到能源紧张；从那年起，中国成为一个石油产品进口国，随后在 1996 年又成为石油净进口国。石油供应安全已不可避免地成为中国发展最大的绊脚石。

然而，这更多地是一种看法而非现实。为了满足 13 亿人口的能源需求，中国的石油公司在过去的 20 年里一直在发展寻找石油的战略布局，而这或多或少得到了中国政府的帮助。在某种程度上，我们可从"走出去"战略中窥见中国对外能源政策的雏形，而"走出去"战略正是在 20 世纪 90 年代末中国刚成为石油净进口国时提出的。

不论是在中东、非洲、美洲、欧洲、亚太、中亚或是俄罗斯，中国都在能源合作上面临着种种机遇与挑战。长期展望则是，能源合作将会有明确的战略目标、可行的方针以及高效的政策，更多利益相关者会加入其中，并以多样化的形式进行合作。在此背景下，中国的能源外交关系将得到进一步强化而非弱化，同时对伙伴利益将更为包容。

迄今为止，能源外交是中国对外能源政策的核心内容，而"走出去"则是实施政策的关键手段。作为世界上最大的发展中国家以及发展最快的新兴国家，中国始终竭尽所能地发挥其影响力，充分利用其在资金、技术、制成品及劳动力等方面的相对优势。中国一直积极参与到各大区域组织当中，如上海合作组织（SCO）、中非合作论坛（FOCAC）、东盟10+1（ASEAN 10+1）等，以此与各能源资源国发展合作能源关系。

中亚地区与俄罗斯

在资源富有国家所在的各大区域里，中亚地区与俄罗斯是中国的首选。这不仅是因为这些国家是中国邻国，且同为发展中国家，同时还因为中国将它们置于外交优先位置，俄罗斯也特为中国的主要战略伙伴。

机遇

自苏联解体以来，相对有利的国家关系为能源关系奠定了一定基础。发展与中亚国家及俄罗斯的能源关系对于满足合作伙伴的政治经济需求同样具有重要意义。中国是世界上最大的能源消费市场之一，而中亚及俄罗斯则是世界上最大的能源资源地区之一，两者结合是不可避免的。将能源作为商品、能源管道作为链条发展经济，经济繁荣则有助于稳定地区安全及社会安全，这就是习近平主席所提出的新丝绸之路经济带倡议的关键目标。

挑战

世界强国以及主要能源进口国之间对里海能源资源的地缘战略竞争日益激化。与拥有大批高质量油田的中国公司相比，西方国家的跨国公司在该地区更具影响力。中国在该地区秉持"有所作为"的对外政策理念，可是由于中亚国家有可能政权不稳，各种族群体及宗教派别之间的差异导致该地区社会矛盾根深蒂固，这一切都给中国带来了种种地缘政治风险。

政策选择

为了能够充分利用上海合作组织（SCO），中国将推动 SCO 多边能源合作机制转变，如建立 SCO 能源俱乐部，并将落实新丝绸之路构想，其政策核心包括以下五点：政策沟通、运输连通（公路、铁路、航空）、贸易畅通、货币流通以及民心互通。此外，中俄天然气管道、铀资源共同利用、跨国电力网络建设以及煤炭勘探开采合作等都是中国在该地区能源政策的重点内容。

非洲地区

在很长一段时间里，中国都将非洲视为其石油进口的一个主要来源。事实上，北非在中国石油进口名单中仅次于中东。中国所采取的不干预非洲国家内部事务的政策深受非洲国家好评。而中非合作论坛的建立及高效运行也为中国参与中非能源关系提供了一个重要平台。中国在非洲的石油开发取得了重大进展：一方面是通过贸易获取能源，另一方面则是通过直接接管或与其他跨国能源公司联合收购非洲的本地公司来生产股本油。

机遇

目前有许多地区已探明蕴藏着丰富的油气资源，有待勘探生产。非洲经济展示着强劲的增长势头，2012 年增速约为 5%，撒哈拉地区甚至超过了 5%，与世界上其他地区对比显著。毕马威（KPMG）统计数据显示，非洲国家的国内生产总值（GDP）到 2020 年可望达到 2.6 万亿美元。非洲的基础设施正不断升级，外国直接投资也日益增多。政治与经济方面的积极转变也给非洲带来了巨大的投资潜力：通过出口获得资本积累，非洲的政治经济形势一直在逐步改善。资源产业、金融业、能源业、通信业及其他非资源产业的发展同样显著。中东地区曾是传统燃料的供应中心，而北美地区则是非传统燃料的新供应源，非洲则成为重新平衡这两大地区的能源格局的一个重要变量，同时非洲也平衡了 OPEC 与非 OPEC 国家之间的能源格局，由此可见非洲在全球能源体系中发挥着愈发重要的作用。

挑战

尽管中国与非洲国家在煤炭、石油、天然气以及诸如太阳能等非再生能源的合作上取得成功，但仍然存在着一些不确定性。语言和商业实践上的文化多样性是双方需要克服的主要障碍。部分非洲国家的政治动乱仍将持续很长一段时间。非洲经济体仍不稳定，而且其中大部分仍处于欠发达水平，资金技术短缺，基础设施落后。以上种种不利因素皆有可能增加投资成本。与早期进入非洲的其他国家相比，中国并无竞争优势可言。

政策选择

中国应以一种互利体面的姿态进入下游的炼油化工领域，从而更多地参与非洲的基础设施建设。

中东地区

海湾地区拥有着最为丰富的油气资源，这对于中国能源安全来说具有重大战略意义，因此，加强与海湾地区国家的油气合作可谓是"重中之重"（图35）。

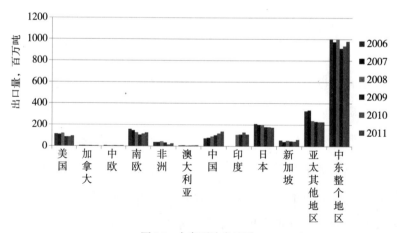

图35　中东石油出口国

机遇

将近 20 年来，中东地区一直是中国最大的油气供应商。中国主要是与科威特、沙特阿拉伯、伊拉克、伊朗、卡塔尔、阿曼、安哥拉以及阿拉伯联合酋长国进行能源合作，这些国家与中国的能源关系自伊拉克战争以来便处于稳定、持续的状态。2012 年，科威特超越卡塔尔成为中国进口液化天然气的最大供应商。伊朗已签署协议，对华石油出口提高至每日 50 万桶，尽管由于美国的经济制裁，伊朗无法直接从中国获得收入。2013 年中国从沙特阿拉伯进口石油也增加至每日 117 万桶。中国已与阿拉伯联合酋长国建立了一个长期全面的战略合作机制，深化勘探开采工作，参与储备设施建设，开展油气精炼方面的多层次合作，并尝试在能源交易中使用双方国家货币进行清算。

挑战

北美地区的能源依赖正改变着美国对中东的政策。中东已进入了一场新的地缘政治游戏，并且该地区各国间存在着冲突。而阿拉伯之春、美国"再平衡"战略以及伊朗核危机都激化了各种族群体和宗教派别间存在的种种矛盾。

政策选择

中国应谨防扩大与中东能源合作可能带来的代价，以免类似于伊拉克战争和利比亚内战的冲突再次爆发。为避免冲突发生，中国应为相关机构拟好反危机措施。

美洲地区

北美地区（尤其是加拿大）和部分拉丁美洲国家储藏着丰富的石油资源。近年来，中国从巴西、厄瓜多尔等拉丁美洲国家，特别是委内瑞拉，进口大量石油，在能源合作上取得了重大进展。拉丁美洲已成为了中国石油进口的第三大供应商。自中国石油和中海油于 2012 年底成功接管加拿大的页岩气田后，加拿大成为了开放其上游资源给中国公司进行对外直接投资的少数发达国家之一，尽管这也引发了中国会否从加拿大土壤中提取到其他原料的相关争论。美国在墨西哥、加拿大及拉丁美洲的外交政策中扮演着一个相当重要的角色。因此，我们很有必要对中美能源关系进行判断。

机遇

自 1978 年首位美国代表詹姆斯·施莱辛格出访北京以来已有 30 多年了。中美能源合作经历了四个阶段：探索、停滞、团结发展、深化及制度化。致密油气、页岩油气等非常规能源的开发速度已加快。中美天然气贸易以及清洁能源技术转让使得中美关系破冰，两国合作步入正轨，目前正快速进行能源结构调整、发展清洁能源、保护石油安全和提高能源效率。

挑战

中美两国皆是世界上最大的能源生产国和消费国，既有着相同的利益与责任，也面临着相同的挑战。然而，由于中美两国实行不同的政治制度和经济制度，并且处于不同的社会发展阶段，双方的合作目标并不总是一致的。比如说，美国有三大目标，即能源安全、生态可持续性以及商业利益。美国政府希望中国政府能够开放其上游资源，而中国则希望美国能够提供核心技术和深海钻井技术。不过，两个合作伙伴都给予了对方充分的信任。

政策选择

迄今为止，中美两国签署了数十份政府间与部门间合作协议，这其中包括关于地质储量的两大双边机制、美中政策对话和可再生能源论坛、全球核能合作伙伴三大多边机制、国际先进生物燃料论坛等，中国、印度、日本、韩国及美国的五位能源部长进行会晤签署公约，还建立了中美清洁能源联合研究中心以及一个企业合作平台。不过，如何在政府及企业的共同努力下通过制度化实施双边合作政策是关键所在。

亚太地区

亚太地区是指东南亚及南亚国家。中国在此能源关系中的主要考量是，这些国家与中国陆地接壤或隔水相邻，并且它们都是东南亚国家联盟（ASEAN，简称东盟）的成员国。

机遇

中国与东盟的"10+1"合作对于中国与其邻国外交有着重要意义。积极扩大与东南亚及南亚国家的能源合作有助于缓解南海主权争端。中缅油气管道工程则是中国在亚太地区对外能源政策的一个范例。该工程于 2013 年 11 月圆满竣工，预计能够实现每年运输 2000 万吨原油的既定目标。亚太地区的能源资源储量相对丰富，生产油田与中国东部邻近，而中国东部是主要的经济发达地区，不仅能源消费巨大，而且对东盟经济体开放。此外，到中国大陆的陆路运输比水路运输更为便捷安全。

挑战

该地区的部分国家对中国持抵触情绪，在南海诸岛主权以及中国在南海区域进行油气开发的权利和利益等问题上一直存在争议。

政策选择

考虑到外交战略要求及地理环境，中国必须重视发展与亚太地区的能源富有国家的合作关系。此外，同样储藏着丰富煤炭及铀资源的澳大利亚亦十分渴求与中国发展能源合作关系，并已为双方未来合作打下了良好基础。

欧盟

中国与欧盟在能源上既是合作关系也是竞争关系。中国与欧盟在稳定国际市场及新能源研究开发上是合作伙伴，而在寻求获取俄罗斯和里海的油气资源时则为竞争对手。

机遇

中国与欧盟之间的长期合作保持着一种相对稳定的模式。大部分欧盟成员国在 CCS 等清洁能源生产技术方面领先,具有相对优势。由于许多欧盟成员国都是国际能源署的成员,一部分还是 G8 集团成员国,在国际能源管理机构中相当活跃,因此欧盟对国际能源规则的制定有着重要影响。欧盟有着统一的经济和市场,采取共同的能源战略,这对于中国企业来说也是很有吸引力的。

挑战

自 2008 年金融危机以来,欧盟在对华贸易上的保护主义倾向越发明显。欧盟不仅对中国光伏产品实施高惩罚性关税,还试行征收航空碳税。欧盟在气候变化等问题上的强硬立场导致其与中国之间关系不相调和,使得双边能源合作受损。

政策选择

在与欧盟传统的能源合作中,中国更偏向采取股票收购和联合项目的方式,而在技术合作层面,双边合作往往是以高水平对话或论坛的方式进行。

评论

如果我们用能源安全的 4A 性来对上述六大区域进行分析,我们则能够理解为何中国会在其对外能源政策上优先选择中亚和俄罗斯。从可用性来看,中亚地区和俄罗斯能源资源储藏量庞大。从可取性来看,该地区的油气资源皆可通过管道、铁路、电网、水路等途径直接运输到中国。比如,俄罗斯向中国输送液态天然气安全又高效。从可购性来看,中国在与邻国合作中能够灵活地采取易货、贷款、预付等不同的交易方式,无须总以美元结算,人民币和卢布同样适用，并且更为经济实惠。从可接受性来看，鉴于中国与该地区有着亲密的民族关系，相对而言中国人民更能接受该地区的能源资源。倘若没有土尔库斯坦提供的天然气，那么北京冬天的空气质量可能会比燃料源尚未从煤炭转为天然气时还要糟糕。基于上述发展趋势，我们认为，图36所显示的此前的石油进口区域结构将逐渐改变。

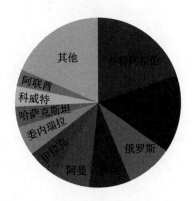

图36 中国从各地区进口石油情况

来源：中商智库（数据）

尽管发达国家和中国一样都是能源消费国家，但是中国也会重视发展与其能源关系，共同维护全球能源市场稳定。作为能源消费国家，发达国家在多方面拥有相对先进技术，用以进行能源勘探开采、能源储存及成本节约、新能源开发、环境保护和现代商业管理实践。

CHPATER 6

第六章

6

"一带一路"倡议下的能源合作

全球石油市场的重大转变及其对中国的影响

石油价格自 2014 年底以来持续下跌，因而 2015 年被认为是非同寻常的一年，这对于中国而言更是如此。其非同寻常之处在于能源史上的第三大转变，即从化石能源，如传统的石油、天然气和煤炭，转投到新能源和可再生能源；再者就是从 2014 年 11 月起油价下跌，并在 2015 年再创新低。

从化石能源到非化石能源的转变始于北美页岩气革命，较之能源史上前两次转变（即从木柴到煤炭的转变以及从煤炭到石油的转变），此次转变所需时间更长。然而，与此前两次能源转变相似的是，此次转变将从根本上改变全球能源结构。几乎所有国家都必须在这个过程中有选择地制定政策，并开展一场新能源导向型的能源革命或战略转型。

煤炭仍是中国的主要能源。能源革命将基于目前的全球能源情况及调整需要而启动。

中国专家对低油价的看法[①]

中国石化顾问委员会副主任张康表示：从 20 世纪末到 21 世纪初，全球的油气供需情况经历了根本性的改变，供需情况从原来的平衡状态转变到

①在 2015 年 1 月 11 日，这些能源领域的专家们相聚在中国人民大学国际能源战略研究中心，共同分析此次油价下跌的原因、对全球能源状况的影响以及中国的战略对策。国家能源局共设有 16 个研究咨询基地，中国人民大学国际能源战略研究中心则是其中之一。此次座谈会由中心主任许勤华教授主持，会上代表们针锋相对，各抒己见，围绕能源与国际冲突、国际关系、国内能源与国际能源、中国能源如何国际化等议题展开了激烈讨论。

135

供应明显过剩。而在世界油库不断经受战争动荡的背景下，一直存在着油气产能过剩的情况，对炼油能力过剩的战略储备也已大大增加。自21世纪初开始，非常规油气资源特别是页岩油和页岩气都快速增长，而这影响到了常规石油的价格，导致其价格暴跌。我们正经历着一场从化石能源到非化石能源的能源结构转变。我认为，在21世纪两者同等重要，而并非非化石能源正在取代化石能源。有史以来，世界经历了数次战争与和平的交替时期，而这也可从石油价格的波动中反映出来。一般来说，倘若世界石油能够处于一个供需矛盾缓和、价格轻微浮动的状态，那会有利于中国的发展。我想这样的一次价格修正对于中国的发展来说是一个更为有利的环境，我们应该充分利用它来开展中国的能源革命。

中国国际战略学会高级顾问、少将王海运表示：若将油价波动看作一种仅隶属于市场化资源配置的正常表现，这是错误的。油价下跌的原因包括地缘政治所导致的国际资本投机及放大效应。有人说地缘政治因素已不再相关，我并不认同；也有人说地缘政治因素是一种典型的"冷战思维"，同样，这种看法我也无法苟同。我们不应忽视地缘政治因素。如果我们忽视这些因素，认为它们不相关，那么我们恐怕是要吃大亏的。我认为相当有必要提醒我们国内研究界这一点。至于美国超越俄罗斯会否同样影响美国的跨国石油公司，这就得看是优先考虑短期目标还是长期目标。尽管如此，低油价时代仍将持续一段时间。在接下来的30年里，石油将仍是一种具有重要战略意义的能源，石油消费扩大是一个长期的过程，甚至需要花更长时间才能从煤炭时代过渡到石油时代，再逐步过渡到清洁能源或新能源时代。再者，从军事角度看，目前石油被大规模取代仍是遥遥无期。因此，市场将进行调整修正，不久后油价便会反弹。

国家应对气候变化战略研究和国际合作中心主任李俊峰表示：我们不能忽略低油价背后的政治因素，不过这并不是一个阴谋论。俄罗斯卢布贬值不单单是美国施加的经济制裁所导致的，俄罗斯经济对石油的过分依赖以及其糟糕的抗打击能力才是罪魁祸首。通过推广混合燃料汽车，美国、日本等国家可将其石油消耗降低40%。然而,中国及印度等国家在节能技术上发展落后,这些国家的能源消费将成为油价上升的最大因素。本土石油公司无法根据其自身的生产能力对全球市场做出预测。现在若要对石油的长期需求进行评估,那么全球发展问题也需考虑在内。全球化进程中有两大因素限制着石油发展。一是减排,在过去这只不过是虚张声势,可现在却已落到实处。二是地缘政治形势。我们切不可低估世界大国之间的地缘政治较量,石油是一种商品,其本质是不可忽略的。

中国能源网首席信息官韩晓平表示:油价的基本问题就是老革命和新革命的问题。老革命是指页岩油气革命,而新革命则是指节能技术革命。沙特阿拉伯等 OPEC 国家之所以能持续石油生产是因为这些国家在许久以前已收回成本,即使目前石油价格低于 60 美元 / 桶,它们仍会继续生产,否则就会失去市场份额。美国是页岩油气革命的发起者,因此也不会放弃生产。俄罗斯亦然。历史正不断重演,而俄罗斯可能会在某个时候带来一些变数。1929年金融危机与 2008 年金融危机极为相似,导致两者的一个原因是结构性转型的潜藏问题。1929 年金融危机发生于煤炭到石油的转型期,最后导致了经济大萧条。而最近的情况与此相似。东得克萨斯油田的发现致使全球油价暴跌,进一步推动了结构转型。随后,内燃机的需求又使得以煤炭为基础的能源结构被进一步淘汰。

新华社高级记者杨元华表示:发展、调整、不稳定、扭曲和混乱是油气市场发展的关键词。中国观点倾向于跟随西方主流媒体的步调,这是相当危险的。在分析石油市场时不应忽视金融因素,因为金融是现代经济发展的核心,正是金融决定了未来全球发展。地缘政治因素十分复杂,我们应对低油价及何为阴谋进行分析,而不可将两者混为一谈当作阴谋论来解读。现在我们可根据供求规律、竞争规则及价值规律进行分析。这三者适用于不同时期,有时其中一条作为主要参考。因此,在分析目前的问题时,我们不应过多关注供需问题,而应考虑更多因素。

中国海洋石油公司能源经济研究院首席经济学家陈卫东表示：美国的页岩油气革命改变了目前的能源结构。此次油价下跌期间，石油输出国组织（OPEC，又称欧佩克）坚持不降低价格和减少生产，并尝试维持市场。这反映了什么问题呢？显然，它们已意识到能源转型正在进行，而低油价或者油价小幅上涨可能是对石油生产国最为有效持久的保护。高油价会推动可再生能源的发展，我们也已看到了替代石油技术的迹象。一方面，美元对黄金汇率对油价起着决定性作用。数据显示，一桶石油等于1.5克黄金，变化不大。我们分别在1986年、1998年及2008年经历了三次油价波动，可并无迹象显示石油会被取代。然而，在最近这次油价下跌里，我们却看到了技术进步所带来的石油替代品或是其他会大大减少石油消费的产品的身影。这里的技术进步并非是开采及加工自然资源后提供给市场的东西，而是一种知识爆炸。另一方面，倘若中国现象不存在，那么煤炭就不会再进入到市场，也不会发生天然气放缓。中国对全球能源趋势及全球能源结构带来了实质性冲击。我们不必讨论油价、地缘政治或者中国的能源战略应如何发展等问题。我认为我们当中应有这么一群人能够关注着能源转型及文明进化问腿并琢磨一下中国在此时应当做些什么。

中国国际问题研究院下属的国际能源战略研究中心主任石泽表示：我们应该研究"一带一路"政策对能源的影响。"一带一路"政策是促进能源合作的起点。其框架涵盖了方方面面，包括能源安全、能源软环境以及能源合作制度的建设。

中国石化前总地质师曾兴球表示：中国的能源革命考虑以下四个因素：一，低碳发展成为了全球目标，而从低密度到高密度的转移也是不可逆的。二，石油、天然气以及煤炭等化石燃料仍在一次能源中占很大比例，如果我们忽视这个问题，那么我们则会遭殃。三，技术发展是发展中国家实现发展的关键。新技术将带来一个新阶段、新发展，能够决定一个国家的竞争力。中国需要在此问题上制定长期计划。四，改革是一个全球性趋势。政府改革与企业发展都应利用好低油价窗口，下决心发掘潜力、实施改革、探索潜能。改革意味着我们得彻底地改造自己，重建我们的企业架构，从思想和制度方面重新开始。特别是思想方面要从头开始，因为如果不改变想法的话，那么一切都无法改变。什么想法是最重要的呢？主要有两个想法：一是要尊重和相信市场；二是要清楚认识法律制度、法则和纪律。

对中国对外能源政策的影响

全球石油市场的巨变会在多方面改变中国的对外能源政策。

改变对外能源政策的相关理念

正如我们所见，油价当前的下滑与之前 1986 年及 2008 年的暴跌有所不同。此次油价下跌发生在一个能源转型期，是在供需基础上对常规及非常规油气（页岩/致密油气）资源上争取更大的市场份额。常规油气及非常规油气的总产量高于消费量，经济依旧疲软，尤其因为发展中经济体（包括中国）的虚弱态势正影响着世界经济，因此下行压力进一步增大。应该说，北美页岩气革命的成功是目前此次油价下跌的主要导火线，同时也正拉开新能源时代的序幕。

低油价实际上是一种新常态，在油价泡沫破裂后，油价会逐渐向一个合理价格靠拢。适应新常态低油价就是要尊重国际能源市场的经济规律。对于中国而言，倘若要在低油价新常态下建立一个新的国际能源合作制度，中国有必要本着国际能源市场经济规律的相关精神更多地推动国际能源合作。

促使中国清楚认识其在全球能源秩序中的地位与角色

石油价格走低预示着一个所谓的"大能源时代"即将到来，这使得中国在国际能源市场中更具分量。在大能源时代，煤炭和常规油气资源将不再独占鳌头，致密油气、页岩油气、煤层气等非常规油气和新能源都将蓬勃发展。核能与太阳能、风能、潮汐能等各种可再生能源方面的技术都将日益成熟。从能源开发领域来看，在大陆架油气勘探开发上的关注将会减少，而近海油气勘探开发的力度将有所加大。从能源与自然环境的关系来看，能源开发将更多地受到气候变化等因素的制约。

在大能源时代，能源大国将会重建，石油大国将不再是能源大国的核心，并将引入诸如能源供给大国、能源需求大国、能源技术大国、能源金融大国及相应的低碳大国等概念。鉴于各自在能源大国中的优势，世界上多个区域/经济体将会在全球能源权力结构中的某个领域占据统治地位。能源供给大国是指一个能源资源国在世界能源市场中拥有绝对的能源资源供给能力，比如沙特阿拉伯。能源资源国及能源生产国借助其能源供给能力在全球能源权力结构中始终处于金字塔尖的位置。能源需求大国指的是一个国家由于其庞大能源消耗量而对能源资源需求强大，拥有强大市场力，比如中国。能源技术大国指的是一个国家在第三次工业革命中拥有先进技术并对世界未来发展具有影响力，比如德国。能源金融大国指的是一个国家因拥有发达金融体系且对全球金融市场具有影响力，使得其对能源价格的影响超出预期，比如美国。低碳大国指的是，因其对能源产品碳含量的计算方法和其在碳政治中的话语权，一个国家在低碳经济秩序中有着相对权力，比如欧盟。

全球能源需求的核心已逐步从发达国家过渡到发展中国家，尤其是亚太及中东的新兴国家和地区。中国已成为世界上最大的能源消费国和原油进口国；因其巨大消费力与庞大市场，中国不仅影响着能源价格，而且也正改变着其对外能源关系。

提升中国在对外能源政策中的地位

中国石油消耗上的增多或减少以及中国经济增速对于全球石油市场的波动，尤其是油价，有着一定冲击力。当前的油价下跌也预示着两点。一，现代石油工业已经运行 100 多年，运行机制已变得复杂；任何试图操纵国际石油市场的政府或国家只能在某些特定场合（如地缘政治冲突）利用某些手段，比如说金融资本，而在世界政治经济秩序中，操纵油价最终不可避免成为一把双刃剑,带来的不过是一场不完全的胜利罢了。二,由于中国庞大的消耗量,中国在能源市场上获得了更多权力。历史上,具有最大能源消耗量的国家都变成了霸权国家,比如说木柴时代的荷兰与西班牙、煤炭时代的英国、石油时代的美国等。中国将如何通过国际能源合作来提升其在全球资源方面的话语权,且在国际政治意义上如何将其市场力转变成国力,这是值得考虑的。

因此,中国会提升其在对外能源政策中的地位。在保证国内发展的前提下,中国将加大国际投资力度,在涉及能源生产及消费的各个方面有效地利用国际资源。同时,在国际政治意义上如何将市场力转变成国力也许是中国目前面临的最大的目标和任务。

重新布置对外能源政策的战略重点

自 1993 年中国成为石油产品的净进口国以来,中国对外能源政策的重点一直是更多地参与全球事务,成为一个全球玩家。通过与世界各地主要能源生产国之间的协议,中国已逐步建立了上游勘探和开发的五个板块,也建立了一个陆上油气管道国际网络。鉴于全球能源形势的重大变化,中国对外能源政策的战略重点可能会重新布置。

第一,一个新重点是在坚持全球参与及引进新技术、资本及人才的同时着重"引进来"。第二,可能需要调整国际能源合作的战略重点。以前的战略重点是石油、天然气和煤炭等原材料的采购,现今应调整为通过国际合作的方式,加快新能源、清洁能源及低碳能源等方面的技术转移,培养累积管理经验,建设能源金融市场,以及扩大人才库规模。

总的来说,低油价时代的到来对于中国而言是一次开展能源生产及消费革命的战略契机。中国将尽力适应全球能源形势的变化,调整其对外能源政策,并在多方面加强国际合作,从而更为有效地实现能源国际化。2015 年是以创造更绿色 GDP 为目标进行能源政策调整的关键一年,是习近平主席倡导能源革命后的第一年,同时也正是在 2015 年中国向世界做出了排放达标的承诺。

中俄石油及天然气合作：地缘政治影响

历经约十年谈判后，中国与俄罗斯终于在 2015 年 5 月 21 日签署了一份长达 30 年的天然气供气协议。根据协议，自 2018 年起，俄罗斯将通过中俄天然气管道向中国出口天然气。出口天然气总量将逐年上升至 380 亿平方米，总价值为 4000 亿美元（折合人民币 2.5 万亿元）。在签署天然气协议前，中国早在 2009 年 4 月便同意分别向俄罗斯石油管道垄断企业俄罗斯石油运输公司与国有石油巨头俄罗斯石油公司提供 100 亿美元及 150 亿美元贷款，作为交换，俄罗斯需在逾 20 年内提供 3 亿吨石油。中俄原油管道于 2010 年 9 月竣工，每年向中国输送约 1500 万吨原油。我们将探讨中国与俄罗斯之间的油气合作：为何此前失败的合作突然成功了？谁是合作中的赢家？如何才能延续合作？其地缘政治影响是什么？

经济评估（双边合作）

2015 年 5 月中国从俄罗斯进口原油增加了 20%，高达 392 万吨，日均 92.7 万桶。同时，中国从沙特阿拉伯进口原油减少了 42%，仅为 39.2 万桶。俄罗斯取代沙特阿拉伯，首次成为中国最大的原油进口国。2009 年以前，俄罗斯出口中国的原油总量仅约 2500 万吨，并主要通过铁路运输，而此次中国从俄罗斯进口总量突增表明，中俄能源合作正迅速发展。

双边合作的变化不仅仅体现在交易量上，如新贷款方式等交易模式也反映了变化。此外，运输方式更为多元化，其中包括管道、铁路、公路货运、水运等。俄罗斯欢迎中国能源企业对其上游能源产业进行投资。这其中必然有某些关键因素驱使着中国和俄罗斯开展紧密合作，毕竟此前双方尤其是俄罗斯一方并无如此热切地开展密切合作。现在我们先来进行一下经济评估，看看中俄两国通过能源合作可获得何种经济效益。

英国石油公司（BP）发布的数据显示，截至 2013 年底，俄罗斯已探明的石油储量已达 127 亿吨，占据全球储量总量的 5.5%，其石油生产以 1.3% 的增长率逐年递增，已达 5.21 亿吨。此外，俄罗斯已探明的天然气储量为 3.13 万亿立方米，占据全球储量总量的 16.8%，其天然气年生产增长 2.4%，达 6.05 亿立方米。显然，俄罗斯是一个能源资源丰富的大国，也是世界领先的油气生产商和出口商。

在俄罗斯方面，能源安全意味着有足够的外国消费市场来购买其油气从而获取资本。众所周知，俄罗斯约 30% 的预算收入来源于其油气销售。俄罗斯目前的能源安全有两点核心：一是拥有一个国际油气市场；二是将其出口重点移向亚洲，因为亚洲地区是全球最大的能源消费区，有中国、印度、日本及韩国等主要油气消费国。近年来，俄罗斯的欧洲市场需求减少。比如说，俄罗斯所供应的天然气在欧盟天然气消费中的比重已从 2003 年的 45% 下降至 2012 年的 31.9%，跌幅明显。在这种形势下，俄罗斯开始更多地重视向东出口油气。

因此，俄罗斯在 2014 年发布了其 2035 新能源战略，大致提出 2035 年应达到的新战略目标。俄罗斯将提高其能源公司的竞争力，增加其出口源及能源产品，提高其产品质量，维持其在全球能源市场中的市场份额。在此需要强调的一点是，该新战略强调亚太市场将是俄罗斯最具有发展潜力的能源市场。俄罗斯将扩大其在亚太地区的能源出口份额，至少应提高 28%，俄罗斯所产 23% 的油气产品、32% 的原油和 31% 的天然气将出口至亚太地区。这是俄罗斯首次意识到并且公开承认推动与中国的能源关系是最为重要的。

与俄罗斯的油气贸易同样是中国能源外交及对外能源政策的头等大事。中国近年来经济增长强劲，使得其石油消费激增。诸多因素导致了石油消费及进口增长，如国内生产总值的快速增长、能源密集型产业、汽车数量剧增以及减少低效率且极不环保的煤炭在能源消费中比重的需求。中国正积极向国外寻找石油，特别希望能使其能源供应源更为多样化，从俄罗斯、中亚、北美和拉丁美洲等地区进口更多石油，也正努力保护其原油进口运输通道。

在 2014 年，中国石油的对外依存度已达 60.6%，远远超过了 50% 的国际警戒线。天然气对外依存度为40%。油气供需不平衡给中国能源安全带来挑战。在温室气体减排这一目标的压力下,"十二五"规划提升了发展清洁能源的重要性,这将推动天然气消费。国际能源署预期天然气需求年增长约为7.8%。不同于俄罗斯的能源安全情况,中国的重点主要是能源供应安全问题,如四个标准(资源可用性、可取性、可购性及可接受性)以及陆上油气管道及海外航运等能源运输安全问题。

国内的供需差距可用以下方案解决:一,储存能源,提高效率;二,重视自给自足,扩大国内资源开发;三,通过技术研究及开发,推动新能源及可再生能源发展;四,充分利用国际油气资源。

通过以上分析,我们发现俄罗斯这一出口大国满足了中国这一进口大国的能源需求,而这也是促成中俄两国油气合作获得成功的关键驱动力。然而,尽管中国已从世界各地进口了足够其接下来十年消费的天然气(通过中亚天然气管道从中亚地区,主要是从土库曼斯坦获取管道天然气,从中东地区,主要是卡塔尔,以及印度尼西亚和澳大利亚获取液化天然气),中国依然在低油价形势下签署了这份价格相对高昂的协议。因此,肯定存在着影响合作的其他因素。

合作诱因(经济因素和政治因素)

即使通过对中俄两国能源发展的描述,我们仍无法完全理解为何俄罗斯在与中国的能源合作上变得如此积极,甚至将此合作置于"一带一路"框架下。尽管我们知道欧盟国家的油气消费已达顶峰,并且由于新能源、可再生能源以及其他替代资源,它们的油气需求将会逐渐减少,然而欧盟依然是俄罗斯油气的最大市场。因此,需求减少并不是中俄能源合作的唯一诱因。

有趣的是,在历经十年的失败谈判后,中俄能源合作居然在金融危机期间取得了重大进展。当国际油价开始下跌,两国能源合作更进一步。自乌克兰危机以来,普京政府似乎在推动两国全面合作方面态度更为坚定,并最终使得俄罗斯加入了中国的"一带一路"战略。尽管两国在很久之前有过合作,然而促使普京政府采取进一步行动的正是金融危机、油价危机和乌克兰危机等一系列危机，这是毋庸置疑的。

如表 27 所示，中俄合作的长期展望有三个阶段。第一阶段是 1994 年至 2003 年，两国高层试图开展双边能源合作并建立了一个统筹委员会。最初的合作项目包括核能和石油管道。第二阶段是 2003 年至 2009 年，这是双方能源合作的启动时期。两国政府展开了关于天然气贸易的商讨并建立了副总理级能源合作机制。此外，两国的国有企业即中国国家开发银行和俄罗斯的石油公司以及石油运输公司开拓了一个全新的合作模式——"贷款换石油"。中国向俄罗斯提供 250 亿美元贷款，而俄罗斯将以供应石油的形式来偿还贷款。第三阶段是 2009 年至 2015 年，合作进入实施阶段，中俄原油管道竣工。2015 年 5 月中国国家主席习近平出访莫斯科期间，双方政府在中俄天然气合作项目备忘录上达成共识，结束了两国在天然气供应问题上的十年谈判。第四阶段则是中俄全面深入开展能源合作的时代。俄罗斯的目标能源市场正转向东亚地区，而中国则从 2013 年开始实施其"一带一路"新战略，因此两国的能源合作正从石油和天然气领域延伸至核能领域，从中下游产业延伸至上游产业，从能源领域延伸至石油服务及设备领域，从常规能源拓展至非常规能源及可再生能源，从资源层面拓展至技术层面。还有一点需要说明的是，尽管能源合作依旧是双边贸易的重点，但两国合作自 2015 年起已不再局限于能源领域，而是上升至战略层面，能源则开始扮演一种工具的角色。

表27 中俄油气合作大事记

日期	关键人物 / 事件	重要文件	重要成就
阶段一 （1994—2003）探索阶段			
1996 年 4 月	叶利钦 （俄罗斯总统）	《关于共同开展能源领域合作的政府间协定》	拉开中俄能源合作序幕
1996 年 12 月	李鹏 （中国国务院总理）	《关于共同开展能源领域合作协定》	建立中俄能源合作委员会
1999 年 10 月	田湾核电站启动		

日期	关键人物/事件	重要文件	重要成就
2001年9月	中俄两国总理	《关于开展中俄原油管道工程预可行性研究工作的协议》	中俄安大线石油管道项目启动
阶段二 （2003—2009）启动阶段			
2003年5月	中俄天然气公司	《关于"中俄原油管道原油长期购销合同"基本原则和共识的总协议》	开展天然气领域合作
2006年3月		《关于从俄罗斯向中国供应天然气的谅解备忘录》	天然气领域有实质性发展
2008年	胡锦涛与梅德韦杰夫		建立副总理级能源谈判机制
2008年	王岐山与谢钦	《中国石油天然气集团公司和俄罗斯管道运输公司关于斯科沃罗季诺—中国边境原油管道建设与运营的原则协定》	中俄能源谈判
2008年	中国国家开发银行、俄罗斯石油公司及石油运输公司	贷款换石油	中国同意提供250亿美元贷款换俄罗斯石油供应
2009年4月	中俄能源谈判代表第四次会晤	《中俄石油领域合作政府间协议》	达成一揽子合作协议
2009年10月	中俄能源谈判代表第五次会晤	《关于天然气领域合作的谅解备忘录》	进入长期战略合作阶段
阶段三 （2009—2015）实施阶段			
2011年1月	梅德韦杰夫访华		中俄原油管道投入运营
2012年6月	中俄能源谈判代表第八次会晤	《中俄能源谈判代表第八次会晤纪要》	
2012年9月	中俄能源谈判代表第九次会晤	中俄签署四份文件	
2013年3月	习近平主席访俄	《〈中俄睦邻友好合作条约〉实施纲要（2013—2016年）》	多领域合作
2014年5月	习近平与普京	中俄关于全面战略协作伙伴关系新阶段的联合声明	进一步深化石油领域合作
2014年5月		《中俄东线天然气合作项目备忘录》	中俄天然气十年谈判结束
2014年5月	中俄天然气公司	《中俄东线供气购销合同》	从2018年起，俄罗斯开始通过中俄天然气管道东线向中国供气

日期	关键人物/事件	重要文件	重要成就
阶段四 "一带一路"阶段			
2015年9月		俄罗斯第二大天然气生产商诺瓦泰克公司与中国丝路基金签署了关于购买该亚马尔液化天然气项目9.9%股权的框架协议	

来源：中国石油、中国日报

中俄油气合作大事记说明了一件事：不论俄罗斯在何时遭遇经济或政治难题，如金融危机（2008—2009）和乌克兰危机（2014—2015），俄罗斯都会向中国靠拢。卡洛斯·帕斯夸（Carlos Pascual）先生是美国 IHS 公司高级副总裁，曾任美国驻乌克兰及墨西哥大使，美国国务院能源资源局的创始人。2015年8月13日，他在 IHS 博客谈论起全球政治及经济对油价下跌的影响时写道：

> 国际社会对石油出口国实施制裁，阻止其进入资本市场，而石油出口国只能自寻出路，利用自身资金走出金融危机，油价下跌与此不无关系。对于俄罗斯来说，其关键问题是过分依赖石油来获得出口收入。石油占俄罗斯出口收入的70%，石油及天然气总共占其财政预算的52%（可重新计算已确认数据）。乌克兰危机使得俄罗斯无法获得新技术及资本市场，此后的国际制裁与油价暴跌都使得俄罗斯陷入了糟糕的财务状况。卢布贬值50%，人们和公司都失去了一半的真实收入。公司陷入运营困境，它们没有经济能力将设备和外资引进国内，也无法保证用当地货币卢布换算成本后产品仍具有竞争力。

另一方面，向俄罗斯靠拢是中国不可避免的一个战略选择。首先，俄罗斯是接壤中国的一大邻国；其次，中国目前正处于俄罗斯此前经历过的经济转型当中；再者，中国与俄罗斯在国际政治及经济体系中处于相同位置，同样遭受着西方阵营国家的竞争，正如我们从历史中看到的，中俄两国均属于社会主义东方阵营。

简而言之，中俄两国的油气合作显然是资源与市场的一次成功联姻。这种油气合作对于中国来说更多的是一种战略考量，不过，对于俄罗斯来说则是出于经济及战略两方面因素的考虑。

地缘政治影响

亚洲内部目前已逐步形成了一个完整的循环供需体系。该体系由三类国家组成：出口国、进口国及中转国，这有助于降低亚洲天然气溢价和缓和高油价。出口国主要包括俄罗斯、中亚国家（哈萨克斯坦、土库曼斯坦和乌兹别克斯坦）和澳大利亚，进口国包括中国、日本、韩国、印度和新加坡，中转国包括缅甸和中亚国家。如前所述，历经十余载谈判后，中国与俄罗斯终于在2015 年 5 月 21 日签署了一份 30 年天然气供气协议。根据协议，自 2018 年起，俄罗斯将通过中俄天然气管道向中国出口天然气。

目前一个坚固有效的供需网络已形成：俄罗斯油气通过中俄原油和天然气管道运输，中亚油气通过中哈原油管道及中亚天然气管道运输，缅甸天然气及中东石油通过中缅原油和天然气管道运输，澳大利亚液化天然气通过航运运输。油气管道有效地连接了亚太地区的各出口国、进口国和中转国。对于东亚地区其他两大消费国——日本和韩国而言，该地区相对富裕的能源供应也是好消息，毕竟它们亦可通过中俄油气管道享受到更低价格的俄罗斯石油及天然气。近日，中国、日本和韩国之间的三边协议生效以推动三国投资。尽管中日之间存在着领土及政治争端，但是该协议依然加强了三国合作。

正如 19 世纪那样，俄罗斯将继续与美国竞争各大市场。出于种种原因，欧盟市场对于美国液化天然气出口而言并非十分具有吸引力，不过拥有着诸如日本、韩国、中国及印度等主要能源消费国的亚洲无疑是一个目标市场。对于俄罗斯是否能够在美国液化天然气基础设施落成前确保亚洲市场，2015

年5月中俄两国天然气协议的成功签署则很好地回应了这一问题。

该份天然气协议也显示了，一个坚固有效的内部能源供需循环网络已在亚洲地区形成，现在还有可能形成未来的亚洲液化天然气中心。在日本、韩国及中国看来，建立一个面向亚洲天然气及液化天然气需求的定价机制，且定价比日本海关清关价格更有竞争力，都是理想且持久的政策目标。不过，在中期内也许需要面对亚洲天然气中心定价的挑战。无论如何，参考北美及欧洲的定价转型经验，我们清楚这个过程并不会一帆风顺。

这份天然气协议同样意味着世界地缘政治的一次巨变。通过满足中国、日本、韩国及印度等主要能源消费国的能源需求，欧亚大陆充分展示了其地缘政治力量。这正如哈尔福德·麦金德的"大陆腹地说"所言，区域供需一体化帮助欧亚大陆重拾其重要地位。理论中的"世界岛"或"核心"由欧亚大陆和非洲构成，包含富裕的自然资源，可供发达经济体利用。

结论

俄罗斯从与中国的油气合作中获益良多。尽管石油及天然气价格持续下跌，但是俄罗斯确保了中国的巨大市场及能源投资。由此可见，在俄罗斯对抗西方制裁压力中，中国起到了缓冲作用。

"一带一路"倡议下能源合作的预期利益与潜在风险

中国国家主席习近平在2013年9月及10月出访中亚和东南亚时提出了共建丝绸之路经济带与21世纪海上丝绸之路的构想，这也被称为"一带一路"倡议。在2013年中国东盟博览会上，中国国务院总理李克强强调需要铺就面向东盟的海上丝绸之路，打造带动腹地发展的战略支点。根据倡议，加快"一带一路"的建设进程有助于推动沿线国家经济繁荣以及区域经济合作。这一部分则用能源合作进行案例分析，通过经济评价来解读"一带一路"倡议的预期利益与潜在风险。

"一带一路"地区能源合作的背景

能源是人类生存的五大必需资源之一，也是一个国家经济发展的战略物资。随着全球化推进，能源安全已从 20 世纪 70 年代石油危机后的寻求独立过渡到今日的适应相互依存，从强调供应安全过渡到在经济增长、能源可持续发展及环境可接受性三者间达到平衡。然而，由于经济与环境关系密切[①]，能源安全已成为全球共同的安全挑战以及所有经济活动的重点。

> ①正如戴维·麦凯（David J.C. Mackay）在其《可持续能源：事实与真相》（2009）一书中所言，2/3 的温室气体来源于能源消费。

到目前为止，该倡议已发展成中国的一项对外战略并得到了 64 个国家的响应。因此，"一带一路"合作框架下目前共有 65 个国家，可分为中国及 6 个地区：东南地区（11 个国家）、独联体（6 个国家）、南亚地区（8 个国家）、西亚北非地区（16 个国家）、中东欧地区（16 个国家）以及中亚地区（5 个国家）。考虑到这些国家能源储存的重要性及对中国的地缘经济影响，该倡议将蒙古及俄罗斯两个国家单独列出。

"一带一路"方略下不同地区的角色

在 65 个国家当中，我们发现有三类能源国家。第一类为能源出口国，主要分布在东南地区、西亚北非地区、中亚地区，如俄罗斯、蒙古、哈萨克斯坦、沙特阿拉伯、伊朗、印度尼西亚等；第二类为能源进口国，主要分布在中东欧地区和南亚地区，如中国、印度、波兰、捷克等；第三类为管道路线沿线国家，主要是独联体国家，如乌克兰、阿塞拜疆等。

> ① BP (2015). *Statistical Review of World Energy June 2015*. Available at http://www.bp.com/en/global/corporate/energy-economics/statistical- review- of-world-energy.html.

根据英国石油公司（BP）数据，我们可通过以下图表根据不同燃料类型来描述"一带一路"方略下各个能源产业在地区所发挥的作用[②]。

表28至表31所展示的是"一带一路"方略下不同地区的角色。比如说在表31中，南亚国家是最大的煤炭进口国，而东南亚国家则是最大的煤炭出口国。应该注意的是，当不考虑中国时，所有的三种能源类型居然都呈现盈余状态。而在表32里，我们则讨论了包括中国在内的情况。

我们看到，尽管中国在2014年"一带一路"能源产业中属于纯进口国，不过在"一带一路"国家中所有三种燃料资源过剩。特别是石油及天然气仍有富余，而这正是中国发展"一带一路"方略的主要动机，因为燃料富余能够加强中国能源安全，促进经济发展。

表28　"一带一路"国家的地区划分

地　区	国　　家
中东欧	阿尔巴尼亚、波黑、保加利亚、克罗地亚、捷克共和国、爱沙尼亚、匈牙利、拉脱维亚、立陶宛、马其顿、黑山共和国、波兰、罗马尼亚、塞尔维亚、斯洛伐克、斯洛文尼亚
中亚	哈萨克斯坦、吉尔吉斯斯坦、塔吉克斯坦、土库曼斯坦、乌兹别克斯坦
中国	中国
独立国家联合体	亚美尼亚、阿塞拜疆、白俄罗斯、格鲁吉亚、摩尔多瓦、乌克兰
蒙古	蒙古
俄罗斯联邦	俄罗斯联邦
南亚	阿富汗、孟加拉国、不丹、印度、马尔代夫、尼泊尔、巴基斯坦、斯里兰卡
东南亚	文莱、柬埔寨、东帝汶、印度尼西亚、老挝、马来西亚、缅甸、菲律宾、新加坡、泰国、越南
西亚北非	巴林、埃及、伊朗、伊拉克、以色列、约旦、科威特、黎巴嫩、阿曼、巴勒斯坦、卡塔尔、沙特阿拉伯、叙利亚、土耳其、阿拉伯联合酋长国、也门

注：截至2017年4月数据，"一带一路"沿线国家还包括埃塞俄比亚、新西兰、南非和韩国

表29　2014年"一带一路"地区石油情况统计

按日均千桶计算

地区	角色	产量	消费量	剩余量
中亚	出口	2007	480	1528
俄罗斯联邦	出口	10838	3196	7642
东南亚	出口	28342	7842	20500

续表

地区	角色	产量	消费量	剩余量
独联体	中转	848	545	304
西亚北非	进口	85	1240	−1156
中东欧	进口	895	4419	−3524
南亚	进口	2463	5722	−3259
总计（不包括中国）		43015	17721	25293

表30　2014年"一带一路"地区天然气情况统计

按十亿立方米计算

地区	角色	产量	消费量	剩余量
中亚	出口	146	82	64
俄罗斯联邦	出口	579	409	170
东南亚	出口	221	157	64
独联体	出口	593	469	124
西亚北非	中转	36	66	−30
中东欧	进口	16	53	−37
南亚	进口	97	116	−19
总计（不包括中国）		1687	1352	335

表31　2014年"一带一路"地区煤炭情况统计

按百万吨油当量计算

地区	角色	产量	消费量	剩余量
中亚	出口	57	37	20
俄罗斯联邦	出口	171	85	86
东南亚	出口	310	126	184
独联体	中转	32	34	−3
西亚北非	进口	18	45	−28
中东欧	进口	84	87	−3
南亚	进口	245	366	−121
总计（不包括中国）		915	780	135

表32 2014年"一带一路"能源行业中国情况统计

能源行业		产量	消费量	剩余量
石油 （日均千桶）	总计（表29）	43015	17721	25293
	中国	4246	11056	−6811
天然气 （十亿立方米）	总计（表30）	1687	1352	335
	中国	135	186	−51
煤炭 （百万吨油当量）	总计（表31）	915	780	135
	中国	1845	1962	−118

不同能源安全策略

　　每类能源国家对能源安全都有着自身特定的理解。对于能源出口国，即通过出售能源资源及产品获取收入的国家，如俄罗斯、沙特阿拉伯、科威特、印度尼西亚、哈萨克斯坦、土库曼斯坦等，能源安全意味着有足够的市场以及有利的能源价格来覆盖其预算；对于那些能源进口国，如中国、印度、捷克、波兰、塔吉克斯坦等，能源安全就是有足够的经济及环保的能源来维持其国民经济；对于能源中转国，如乌克兰、格鲁吉亚等，能源安全则是充分享受从运输能源中所获得的回报。

　　某些国家就像中国那样，既是能源出口国，同时又是能源进口国以及中转国。目前中国已成为世界上最大石油进口国、最大能源生产国（68% 的煤炭）以及第二大能源消费国。同时，中国的碳排放量为世界第一，反过来中国在可再生能源的安装及消费上的投资同样居全球首位。

　　这就是中国为何会带头引领"一带一路"倡议，因为中国体会到了大多数"一带一路"国家遭遇的经济安全挑战，尤其是能源安全挑战。下面则用能源合作作为案例进行分析，通过经济评价来解读"一带一路"倡议带来的预期利益与潜在风险。

"一带一路"能源安全的未来版图

世界能源发展的巨变

在过去的几十年里，两个地区显著改变了全球能源版图。其一是北美地区，其对世界能源版图的影响主要源于页岩气革命的成功，而页岩气革命主要是在美国进行。其二则是亚洲地区，该地区正不断壮大，是当前世界上发展最快的能源消费中心。由于亚洲地区主要有中国、日本、韩国及印度等国家，人们普遍预期该地区在接下来几年里将会继续在能源消费市场中发挥关键作用。在上述四个国家中，中国和印度是两个新兴玩家，而日本和韩国早已公认为是能源消费大国。两个地区近期的发展状况向全世界传达了一个明确的信息：全球能源市场经历了一场剧变，而且势头仍将继续。

一方面，全球方略中非常规油气资源的影响与日俱增。目前的一个明显趋势是石油及天然气出口中心正从波斯湾转向墨西哥湾；同时，非洲大陆的能源开发也吸引了世界各地的众多关注。另一方面，中国及印度持续增长的能源需求使得亚洲地区成为主要能源消费区，这意味着主要的石油及天然气进口市场已逐步从欧美地区转移到亚洲地区。这些变化皆对全球能源秩序带来了直接冲击。

① 此处的能源并非独指煤炭、石油及天然气等常规能源，同时还包括如页岩油气、致密油、核能等新能源与可再生能源。

随着能源技术发展，世界已进入一个真正的能源时代①。能源地缘政治与石油地缘政治从不相像，尽管石油和天然气目前依旧占据优先位置。在主要能源消费国对非常规能源及可再生能源开发的不懈努力下，目前的全球能源消费结构会经历一次巨大的调整。能源消费的常规能源结构正面临着非常规能源的挑战，这将影响两者的全球供需情况。

供给方面，常规油气国阵营高度整合并形成巨大的市场影响力，这是二战后全球油气资源供给秩序的重要特征。然而，随着非常规油气资源商业化的不断成熟，常规油气资源面临着来自外力的威胁，为保持竞争优势，其势必对消费端的需求更为关注，及时调整自身策略。

需求方面，中国与印度等新兴经济体在全球能源消费所占比重日益增大，使其成为新时期全球油气市场的大买家和重要玩家。随着购买力及市场影响力不断增强，国际企业地位不断提升，这些新兴国家的企业将会扮演一个更为重要的角色，其进口选择也将对世界能源产业的未来发展产生重要影响。

"一带一路"地区对全球能源秩序的影响

在 65 个"一带一路"国家当中，除去 16 个中东欧国家与埃及之外，共有 48 个亚洲国家。换言之，"一带一路"国家中亚洲国家占比 74%。因此，亚洲地区（"一带一路"国家加上日本以及韩国）及其他"一带一路"国家都在方方面面改变了全球能源秩序。

首先，油气资源需求的持续增长使亚洲地区成为最近世界能源消费激增的最大贡献者。以石油消费为例，2011 年中国和印度分别从中东地区进口石油 1.378 亿吨和 1.107 亿吨。如果将日本进口的 1.751 亿吨计算在内，那么这三个国家进口的石油量将占去约一半的石油总出口量（9.794 亿吨）。同时，北美与欧洲进口的石油总量仅为 2.268 亿吨。详细数据见表 33，可供对比。

表33 从中东进口石油情况统计

单位：百万吨

年份 国家	2006	2007	2008	2009	2010	2011
美国	113.2	110.4	119.7	86.9	86	95.5
加拿大	6.8	7	6.3	5	4.3	5.3
欧洲	159.3	146.6	127.6	105.9	116.7	126
中国	73.9	78.8	92	103.2	118.4	137.8
印度			107.6	110.1	129.6	110.7
日本	209.1	199.9	196.9	179.4	179.9	175.1
中东总计	1001.3	975.3	1000.7	913.8	935.9	979.4

来源：英国石油公司，2015 年

如图 37 所示，中国、日本、韩国和印度四国 2013 年能源消费份额约占全世界 35%，1993 年至 2013 年间四国占全球一级能源消费总增长的 59%。这表明这四个国家对世界能源市场的影响正日益扩大，愈发重要。

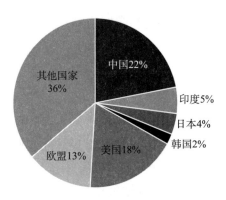

图 37　2013 年世界一级能源消费份额

中国自 1993 年起首次开始进口石油产品，此后便对石油进口越发依赖。中国在此期间的能源政策着重强调"走出去"的过程。换句话说，中国经历了全球化历程，改变了其政策重点，利用海外燃料市场来满足其能源需求。不过中国依然相当依赖其国内资源。由于国内煤炭产量充足，中国对于国外碳氢能源依存度较低，仅为 11%。然而，其进口石油及天然气依存度显著。并在持续增长。中国是目前世界上最大的能源生产国，同时也是最大的能源消费国，2013 年中国一级能源消费占全世界 22%。印度也有类似经历，也正扩大能源需求来支持经济发展。

总而言之，当今世界能源发展的巨大变化给中国带来了能源安全方面的机遇与挑战。而作为全球第二大经济体，中国应当满足世界经济增长的需求，因此，"一带一路"倡议是一个为中国而设的良好平台，中国可以通过该平台满足包括自身需求在内的不同的能源安全需求。

能源合作的预期利益

中国在未来几年将仍是"一带一路"地区主要能源消费国和供应国之间

能源合作的引擎。石油需求预期仍将持续增长，这促使世界石油及天然气公司加大了对上游油气的投资力度。加强能源安全已成为一项广泛共识的政策议程，这一现象在国有石油企业中尤为明显。中国三大国有石油企业——中国石油、中国石化、中海油在海外上游投资股权收购中表现瞩目，且考虑到未来中国石油需求规模庞大，中国石油、中国石化及中海油常被看作全球上游油气投资当中的领头羊。

根据中华人民共和国国家统计局发布的数据，2015 年中国天然气消费达到 1932 亿立方米。可是根据国家能源局的估算，国内供应仅为 1000 亿~1500 亿立方米，显然是无法满足中国的消费需求的。因此，需要通过增加进口量来满足需求。液化天然气和管道天然气现在已是主要的进口来源。2011 年中国分别从澳大利亚、卡塔尔以及印度尼西亚进口了 50 亿立方米、32 亿立方米、27 亿立方米液化天然气，总进口量达 109 亿立方米。中国也开始与哈萨克斯坦、土库曼斯坦和乌兹别克斯坦等中亚国家、缅甸和俄罗斯合作，完成其在东北及西南地区的国际天然气管道建设。2009 年中亚天然气管道开始运输天然气。2013 年 10 月中缅油气管道也投入运营，每年运输天然气 120 亿立方米。

能源供应安全的共同利益促进了诸如中国和印度等"一带一路"国家之间的合作，也推动了"一带一路"国家与美国、日本、韩国及西欧国家等非"一带一路"国家之间的合作。印度经济近年来发展迅猛。预计印度在 2020 年将需要进口超过 2.5 亿吨石油，并将超过韩国成为仅次于中国、美国及日本的第四大能源消费国。国际能源署预计，到 2040 年，印度将取代中国成为亚洲地区能源消费增长最大的国家[①]。早在 2005 年 5 月，印度国民大会党已表示，如果印度不能及时发现新油田，那么目前已探明的石油储量只能用到 2016

①国际能源署：《世界能源展望 2015》

年。因此，印度采取了保护性的天然气勘探措施，并为其海外能源拓展制定了一个全面的供应计划。

印度在其外交能源勘探战略上开创了一套"T"模式：其北，从俄罗斯处获得油田勘探权；其西，建立一条从伊朗至印度的安全石油运输通道；其东，获取缅甸最大配额的石油出口。此外，印度还将范围进一步延伸至非洲和拉丁美洲。而相同的对外能源战略促使中国与印度走到了一起。例如，中印两国已联手开发了哈萨克斯坦的石油资源，并共同进入了苏丹石油勘探计划。

通过在能源基础设施建设和能源贸易等方面充裕的资本投资，这些"一带一路"国家的能源企业所扮演的角色将影响其国家能源安全。直接投资是"一带一路"地区主要的能源合作方式，主要参与者将是企业而非政府。投资将流向油田和天然气田开发，也会流向诸如风能、太阳能、地热能等新能源及可再生能源产业及相关技术开发。

中国和印度等"一带一路"国家的全球能源消费增多，并且由于国民经济发展需要，预期其对能源需求仍会持续增长，使得它们也已加入日本和韩国，成为能源市场的大买家。预期这些国家在能源市场会继续不断壮大，其影响力也会不断提升，迟早会成为全球油气市场的关键玩家。消费端在能源进口上选择多种多样，这无疑直接影响了在价格、进口资源以及常规与非常规能源发展等方面的全球能源竞争。

2008年金融危机爆发后，全球资本市场受到剧烈冲击，欧美能源企业在融资方面陷入了不小的困境，这使其商业运营活动大受影响。在此背景下，中国、印度以及其他"一带一路"国家的国有能源企业拥有相对充裕资本，而原本对其设有很高进入门槛的能源资源市场开始松动，使得这些企业在该地区的并购行为日益活跃。比如说，随着海外进程推进，中国和印度效仿曾经的日本和韩国，正不断在这一过程中积累大量的国际经验。通过与全球领先企业的深入合作，中国及印度企业已具有一定国际竞争力并具备成为全球顶尖能源公司的基本素质。

能源合作的潜在风险：投资与不干涉原则

首先是地缘政治风险。亚洲内部已逐渐形成一个完整的供需循环体系。

这个体系由三类国家组成，分别是出口国、进口国和中转国，这有助于降低亚洲天然气溢价和缓和高油价。出口国主要包括俄罗斯、中亚国家（哈萨克斯坦、土库曼斯坦和乌兹别克斯坦）和澳大利亚；进口国包括中国、日本、韩国、印度和新加坡；中转国包括缅甸和中亚国家。

俄罗斯油气通过中俄原油和天然气管道运输，中亚油气通过中哈原油管道及中亚天然气管道运输，缅甸天然气及中东石油通过中缅原油和天然气管道运输，澳大利亚液化天然气通过航运运输，从而形成了一个坚固有效的供需网络。原油及天然气管道有效地连接陆上丝绸之路及海上丝绸之路上的各出口国、进口国及中转国。对于东亚地区其他两大消费国——日本和韩国而言，该地区相对富裕的能源供应也是好消息，毕竟它们亦可通过中俄油气管道享受到更低价格的俄罗斯石油及天然气。中国、日本和韩国之间的三边协议生效以推动三国投资。尽管中日之间存在着领土及政治争端，但是该协议依然加强了三国合作。

"一带一路"地区的世界强国间的地缘政治竞争日益激烈，世界主要能源进口国对能源资源的竞争同样如此。与管理着大量高质量油田的中国公司相比，西方国家的跨国公司可在其地区发挥更大的影响。由于大多数"一带一路"国家拥有丰富资源，且地区里种族群体和宗教派别之间的社会矛盾根深蒂固，因而存在政权不稳的可能性，这对中国形成了种种地缘政治风险。

中国的石油需求增长极大改变了世界能源地缘政治格局，尤其是亚太地区深受影响。中国试图增加并丰富其石油供应及运输路线，这也可能引发与日本以及其他亚洲国家之间的矛盾。不过，这也有可能加强东亚及南亚的大经济体（中国、日本、东盟）、印度、俄罗斯等国家尤其是"一带一路"沿线国家之间的合作。究竟走向哪种局面很大程度上取决于中国在未来几年做出的战略决策。"一带一路"倡议的使命则是要化干戈为玉帛，化敌意为友谊。

其次则是中国对外国能源投资与外交不干涉原则之间存在着冲突风险。中国对外国能源投资的需求增长，而且中国存在着能源安全方面的担忧，可是不干涉原则却阻止其为此做出行动，此时冲突就会发生。不干涉原则是1953年中国政府和印度政府就西藏地方的关系问题进行谈判时周恩来总理提出的，后来成为和平共存五项原则中的其中一项。作为国家谈判基础，和平共存五项原则分别是互相尊重主权和领土完整、互不侵犯、互不干涉内政、平等互利、和平共处，这奠定了今日中国当代外交及能源外交的基础。

中国与其他六国已在伊朗核问题上达成了历史性共识，有可能会解除对伊朗原油出口的制裁。正如美国兰德公司所言，中国的能源需求是塑造中伊关系的关键因素之一。中国的石油公司预计会大力投资伊朗油田以促进能源合作，同时也会投资铁路等非能源基础建设以推动伊朗融入全球能源市场。另外，因其地缘位置及丰富的油气资源，伊朗会在中国的"一带一路"战略实施中扮演重要角色。考虑到中国为保护其海外能源利益加大了对外能源的投资力度，那么中国的不干涉原则会否有所变化呢？鉴于中国在伊朗基础建设上的投资规模以及伊朗在中国"一带一路"战略中发挥的潜在作用，中国有可能在必要时采取一种更为积极主动的姿态来捍卫其长期利益。然而，在不久的将来，中国更多地会避免参与到伊朗的内部事务中。伊朗的例子表明，中国的大规模能源投资与其外交不干涉原则之间存在着冲突风险。

1

Introduction

1.1 Background and Motivation

As the world's largest emitter of CO_2 (see Table1), China has substantially scaled up its unilateral commitment to emissions reduction: by 2020 carbon intensity will have decreased to 40-45% below 2005 levels. Since this is such an ambitious target, the concern from the international climate community is how this target can be achieved.

Table 1 CO_2 emissions and emissions per capita by country in 2011

Country	CO_2 emissions, in 1,000 tons	Emission per capita, tons per capita
World	33,376,327	4.9
China	9,700,000	7.2
United States	5,420,000	17.3
India	1,970,000	1.6
Russia	1,830,000	12.8

Source: EDGAR (2013)

In the Eleventh Five-Year Plan (FYP), 2006—2010, China reduced energy intensity by 19.4% against a target of 20%, largely by means of direct regulation and top-down administrative orders. Despite the fact that some provinces were forced to shut down their industrial capacity towards the end of 2010 to meet their assigned energy-saving targets, the target of 20% was not achieved. Since China is transiting from a planned economy to a kind of market economy, a national carbon emissions trading system naturally arose on China's national agenda.

An emissions trading system (ETS, also known as the emission cap-and-trade system) is one of the instruments of China's policy, offering incentives to reduce emission. Compared with other taxable economic instruments, an ETS allows government authorities to determine and set the total quantity of emissions for a certain period before the introduction of the system. The initial concept of emissions trading can be found in Crocker (1966) who referred to "air pollution permits". The main idea behind emissions trading is to initially allocate emission permits to firms either by auction or by a free-of-charge grandfathering mechanism. Firms are then allowed to trade permits among themselves, with the intention that a firm should hold a number of permits at least equal to its emissions. Hence, firms that have surplus permits can sell them on the market, whereas firms that need additional permits can purchase those available on the market. Obviously, firms need to make their abatement decisions by considering the difference between the marginal abatement costs and the market price of the emission permits.

The first large-scale ETS was implemented in the United States electricity sector concerning SO_2 emissions under the 1990 Clean Air Act Amendments. Emissions trading was later adopted in the U.S. for NOx. In Europe, the Kyoto Protocol (1997) allowed burden sharing among the fifteen European Union (E.U.) countries with a total emissions reduction target of 8% compared with the emissions level in 1990. The E.U.'s current reduction target is 20% by 2020. To meet these goals, the E.U. has adopted an ETS for the greenhouse gas CO_2. There are three periods of emissions trading: 2005—2007, 2008—2012, and 2013—2020. The E.U. is now proposing a 40% reduction by 2030. All countries participating in the ETS present their individual national allocation plan, which determines the emission allowance a major emitter, such as an electric power plant, will be allotted in this period. It should be noted that the volumes of other greenhouse gases are rated with a weight reflecting their potential global-warming damage compared with CO_2.

Carbon trading is one of the key energy and environmental policies of the Twelfth FYP. The short-term goal was to establish a small-scale multi-regional ETS (Beijing, Chongqing, Shanghai, Shenzhen, Tianjin, Guangdong, and Hubei) in 2013 which would transition to a national scheme by 2015. The idea was that this small-scale ETS would be used to resolve some vital issues concerning the design of emission allocations systems, including transparency, transaction cost, the effect on the international competitiveness of affected industries, mechanisms designed to stabilize prices such as price ceilings, the value of "banking" schemes to buffer annual variations in emissions, and efficiency implications of different ways to dispose of auction revenues. In practice, the first cross-region emission trade was carried out in the end of 2014 between Beijing and Hebei and a national ETS is now expected to be functioning in 2017.

Until it has established a reliable national ETS, however, China still needs to rely on direct regulations and top-down administrative orders to achieve energy conservation and CO_2 emissions targets. In the Twelfth FYP, China aimed to change its energy-mix by using more clean primary energy to achieve the targets of energy security and environmental protection simultaneously. The belief was that changing the energy mix alone could not achieve the CO_2 emissions reduction targets. However, changing the energy mix seems to be the most suitable strategy until the national ETS is ready to be implemented.

In this book we summarize the energy policies and the environmental policies related to the energy mix with some observations and discussion.

We start with the results of the energy policies from the Eleventh FYP and then describe the energy policies of the Twelfth FYP, while analyzing the environmental effects of these policies. Since the changing energy mix makes China more reliant on importing primary energy sources, like oil and natural gas, it may also affect the energy security of other nations. The international relations issues in the energy field are also addressed as an important part of this book.

1.2 Preliminaries

1.2.1 "Visible Hand" and "Invisible Hand"

To understand China's energy policies, we need to recall the critical time when China was transforming its planned economy to a socialist market economy after the economic reforms of 1978. During his Southern tour in 1992, Deng Xiaoping (the architect of the Chinese economic reforms) said, firmly and confidently:

Planning and market forces are not the essential difference between socialism and capitalism. A planned economy is not the definition of socialism, because there is planning under capitalism; the market economy happens under socialism, too. Planning and market forces are both ways of controlling economic activity.[1]

① *People's Daily*, February 3, 2012

The core of the socialist market economy is the harmonious combination of the "visible hand" of government with the "invisible hand" of the market. Hence, the evaluation of China's energy policies follows the proportion of the combination of visible hand and invisible hand. This will change with the degree of economic development. In the energy sector, it has changed with the development stages of successive FYPs.

1.2.2 Energy Security, Economic Growth and Environmental Protection

Following the economic growth trend, energy policies were designed to support economic growth (EG), and then when the energy sector could not be self-sufficient, energy security (ES) became an issue. Finally, environmental protection (EP) came to be an important factor in the energy policies due to too much energy consumption. Of course, the weighting of EG, ES, and EP depend on the stage of economic development.

1.2.3 Areas and Administrative Regions in China

"Region" is a general term used to refer to geopolitical units in China, including provinces, counties, cities, and districts. It should be noted that this specific geopolitical unit in China includes provinces, autonomous regions and the municipalities directly under the national government. These regions can be classified into three areas, as shown in Table 2.

Table 2   The distribution of thirty–one administrative regions

Area	Administrative regions (i.e., provinces, autonomous regions and municipalities; Hong Kong, Macau and Taiwan not included)
Eastern	Beijing, Tianjin, Hebei, Liaoning, Shanghai, Jiangsu, Zhejiang, Fujian, Shandong, Guangdong, Hainan
Central	Shanxi, Jilin, Heilongjiang, Anhui, Jiangxi, Henan, Hubei, Hunan
Western	Sichuan, Chongqing, Guizhou, Yunnan, Shaanxi, Gansu, Qinghai, Ningxia, Xinjiang, Guangxi, Inner Mongolia, Xizang

It should be noted that there are different classifications in the literature. For instance, Chen and Fleisher (1996) divide China into two areas, coastal and non-coastal, to study regional income inequality and national economic growth. Hu and Wang (2006) adopt the old "three belts" scheme (eastern, central and western China) of the Seventh FYP to examine the energy efficiency of China's different regions. Gelb and Chen (2004) use the designation of the official western area to provide a progress report of the

Great Western Development Strategy promoted by the Chinese government.

In order to make the results more relevant to policymaking, we adopt the official classification from Hu and Wang (2006). That is, the classification of the thirty one administrative regions to be investigated is shown in Table 2. Using the three belts scheme, we can simplify our discussions when necessary.

1.2.4 Geographies of Economic Development

There are significant differences between the various parts of China. In the Seventh FYP (1986—1990), the three belts scheme was used to classify the three major areas in China: eastern, western, and central. Each area consists of different administrative regions (i.e., provinces, autonomous regions, and municipalities). The three areas are characterized as follows: (1) the eastern area has a higher growth rate and more direct foreign investment than most of the central and western provinces; (2) the central area is largely rural and agricultural and is the home base for a large sector of the population; and (3) the western area has comparatively low population density and is the least developed area.

1.2.5 Administration

Traditional Chinese institutional structures are flexible enough to accommodate local contexts, and were constructed to seek compromise between top-down policy approaches, and local, social and business interests. The objectives of Chinese energy efficiency and conservation (EE&C) policy have been transformed, adapting to governing purposes, combining commitments to the general political and social goals with local interests and business incentives.

1.2.6 Energy Efficiency

Technical improvements have been proceeding successfully over the past two decades, spread over hundreds of companies in China. The broader use and lower cost of investments in energy efficient developments will be decisive in achieving greater energy efficiency. Two sets of factors—the need to be competitive on a world level and the necessity to comply with the government-set energy intensity standards—are the impetus for Chinese firms to increase efficiency.

1.3 Gaps in Understanding Key Notions

There are big gaps in understanding key notions in energy between outsiders, especially Westerners, and the Chinese. China has its own energy culture with distinct characteristics based on its specific cultural viewpoint, its stage of development, political system and institutions of ownership.

Removing these gaps in understanding can facilitate research in the international arena of the energy and environmental issues of China, and shape a more accurate perception of an energy culture with particular Chinese characteristics. This section tries to clarify some of these gaps in understanding in energy between Chinese people and foreigners, taking the notion of energy security as an example.

1.3.1 Energy Security & Energy Safety

As mentioned in APERC (2007)[1], the definition of energy security has changed over time. After the oil shocks of the1970s, the definition of energy security was related to the risk of oil supply from the Middle East. With the diversification of energy sources, oil security evolved into energy security, however, the security of supply was still the priority. According to the International Energy Agency (IEA), "Energy security, broadly defined, means adequate, affordable and

[1] Asia Pacific Energy Research Centre, 'A Quest for Energy Security in the Twenty-First Century'. Paper presented by Institute of Energy Economics, Japan. Available at www.ieej.or.jp/aperc, accessed 27 August 2008.

reliable supplies of energy," and many Westerners have the same point of view as the IEA.

APERC classifies the elements relating to security of supply into: availability (elements relating to geological existence), accessibility (geopolitical elements), affordability (economic elements), and acceptability (environmental and societal elements). A similar definition is provided by Muñoz Delgado (2011): "Energy security can be classified into security of energy demand for energy exporters and security of supply (SOS) for energy importers."

After the 1970s oil shortage, most of the then developed nations endeavored to reduce their national dependence on external supplies, through diversifying supply sources, energy conservation and using alternative fuels as much as possible. With the self-sufficiency rate increasing, the key point of energy security has moved from supply security to the balance of the 3Es, which is the balance between economic development and energy, the balance between energy and the environment, and also the balance of environmental concerns and economic development, which creates a triangle.

A revolution in understanding happened after the Fukushima tsunami catastrophe awoke even advocates of nuclear energy to the realization that there is a serious safety issue. Yamashita (2011), from the standpoint of safe nuclear power, pointed out in 2011 that there are four elements of energy security, i.e., 3E+S (Safety).

For China, the concept of energy security has also been evolving as above, from oil supply to energy supply with 4As, and from 3Es to 3E+S, however, the current understanding of energy security is more akin to energy safety and officials of the Chinese government use this term instead of "energy security." "Energy safety" includes the concept of energy security. China is committed to the development of renewable energy in order to ensure the safety of national energy.

After more than half a century of development of the energy industry in China, a new vision of energy security has matured. At the G8 summit in St Petersburg in July 2006, China's former president, Hu Jintao promoted this new vision in these terms:

The fundamental content of energy strategy of China is that keep making energy use efficiency as the top priority, center on the domestic condition, make diverse development, protect environment, strengthen the international mutually beneficial cooperation and make effort in building up the stable, economic and clean energy supply system to jointly maintain the global energy security.

Therefore, there are three elements in the new vision of energy security in China:

- energy security: reduction of energy intensity is embraced as the primary means of overcoming energy-related obstacles and is considered of national strategic importance;

- environmental protection: slowing the growth of energy usage and eliminating inefficient and heavily polluting energy users are the cornerstone of China's approach to addressing environmental challenges;

- long-term economic growth: to depart from a resource-intensive growth trajectory, energy efficiency is considered necessary to sustain long-term economic growth.

As Figure 1 shows, energy policy orientation during the period from the Seventh FYP to the Tenth FYP shifted from focusing on the economy to energy itself and environmental protection.

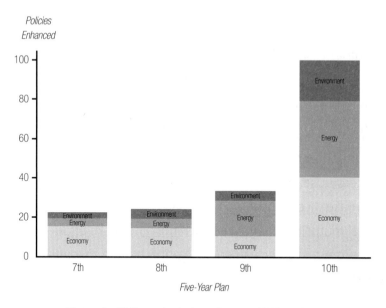

Figure 1   Policy orientation change, 1986—2006

1.3.2   Energy Policy & Energy Law

It is well known that energy policy refers to the statement of national policy regarding energy planning, generation, transmission and usage. Energy policy includes legislation on commercial energy activities (trading, transport, storage, etc.) and fiscal policies related to energy products and services (taxes, exemptions, subsidies; instructions for state owned energy sector assets and organizations, etc.).

Energy laws govern the use and taxation of energy, both renewable and non-renewable, and are the primary authorities for all case laws, statutes, rules, regulations and edicts related to energy. Energy policy is not equivalent to energy law, but can be transformed into law.

In China, up to now there has not been an energy law. There is a draft, but it is still at the review and public hearing stage, though there are laws in place on renewable energy and energy conservation. China's energy development is thus governed by policy but not by energy law. Hence, policies are often ad hoc or temporary.

The differences with other nations are not only between policies and laws. Even regarding the policies, the natures or the objectives of the energy sector, China is not the same as others, for example, the U.S. or the E.U.

1.3.3 Nature of Energy Policy

The energy policy of the U.S. was established in statutory form under the Energy Policy Act of 2005. However, individual states may adopt differing policies that best meet their interests, e.g., the California Global Warming Solutions Act 2006. The E.U. energy policy is based upon the Treaty of Lisbon of 2007, which mandates solidarity in matters of energy supply and changes to the energy policy within the E.U. Hence, E.U. countries adopt uniform regional energy rules.

China's energy policy, in contrast, is a set of goals, objectives and instructions, which may never become laws. If necessary, laws will be amended to achieve the policies. The energy policies are issued following the guidelines of each FYP. The provinces must follow and meet the targets of the energy policies set by the central government.

1.3.4 Objectives of Energy Policies

The basis of the U.S. energy policy is to ensure domestic jobs for the future with secure, affordable, and reliable energy (see Energy Policy Act 2005). The E.U. energy policy aims to provide a sustainable, secure and affordable energy system while protecting the environment and in particular combating climate change and improving energy grids (European Commission 2012). China's energy policy under the Eleventh FYP was to support economic development while considering energy security and protecting the environment.

1.3.5 Energy Efficiency and Conservation (EE&C)

Energy efficiency measures extend to the elimination of outdated plant capacities on a relatively large scale; thus making way to introduce more efficient plants. Energy conservation introduces a cap on the quantity of energy use that may in fact induce energy efficiency.

Energy conservation refers to reducing energy through using less of an energy service. Energy conservation differs from efficient energy use, which refers to using less energy continuously. China is still using the entire suite of policies and activities to meet the objective of reducing energy consumption.

1.3.6 Going Out & International Cooperation

China's Going Out policy contains a double meaning. On the one hand, it means Chinese enterprises going out to make direct investments in other countries; on the other hand, it also means attracting foreign direct investment into China. Misconceptions and misunderstandings about China's quest for energy security exist both inside and outside China.

Inside China, criticisms of investment in overseas oilfields in order to strengthen energy security are: that China's oil imports outpace China's overseas equity oil production; it is not cost effective to transport oil to China; and that there is no evidence that overseas equity oil would be cheaper or more accessible to Chinese consumers in a supply crisis.

Outside China, the unnecessary fear exists that China will exhaust the world's energy supply. This is a misconception, however, for the following reasons:

- China's entire overseas production is less than that of just one of the major oil companies;

• Chinese overseas investments contribute to stability in the global market as they are more willing to take risks and operate in more hostile environments;

• about 75% of the Chinese companies' output is within China. China's domestic oil production is currently the fourth largest in the world.

If the Going Out Policy could be understood as an international energy/resources cooperation policy, there might not be as much domestic criticism or unnecessary fear from abroad.

1.3.7   Energy Dependence Rate & Oil Dependence Rate

Energy dependence refers to a country's reliance on imports of oil and other foreign sources of energy. Different from energy independence, the energy self-sufficiency rate is the ratio between national primary energy output (coal, oil, natural gas, nuclear, hydraulic and renewable energies) and consumption of primary energy in a given year. This rate may be calculated for each of the broad energy types or overall for all types of energy. A rate of over 100% (as is the case for electricity in China) indicates a national production surplus in relation to domestic demand and therefore net exports.

In China, the energy dependence rate is less than 11%, much less than the oil dependence rate which is around 60%. When the oil dependence rate is used to judge China's energy dependence rate, it is not surprising that expressions like "China energy threat" have become popular internationally. We can clarify the matter by comparing Figures 2 and 3.

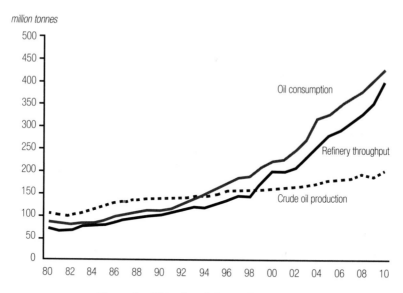

Figure 2   China's oil dependence rate

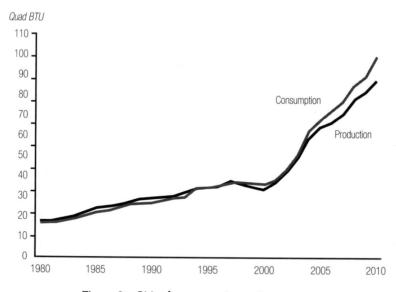

Figure 3   China's energy dependence rate

1.3.8   Energy Independence & Energy Interdependence

Although almost all the economies in the world seek national energy independence, absolute energy independence is impossible. While China, like the U.S., has an interest in becoming less dependent on imported fossil fuels, the two countries share with most if not all countries an interest in stable world energy markets, a more sustainable environment and climate, a prosperous and growing world economy, and peaceful relations with their neighbors. In a word, we are all interdependent, however much any country decides that it would like to be more independent. Policies must therefore strike the right balance between self-reliance and creating the governance arrangements that allow for a stable global economy, energy market and environment.

1.3.9 State-owned Enterprises & National Companies

In China, the system of property ownership is complicated. The main types of ownership include; state-owned/state-holding, collective-owned, cooperative, joint ownership, shareholding, private, joint-venture and sole foreign investment. After 1998, China's petroleum industry split its productive assets from a holding company to create CNPC (PetroChina Ltd.; vertically integrated), Sinopec (Sinopec Ltd.; vertically integrated) and CNOOC (CNOOC Ltd. with initial public offering for 10%~20% of shares). Thus, the three large oil and gas companies do not fall within the traditional meaning of state-owned enterprises (SOE), in which the government has the majority of shares but the company does not always follow the government's orders. The companies' strategy is usually a middle road resulting from negotiation. They cannot be accurately called SOEs as some of them are publicly traded.

1.3.10 Energy Foreign Policy (Energy Diplomacy) & Foreign Energy Policy

Energy diplomacy means the employment of tact to gain strategic advantage or to find mutually acceptable solutions to a common challenge in the energy business and politics. Foreign energy policy means dealing with energy relations in an international context and a range of policies to gain various national benefits by means of deployment of energy supply and demand. China has energy diplomacy but has not established a mature foreign energy policy. Since the new leader, President Xi Jinping, has proclaimed the so-called "Belt and Road Policy," both on land and sea, China seems ready to realise the potential of its foreign energy policy.

2

The Energy System and Policies before the Twelfth Five-Year Plan

2.1 Energy Development by Sector

In this section, we highlight the most relevant findings of the research published by APERC in *Understanding Energy Policy in China* (APERC 2008, 2009) by sectors with some remarks when necessary.

2.1.1 Coal

2.1.1.1 Problems of accessibility and affordability

Owing to the uneven geographic distribution of coal resources, coal transport is a major issue for the continued security of coal supply in China. This is because China's largest coal reserves are located far inland, hundreds of kilometers from the coastal industrial centers where coal is most demanded. Consequently, each tonne of coal shipped from Datong in Shanxi Province to Guangzhou uses an estimated eighteen liters of diesel (Skeer and Yanjia, 2007). At a cost of 6 yuan per liter for diesel, the cost of fuel alone amounts to 108 yuan per tonne of coal shipped from Datong to Guangzhou. Under high crude oil and petroleum product prices, the economics of transporting coal will further limit where customers can afford to purchase coal. However, as Figure 4 indicates, provinces are increasingly reliant on coal from other provinces and regions, and this trend is likely to continue. In short, China is facing great problems in inefficient coal transport in a large volume.

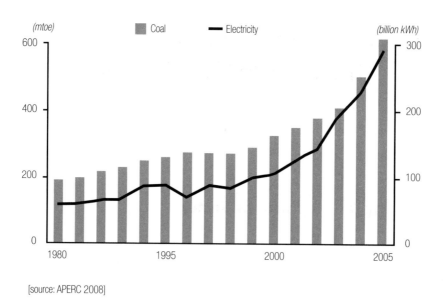

[source: APERC 2008]

Figure 4   Intra–provincial movement of coal

2.1.1.2 Policy: efficient coal transport

The future stability of coal supply will rely heavily on affordable and adequate coal transportation. China will require significant investment in order to upgrade and expand its rail transport infrastructure. Resolving rail transport bottlenecks would also ease pressure on the transportation of coal by truck, a costly and energy-wasteful method. In light of rising petroleum prices and the insufficient capacity of transportation, the cost of transporting coal has been increasing faster than pithead prices for coal consumers in China's coastal provinces.

2.1.1.3 Policy: modification of coal–electricity supply chain

Besides increasing rail freight capacity to meet its coal transport demands, China can improve supply chains through measures that reduce transport needs, for example, by transporting electricity or coal-intensive products rather than raw coal. Efforts to send electricity from resource-rich western areas to coastal provinces are well underway. These enterprises can streamline coal supply chains by reducing the distance between extraction and use, and they have the potential to replace the transport of large quantities of coal in the future.

Current limitations on the development of mine-mouth coal industries and power generation include constrained water resources in coal-rich areas and overburdened power transmission networks. Major grid companies, however, are stepping up efforts to expand transmission and distribution capacity, with particular emphasis on the long-distance high and ultra-high voltage lines of the West-to-East Power Transfer Project. Coal washing at the mine mouth also has the potential to reduce transport demands by improving the energy-density of the transported coal product, but broader implementation of this practice, seldom adopted in China, has faced repeated barriers despite coal industry modernization.

Participation in international coal markets can also help reduce burdens on domestic coal transport. Already, coastal provinces are finding it more economical to import coal from Southeast Asia and Australia, while markets are favorable for continued exports of coal from China's northern ports to neighboring economies. Domestic development of transmission and distribution technologies was also emphasized in the Eleventh FYP guidelines. Increased foreign collaboration, however, may further quicken the speed of development and deployment.

2.1.2 Power Sector

2.1.2.1 Problem: bottlenecks in coal transportation infrastructure

Coal infrastructure and investment is closely tied to that of power in China. About 45% of all coal consumption in China is used for power generation, and 79% of power generation uses coal. The security of power supply therefore relies on coal supply security—namely, timely fuel delivery. In recent years, bottlenecks in coal transportation infrastructure, particularly rail freight, have been blamed for power shortages. More investment is now directed toward rail-based transportation of coal to address this concern, but due to the geography of Chinese coal resources and demand, where coal is often transported long distances from central and western production regions to coastal power generation facilities, this area will continue to be a point for possible stress.

Of all the coal transported in 2005, 16.9% was by water and 24.2% by road, while the majority, 58.9%, was by rail. These modal shares have been stable from year to year since 2000. In fact, coal transport represented 47.9% of all rail transport in 2005, standing at 1.29 billion tonnes.

Capacity shortages along these three major coal transport routes have been reported under normal summer peak-load conditions since 2004, requiring reprioritization of rail freight and passenger needs to ensure adequate supply of thermal coal to generation facilities. Major generators cited inadequate rail capacity as the cause of fuel shortages in 2005. And in early 2008, severe disruptions along railways contributed to depleted fuel stocks for power generators in central and southern China and widespread blackouts.

2.1.2.2 Policy: prioritization of coal transport in rail infrastructure

The central government outlined infrastructure-based strategies to alleviate rail bottlenecks in coal transport under the Eleventh FYP guidelines, including the construction of new freight lines, double-tracking existing lines, separating freight from passenger lines, electrification and increasing receiving capacity at seven ports in Hebei, Tianjin, and surrounding areas which load ships for delivery to southern provinces. While such upgrades are a much-needed response to the current situation, they do not directly address long-term system needs; namely, that developed coastal centers will be unable to meet their growing power demands through local coal-based generation. As coal resources in central China are depleted and production drifts towards the massive northwestern Chinese coal basins, and as efficiency and environmental concerns move to the fore, it will be increasingly attractive to transfer electricity rather than solid fuel to where end users need it by moving power generation to the mine mouth, or even to switch fuels for local generation. Aware of this, and as outlined elsewhere in this study, the central government has prioritized the construction of large-scale mine-mouth thermal power generation plants since 2013.

2.1.2.3 Problem: under–investment in power transmission infrastructure

Under-investment in grid infrastructure has led to an unstable dispatch schedule whereby generators are tasked to compensate for transmission fragility by managing their own loads across a broad range. This not only means that the generators themselves may not be able to operate at their most thermodynamically efficient, but also forces them to maintain economically inefficient fuel reserves. Such uncertainty in generation schedules also makes it more difficult to manage direct power sales beyond the NDRC-contracted annual power purchase agreement.

Grid investment continues to be largely isolated from market signals and is determined through a bottom-up process whereby the central government (through the NDRC) aggregates investment requests made by local governments and other sub-bureaus into a broad investment guideline to be propagated over the course of a FYP. And because transmission and distribution tariffs are not determined competitively or even necessarily cost-based, the two state-oriented grid companies have little direct incentive to increase infrastructure investment.

2.1.2.4 Policy: increased investment in grid

Recent and current policy direction under the Tenth and Eleventh FYPs acknowledges this investment gap and outlines massive increases in grid investment. Economy-wide, grid investment in 2004 increased 30.5% from the previous year, and grew another 40.0% in 2005, reaching 158.6 billion yuan (real 2005 19.36 billion USD).

The Eleventh FYP guidelines (2006—2010) called for an additional 1.2 trillion yuan combined investment by the two grid companies, an increase of 90% over total investment through the period of the Tenth FYP.

There is a strong and growing demand for reliable and high performance power grids in China. Total interregional transmitted electricity demand increased from 8.976 terawatt hours in 2002 to 344.68 terawatt hours in 2006, accounting for 12% of total electricity generation. As a result, much of the new grid investment will be directed towards achieving long-distance interconnection across the country, such as through the west-to-east and south-to-north power transmission projects, which aim to distribute electricity resources more efficiently throughout the economy.

By 2006, the length of 220 kilovolt-and-above transmission and distribution lines was 281,000 kilometers, having grown by 11% per year since 2002. Current efforts, however, aim even higher, namely, the construction and integration of ultra-high-voltage transmission capacity with grids of different sizes and at different levels around the country, something which has not been successfully implemented anywhere over long distances. The first ultra-high-voltage grid demonstration project, a power transmission network with 1,000 kilovolt AC and 800 kilovolt DC, will span 653.8 kilometers and cross both the Yellow and Hanjiang Rivers, transmitting power produced in Shanxi province to Henan province, and then to Hubei province. However, this demonstration project is now facing various challenges regarding safety, economics, technology and reliability.

2.1.3 Petroleum Market

2.1.3.1 Problem: high import dependency

With the growth in demand, petroleum imports have surged. China has been a net importer of oil since 1993 and crude oil since 1996. Table 3 shows that in 2004, before the Eleventh FYP, the import dependency was 44.52%, implying that 44.52% of China's petroleum consumption was dependent upon imported petroleum. The problem is that the import dependency keeps increasing and has been over 50% since 2009.

Table 3   Petro production and demand, 2004—2010

	Unit	2004	2005	2006	2007	2008	2009	2010
Production	10,000 ton	17,587	18,135	18,477	18,632	19,044	18,949	20,301
Demand	10,000 ton	31,700	32,538	34,876	36,659	37,303	38,385	43,245
Net imports	10,000 ton	14,113	14,402	16,400	18,027	18,259	19,436	22,944
Import dependency*	%	44.52	44.26	47.02	49.17	48.95	50.63	53.06

*Import dependency=net imports/demand*100%

2.1.3.2 Policy: overseas upstream investment (Going Out Policy)

The prospect for continued growth in oil demand has pushed the world's oil and gas companies to increase upstream oil and gas investment efforts. This phenomenon is particularly pronounced among state-oriented oil enterprises as the enhancement of energy security has become a broadly shared policy agenda. China's three major state-oriented oil enterprises (CNPC, Sinopec and CNOOC) are often considered to be global leaders in such efforts because of their visibility in a recent surge to acquire overseas upstream investment stakes and because of the sheer size of future needs to meet Chinese petroleum demands.

To fill the gap between a growing appetite for oil and the production from domestic oilfields which cannot meet the demands, Chinese state-oriented oil enterprises have increased efforts to acquire overseas upstream stakes of oil and natural gas. In fact, such efforts are often supported by the central government through tax breaks and low interest payments, leading some to describe such activities as threats to both oil majors and other national oil corporations. For example, the failed attempt by CNOOC to acquire Unocal in 2005 highlighted concerns in the U.S. economy over Chinese oil firms' overseas investment activities and their repercussions.

Indeed, in the Tenth FYP (2001—2005), China had already emphasized the importance of overseas upstream investment due to the increasing dependence on imports. That plan encouraged oil firms to get involved in international operations as part of the Going Out Policy. The strategy was and still is intended not only to acquire upstream stakes, but also to facilitate wider adoption of Chinese technology, equipment, materials and labor in the overseas market.

The Tenth FYP also stated that the need for central government approval for many upstream projects would be phased out in order to allow firms to make their own decisions and take risks. To facilitate the Going Out strategy, the Chinese central government supports oil firms' active involvement in overseas upstream investment in various ways for securing oil from overseas upstream equity production (overseas secured oil). It should be noted that oil security is not the unique objective of the overseas upstream investment. Indeed, the oil firms sell their crude oil on the market rather than supplying it to China.

2.1.3.3 Policy: strategic petroleum reserves

When China became a net importer of petroleum products in 1993 (Figure 5), it needed to establish strategic petroleum reserves (SPR) in order to protect energy security. A decade later, China officially approved the establishment of the national SPR in 2003 with a planned total reserve capacity of 500 million barrels (mb) (about 70 million tons) to be completed by 2020. Establishing the SPR will take about fifteen years to complete and is being undertaken in three phases, incrementally adding reserve capacities of 103.2 million barrels in 2008, 206.9 million barrels in 2013, and 189.9 million barrels in 2020. However, the second phase of SPR construction was delayed and finished in 2015, two years behind schedule (See Table 4).

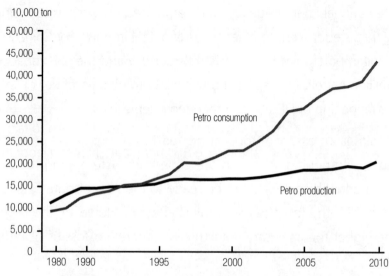

Figure 5   Petro production and demand, 1980—2010

Table 4   Chinese strategic petroleum reserve

Phase	Target		Completion		
	Capacity (mb)	Year	Capacity (mb)	Cumulative level (mb)	Year
Phase I	103.2	2008	103.2	103.2	by 2009
Phase II	206.9	2013*	18.9	122.1	2011
			18.9	141	2011
Phase III	189.9	2020			
Total SPR	500				

* revised to 2015

It is believed that if China had its own SPR, a petroleum crisis would not have occurred in Guangzhou and Shenzhen in August 2005. This event caused significant negative effects on economic development and social stability. In fact, because of this China was late to complete the first phase of the project.

After the 1973 global oil crisis, some industrialized countries set up the IEA (International Energy Agency) and committed themselves to maintain a reserve that is equivalent to ninety days of net oil imports. For China in 2010, the net oil import was 4.5 million barrels per day and the SPR capacity was 103.2 million barrels, corresponding to twenty-three days of net oil imports, which is far behind the IEA's recommended reserve level.

An SPR is an essential tool for decreasing the negative effects of oil shortages, dampening shocks to the economic system and providing an interval during which efforts can be made to mediate disputes. Hence, the larger the SPR, the less the economy is affected. However, the larger the SPR, the higher the inventory holding costs. Therefore, loss of GDP may be incurred.

While building the SPR, China also encouraged domestic oil companies to increase commercial reserves.

Remarks:

Results of import dependence rate after Eleventh FYP

Indeed, the import dependence in Table 3 is a nominal value. If some policies such as strategic petroleum reserves can reduce the nominal net imports, we will have "real" net imports.

Hence, we have the following formulation:

Nominal Net Imports=

Real Net Imports + Strategic Petroleum Reserves +

Overseas Secured Oil = Demand − Production

→ Real Net Imports = Demand − Production − Strategic
Petroleum Reserves − Overseas Secured Oil

$$= D − P − SPR − OSO$$

→ Real Import Dependence = [Real Net Imports/
Demand]*100%

$$= [(D-P-SPR-OSO)/D]*100\%$$
$$= [1 − (P+SPR+OSO)/D]*100\% \quad (RID)$$

From the above expression, to decrease real import dependence, we can

(1) increase domestic production (increase P),

(2) shift away from oil dependence (reduce D),

(3) increase overseas secured oil (by investments) from politically
stable economies (increase OSO),
and

(4) increase the level of strategic petroleum reserves (increase SPR).

It is interesting to see how the combined effects of the SPR and OSO (overseas secured oil) changed the import dependence in 2010. With the settings in Table 5, there are four scenarios according to the levels of SPR and OSO. The results of the different scenarios regarding oil import dependence are calculated by an equation (RID) and shown in Table 6. The results show that the oil import dependence rate drops from 53.05% to 34.94% when China has the SPR and OSO shown in Table 5. If political stability is considered, the dependence rate is 45.43%.

Thus we can see how China uses two policies to handle the problem of oil security.

Table 5   Setting in 2010

	Unit	2010
Demand (D)	million barrels	3,089.00
Production (P)	million barrels	1,450.15
Strategic petroleum reserves (SPR)	million barrels	103.2
Overseas secured oil (OSO)*	million barrels	132.31
Political stability of OSO**	%	29%

* Source: IEA (2012), overseas production of national oil companies (CNPC, Sinopec and CNOOC) was 1.25 million barrels per day in 2010 (0.7, 0.35, 0.2 respectively)

** Source: APERC (2008), Political stability of crude oil import sources=29%

Table 6   Results of oil import dependence in 2010

No OSO		With OSO	29% Political stability
		100% Political stability	
No SPR	53.05%	38.28%	48.77%
With SPR	49.71%	34.84%	45.43%

2.1.4   Natural Gas

When China became a net importer of natural gas in 2007, during the Eleventh FYP, there were no special policies concerning the security of natural gas. However, with the gradually increasing demand for natural gas, and after a gas shortage in the winter of 2009, the NDRC and the National Energy Administration (NEA) started formulating some plans with gas companies in 2010.

2.1.4.1   Problem: decrease in self–sufficiency

The need to improve its environment and to counter climate change, its global commitments and the internal demands for marketization of its energy industry are the major driving forces that are gradually changing China's energy supply from coal to natural gas.

National production increased by 14% annually from 27 bcm in 2000 to 96.8 bcm in 2010. Consumption increased from 24.5 bcm to 130 bcm from 2000 to 2011. Consequently, the foreign dependency rate in 2012 reached around 29% and consumption was forecast to be 500 bcm in 2013 (IEA, 2012). However, the import of natural gas reached 58.4 bcm in 2015 and the consumption of natural gas reached 193 bcm in 2015 (National Bureau of Statistics of the People's Republic of China). The foreign dependency rate was around 30%.

Thus, similar to the development trend of oil, there is a likelihood that natural gas development will also lead to overdependence on foreign supply, which will be unfavorable to China's energy security.

2.1.4.2 Policy: Increase in LNG and pipeline gas imports

According to the calculations of the NEA, by 2015 natural gas consumption was expected to reach 230 bcm, possibly 330 bcm. Although the actual consumption was 193 bcm, the domestic supply capacity of 100~150 bcm still could not meet this. It is clear therefore, that there is a need to increase the import volume by multiplying the sources. LNG and natural gas (NG) pipelines are the main means of importation.

In 2011, China imported LNG from Australia (5 bcm), Qatar (3.2 bcm) and Indonesia (2.7 bcm), totaling 10.9 bcm. This was the first year of LNG imports. Australia remains the main LNG import source for China. With the increase of LNG imports from various sources, new LNG stations have been constructed in China, in Fujian, Shanghai, Dalian and Jiangshu to name but a few, in order to take the growing import volume.

China has also started to cooperate with Central Asian countries (Kazakhstan, Turkmenistan and Uzbekistan), Myanmar and Russia to complete its international NG pipelines towards the northeast and southwest. In 2009, the China—Central Asia pipeline started to transport gas. In October 2013, the China—Myanmar pipeline (12 bcm/year) also started operation.

2.1.4.3 Policy: exploration and development of shale gas

China is trying to reduce its reliance on oil and gas imports through a combination of supply-side and demand-side policies. One way is to develop carbon capture and storage or use (CCS/CCU) technologies to enable China to continue using its domestic coal resources, at the same time as limiting CO_2 emissions. Another initiative is to develop domestic shale gas, which has strong government support due to its strategic importance for China. However, this is likely to be a slow process unless there are technological breakthroughs. China and the U.S. have been in discussion over cooperation on shale gas (Robinson and Qinhua, 2013). PetroChina has explored shale gas in Wanxian, Sichuan province, and has a target of 1 bcm in shale gas production in 2015 in collaboration with Shell. However, at the end of June 2016, Shell withdrew its investment in the exploration and exploitation of shale gas in Sichuan because they considered it unlikely that the projects would lead to large-scale shale gas production [1].

① http://news.xinhuanet.com/
fortune/2016-07/12/c_129138555.htm

2.1.4.4 Problem: geopolitical risks

The geopolitical risks China is facing are on three levels: the first is a bilateral one, referring to the sustainability of long-term natural gas supply agreements; the second is a regional one, which is about the safety of the pipelines it is developing; and the third is a global one, involving China's energy relations with Central Asia, Europe, Russia and others. Among these, the transborder pipelines are most seriously at risk as they face the numerous problems posed by the change of gas reserves in the countries China imports from, financial and economic risks, risk of damage to the energy infrastructure, internal conflicts in those nations, terrorist attacks and worsening of bilateral relations, etc.

Remarks: How to promote natural gas–generated power?

It is well known that natural gas-generated power is showing some promise in China. However, the question remains, how to promote its development? There are three challenges: ensuring the supply of natural gas, ensuring the infrastructure of gas in cities and the less competitive price of gas compared to coal, even to oil.

2.2 Past Five-Year Plans and Energy Policies

2.2.1 The First Stage: Sixth–Ninth Five-Year Plans (1981—2000)

The focus of this first stage was economic development. Hence, energy development and the corresponding policies were made in an ad-hoc manner aimed at supporting economic development.

The Sixth Five-Year Plan (1981—1985) highlighted the fact that a shortage of energy was a significant problem restricting China's economic development. The plan was to increase primary energy production by just 1.4% per year (visible hand) while industrial growth would grow by 4% per year over the same period (visible hand). In addition, energy conservation policies were emphasized to support economic development. The Seventh Five-Year Plan (1986—1990) emphasized expansion of supply to meet the expected rapid growth of demand due to faster economic development. The Eighth Five-Year Plan (1991—1995) included targets for total primary energy supply to grow at 2.4% per year and for economic growth of 6% per year over the period. In terms of energy security, petroleum began to be imported in 1993. The Ninth Five-Year Plan (1996—2000) planned for 8% annual economic growth over the period. Oil petroleum began to be imported in 1996. During these twenty years the expansion of the supply of energy was mainly directed by the visible hand of government to achieve economic growth.

Figure 6 shows that the growth rate of GDP was always greater than that of energy consumption during this stage (1981—2000).

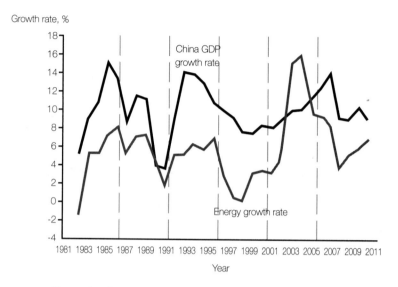

Figure 6　Growth rate of GDP and energy, 1981—2011

2.2.2　The Second Stage: Tenth Five-Year Plan (2001—2005)

Following previous practice, the Tenth Five-Year Plan set 7% and 4.5% as the targets for annual economic growth and the annual decline in energy intensity (energy consumption per GDP) respectively. However, Figure 7 shows us that the energy intensity rebounded from 2001 to 2005, and Figure 6 that the growth rate of energy was higher than that of GDP in 2003 and 2004, which becomes an important issue in that the previous practice did not function very well.

China became a member of the World Trade Organization (WTO) on December 11, 2001. Figure 8 shows that energy consumption increased rapidly in all kinds of energy from 2001, but coal in particular dominated the total increase of energy consumption.

Figure 9 reports the energy consumption by sector, showing that the energy consumption of the manufacturing sector increased rapidly compared with other sectors from 2002 onwards.

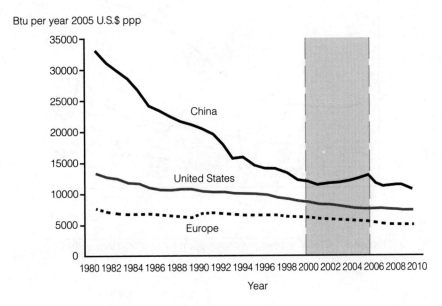

Figure 7　Energy intensity, 1980—2010

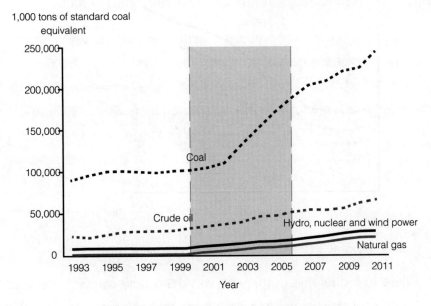

Figure 8　China's energy mix, 1993—2011

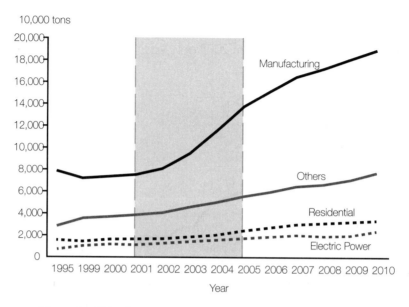

Figure 9　China's energy consumption by sector, 1995—2010

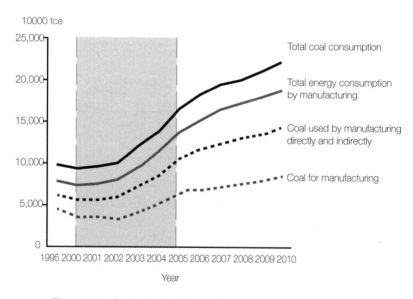

Figure 10　Coal consumption in manufacturing, 1995—2010

Figure 10 further tells us that coal was the major energy source used by the manufacturing sector. Table 7 supports this, showing that in 2005 the proportion of coal used for manufacturing in total energy use was around 77%, and the proportion of coal used for manufacturing out of total coal use was 63.8%. Note that these figures include coal used for electricity generation which was consumed by the manufacturing sector. Hence, they include the direct and indirect consumption of coal by manufacturing. If we look at the contribution to GDP from manufacturing, Table 8 shows that it was 32.7% in 2005. That is, 63.8% of the coal used in China in 2005 was used to generate 32.7% of GDP. We can make similar observations from the use of petroleum by industry sector from Figure 11. Therefore, before the Eleventh Five-Year Plan (2006—2010), China's GDP was generated from non-green sources.

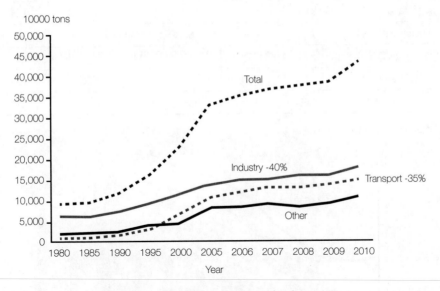

Figure 11　Petroleum consumption by sector

Table 7　Coal used for manufacturing

	Unit	2000	2005	2010
Total consumption	10,000 tce	94,287.6	165,611.2	223,030.5
Electricity generation	10,000 tce	40,541.2	75,920.6	107,975.8
Manufacturing	10,000 tce	36,127.8	65,728.7	84,874.2
Manufacturing, directly and indirectly*	10,000 tce	56,384.1	105,685.5	143,761.4

	Unit	2000	2005	2010
Total energy consumption by manufacturing	10,000 tce	73,824.3	137,140.4	188,497.9
% of coal used for manufacturing in total energy use	%	76.4	77.1	76.3
% of coal used for manufacturing in total coal use	%	59.8	63.8	64.5

Continued

* (Coal for Manu.)+ (% of Elec. used by Manu.)*(Coal for Elec.)

Table 8   Energy efficiency of manufacturing

	2004	2005	2006	2007	2008	2009
GDP (100 million yuan)	51,748.5	60,117.99	71,212.89	87,464.95	102,539.5	110,118.5
% of Manu. in GDP	32.4	32.7	32.9	32.9	32.7	32.3
Energy elasticity*		1.36	0.66	0.49	0.30	0.72
Energy/GDP	2.23	2.28	2.12	1.89	1.68	1.64
Coal elasticity*		1.55	0.71	0.35	0.27	0.58
Coal/GDP	1.68	1.76	1.65	1.43	1.27	1.23

*(ΔEnergy/Energy)/(ΔGDP/GDP)

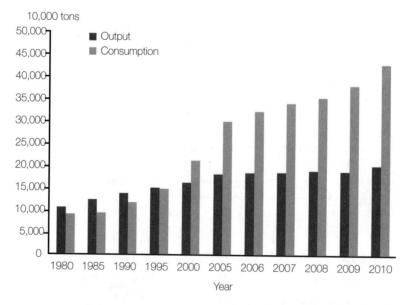

Figure 12   Crude oil output and consumption

Besides increases in coal consumption, we also find that crude oil and natural gas consumption increased by 42.5% and 70.0% respectively from 2001 to 2005 (Table 9). While oil had been imported since 1996 and the import of liquefied natural gas was planned only in the late 1990s, such rapid increases in demand for oil and natural gas made energy security an import issue for China's energy policy from then on. Given the inadequate domestic supply, securing foreign energy supply became one of the energy security policies. To this end, the Going Out strategy was used to encourage the state-owned energy companies to invest in some foreign energy markets and projects and to buy directly from international energy markets (both oil and natural gas). However, the pace of Going Out was too slow to ease the strong demand for oil and natural gas during the Tenth Five-Year Plan. Figure 12 indicates that China was no longer self-sufficient in crude oil after 2000. On the other hand, it was also predicted that energy demand would increase sharply due to China's high economic growth rate target. Hence, the Medium and Long-Term Plan for Energy Conservation policy was launched in 2004 by the National Development and Reform Commission to address the demand side.

Table 9　Annual growth rate of energy consumption by type, 2001—2005

Year	Coal	Crude Oil	Natural Gas	Hydro, Nuclear & Wind Power
2001	2.0	1.5	12.7	21.1
2002	5.5	8.4	6.0	3.2
2003	18.3	9.6	20.1	2.6
2004	15.6	16.7	16.1	19.7
2005	12.6	2.8	15.0	12.2
2001—2005	62.6	42.5	70.0	42.3
2001—2011	131.7	97.4	382.0	146.8

In short, at the end of this stage, China faced the problems of non-green GDP and supply security problem of oil and natural gas. Moreover, the pace of going out was too slow for energy supply security. Although this development stage was mainly directed by the visible hand, due to the Going Out strategy, Chinese enterprises needed to face the invisible hand of the international energy markets with which they were not familiar. As mentioned above, energy policies not only consider economic growth, but also energy security. Table 10 shows that China could not meet the energy intensity target (4.5% annual decrease) set in the Tenth Five-Year Plan.

Table 10   Changes in energy intensity

	2000	2005	2010
Energy intensity*	11,986.4	12,486	10,842.2
% of change		4.1	-13.1
Target %		-20.6	

* Btu per year in 2005 U.S. dollars (Purchasing Power Parities).
Source: BP Statistical Review of World Energy, June 2013.

2.2.3   The Third Stage: Eleventh Five-Year Plan (2006—2011)

China has moved to the third stage of energy development planning, which considers not only economic development and energy security, but also environmental pollution. The pollution problem here is not only CO_2 emissions but also pollution from SO_2, NOx, and coal mining. This is because, on average, coal and crude oil represented 70% and 20%, respectively, of the primary energy consumption in China.

On top of this non-green energy mix, China also faced the problem of non-green GDP and the problem of security of supply of oil and natural gas. Hence, in the Eleventh Five-Year Plan, energy policy became a stand-alone policy in contrast with previous five-year plans. In addition, emissions reduction targets were set in the plan to address the pollution problems. Some highlights of the energy and environmental policies are listed below:

- economic growth of 7.5% per year; decrease in energy intensity of 4.4% per year;

- shift from export-oriented economy to one supported by domestic demand;

- 3.2% reduction of SO2 emissions;

- energy-mix strategy included renewables and natural gas;

- energy pricing reforms (first application of invisible hand in energy sector).

The energy section of the Eleventh Five-Year Plan guidelines was divided into a review of the current energy situation including important problems faced in energy development, overall directions and targets, infrastructure, conservation and environment, technology and other overall policies. The overall philosophy of energy development remained similar to past plans, addressing the need to develop both energy supply and conservation, but with an emphasis on conservation as well as overall energy consumption diversification and optimization of energy supply and demand structure (APERC, 2009).

In short, to support economic development, the objectives of energy policy in the Eleventh Five-Year Plan guideline were (1) to enhance energy infrastructure and systems, (2) to improve energy conservation and efficiency, and (3) to reduce environmental pollution. These objectives address the problem of (1) non-green GDP and (2) the supply security problems of oil and natural gas after the Tenth Five-Year Plan.

Although coal was still described as China's energy foundation, the guideline targets indicated that its overall share of primary energy consumption should fall. Specifically, the plan outlined a decrease in the share of coal by 3% and that of oil by 0.5% over the five-year period, and an increase the share of natural gas by 2.5%, hydropower by 0.6%, renewables by 0.3% and nuclear power by 0.1%. Table 11 shows that the share of natural gas increased by 1.8%, less than the 2.5% target. The share of hydro, nuclear, and wind power increased by 1.8%, which is greater than the overall 1% target.

Table 11   Summary of energy mix, 2005 and 2010

	Coal (%)	Crude Oil (%)	Natural Gas (%)	Hydro, Nuclear, and Wind Power (%)
2005	70.8	19.8	2.6	6.8
2010	68.0	19.0	4.4	8.6
Difference (2010–2005)	-2.8	-0.8	+1.8	+1.8
Target	-3.0	-0.5	+2.5	+1.0

2.2.4   Summation

From the energy mix results shown in Figure 13, Figure 8 and Table 11, we can conclude that there was no big change in the energy mix in the period 2006—2010. We can infer that the problems of non-green GDP and the supply security problem of oil and NG were not really resolved in the Eleventh Five-Year Plan. That is, the Twelfth Five-Year Plan faced the same problems and China is still in the third stage of energy policy development.

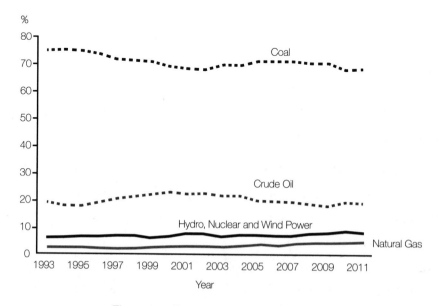

Figure 13   Energy mix in %, 1993—2011

2.3 Changes in Energy Mix, Energy Intensity and Environmental Effects

From the time of the reform and opening-up of China to the end of the twentieth century, the country's economic development has realized the targets of quadrupling GDP while reducing the energy intensity by half (energy consumption/GDP). Since the onset of the new century, the accelerated heavy industrialization and expansion of high energy consuming industries have caused the energy intensity to rebound. However, energy intensity usually decreases year by year. Energy intensity increased by 4.8% and 5.5% in 2003 and 2004. The average annual rate of increase of national energy consumption from 2003 to 2005 was 14%. At this time, GDP increased by 70% from the 1990 level, whereas the total energy consumption increased by 70% from its value at the end of the last century. This three-year continuous increase means that energy intensity in 2005 was higher than the levels in 1999.

Hence, in the Eleventh Five-Year Plan period (2006—2010), the reversal of the increasing energy intensity trend was proposed, with a goal of attaining a 20% decrease. Thus, the target was a 10% decrease in the total amount of major pollutants for this period, and this target was successfully met. It should be noted that this national target of 20% energy intensity reduction was further divided into regional targets and the central government introduced administrative, legal and economic tools to facilitate the regional efforts. The provinces, with these tools and the additional measures that each province could initiate, developed their implementation plans (APERC, 2009). In general, the central government sought to balance economic progress and environmental protection by implementing the most cost-effective measures first. With further economic growth, greater emissions controls and environmental protection will become both more affordable and more necessary.

The use of energy affects the environment in the forms of water pollution, air pollution, and CO_2 emissions that cause global warming. In this second part of Chapter 2, we focus on the policies related to air pollution and CO_2 emissions.

In China, the main air pollutants are sulphur dioxide (SO_2), nitrous oxides (NO_x), particulate matter (PM), and heavy metals. In particular, air pollution is due largely to the dominance of coal in the primary energy mix, of which coal accounts for about 70% (Figure 14).

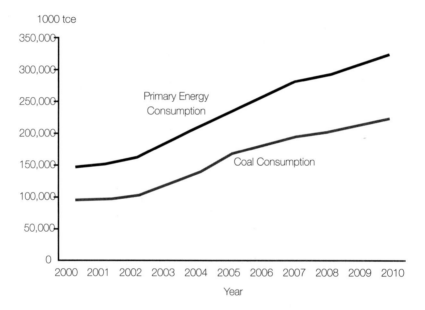

Figure 14　Primary energy and coal consumption, 2000—2010

Coal consumption in 2006 accounted for the majority of SO_2 emissions (about 90%) and also contributed significantly to NOx (67%), PM (70%), and heavy metal emissions like mercury (38%). Between 2001 to 2006, coal consumption grew at an average rate of 11.8% per year, a 74.7% increase over those five years. During the same period SO_2 emissions increased as well, though by a smaller margin, about 5.1% per year, or 28% over the five-year period (APERC, 2008).

In China, air pollution mainly comes from the combustion of coal for electricity and of petroleum fuels for transportation. Hence, we discuss these two sectors in turn.

2.3.1 Thermal Power

2.3.1.1 Air pollution

SO_2 emissions decreased during the Ninth Five-Year Plan and rose steadily during the Tenth as energy demand increased (APERC, 2008). However, China did not achieve its target to reduce major air pollutants, including SO_2, to 10% below 2000 levels. Efficiency improvements and emissions reduction measures taken during the period, though significant, could not fully counteract the rapid growth in fossil fuel consumption (Table 12).

Table 12   Energy mix of thermal power, 2004—2010 (mtce)

Energy	2004	2005	2006	2007	2008	2009	2010
Coal	671.67	755.48	856.09	957.19	983	1015.39	1131.73
Oil	21.76	19.23	13.74	9.71	7.17	4.77	4.4
Gas	18.12	24.25	42.52	61.61	67.48	81.63	122.83
Other energy	4.23	6.95	11.64	15.17	18.07	20.96	18.72
Total	715.78	805.91	923.99	1043.68	1075.72	1122.75	1277.68

In response, the central government stepped up efforts to control SO_2 in the Eleventh Five-Year Plan, requiring the installation of flue gas desulphurization in new and existing thermal power plants. The SO_2 situation is changing as flue-gas-desulphurization (FGD) technology becomes standard in the power sector (APERC, 2009). Despite ambitious Tenth Five-Year Plan targets to reduce SO_2 emissions, the targets for actual flue-gas-desulphurization equipment remained low (15 gigawatts (GW) of installed capacity and with a further 16 GW in construction). These modest targets reflected the estimated high costs of flue-gas-desulphurization systems. During the period 2006—2010 (the Eleventh Five-Year Plan), the SO_2 policy framework was further strengthened, requiring much of the power industry to adopt flue-gas-desulphurization systems as standard. The Eleventh Five-Year Plan guidelines, like the previous five-year plan, adopted a target of a 10% reduction in SO_2.

To implement these targets, the State Environmental Protection Administration of China partnered with the six major power providers to assume 75% of the reduction targets and reduce total SO_2 emissions from coal-fired power plants by 61% to 5 million tonnes. To achieve this, 300 flue-gas-desulphurization systems were installed. As with energy intensity targets, precise SO_2 reduction targets vary by province or region, taking into account each region's industrial structure and ability to pay. From 2006, all new coal power plants were required to install FDG equipment while many existing plants were required to install systems by 2010. Additionally, new economic incentives reinforced efforts to invest in flue-gas-desulphurization: power plants running FGD systems were both assigned higher electricity tariffs (an additional 0.015 yuan/kWh) to offset operating costs and given grid feed-in priority over other generators; both strong incentives in an industry facing high fuel costs and regulated electricity pricing. As a result, flue-gas-desulphurization capacity jumped to over 150 GW, accounting for 30% of total installed capacity by the end of 2006. This meant that China had little trouble in meeting its Eleventh Five-Year Plan goal of adding 137 GW capacity.

Indeed, China witnessed an unprecedented construction of FGD facilities. By the end of 2005 only 14% of coal-fired electricity generating capacity had flue-gas-desulphurization. That percentage rose to 86% by the end of 2010. With the effects of this flue-gas-desulphurization, economy-wide SO_2 emissions increased 28% from 2000 level during the Tenth Five-Year

Plan and decreased 14% from the 2005 level during the Eleventh Five-Year Plan. Table 13 shows the SO_2 emissions by sector, and the right-hand column indicates the percentage change between 2000 and 2010 emission levels.

Table 13 SO_2 emissions by industrial sector in 2000, 2005 and 2010 (million tons)

Industrial Sector	2000	2005	2010	Change 2000—2010, %
Electricity	7.07	11.67	9	27
Mineral products	2.33	1.78	1.69	-27
Chemicals	0.82	1.17	1.04	27
Iron & steel	0.75	1.42	1.77	136
Non-ferrous metals	0.71	0.71	0.8	13
Petroleum/ coking coal	0.38	0.71	0.64	68
Other industries	4.3	2.34	2.13	-50
Non-industrial sources	3.58	5.69	4.8	34
Total	19.95	25.49	21.85	10

2.3.1.2   Energy intensity and CO_2 emissions

The China Electricity Council (CEC) has published a collection of the energy conservation and pollution reduction policies and regulations in the electrical industry dating back to 2002 (CEC, 2012). In 2006, the National Development and Reform Commission and the National Energy Office (NEO) published *The Opinions about Accelerating Shutting Down Small Thermal Power Units*, an implementation policy geared to "encourage large power plants and discourage small energy-inefficient power plants" (National Development and Reform Commission and National Energy Office, 2006). The State Council approved the policy in 2007.

We present here some results from a recent paper (Chung and Zhou, 2013) analyzing emissions from China's regional thermal power. China's electricity generation is mainly dependent on thermal electricity. Figure

15 shows the proportion of thermal electricity generation in total power generation from 2004 to 2010. The proportion decreased from 83.38% in 2007 to 80.51% in 2010 due to the introduction of hydroelectric power. However, coal is still the major fuel in thermal electricity generation in China. Hence, thermal electricity is a heavily-polluting industry and naturally becomes a critical segment for energy conservation and pollution reduction.

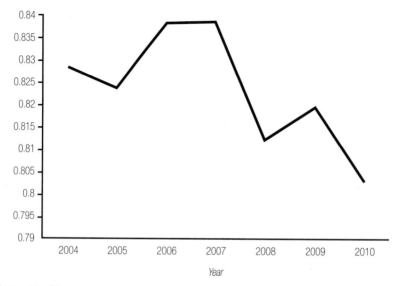

Figure 15   The proportion of thermal electricity to total power generation in China

As stated above, China's power generation is mainly dependent on thermal electricity and coal is still the major fuel. The national target of 20% energy intensity reduction was further divided into regional targets in the Eleventh Five-Year Plan period (2006—2010). Hence, it is worthwhile to study the energy efficiency and CO_2 emissions reduction performance on regional grids from 2004 to 2010. Table 14 summarizes the relationship between provincial power grids, regional grids, and the corresponding two corporations. The North, Northeast, East, Central, and Northwest China Power Grid Companies are under the jurisdiction of the State Grid Corporation of China, while the South and Hainan Power Grids are under the jurisdiction of the China Southern Power Grid Corporation.

Table 14   Seven regional power grids and provincial power grids in China

Corporation	Region/Company	Provincial Power Grids
State Grid Corporation of China	North	Beijing, Tianjin, Hebei, Shanxi, Shandong, Inner Mongolia
	Northeast	Liaoning, Jilin, Heilongjiang
	East	Shanghai, Jiangsu, Zhejiang, Anhui, Fujian
	Central	Jiangxi, Henan, Hubei, Hunan, Chongqing, Sichuan
	Northwest	Shaanxi, Gansu, Qinghai, Ningxia, Xinjiang
China Southern Power Grid Corporation	South	Guangdong, Guangxi, Guizhou,Yunnan
	Hainan	Hainan

Figure 16 shows the changes in energy mix and electricity output of all regional grids, from which the following can be noted:

• coal consumption growth is nearly in line with the thermal electricity output because coal is the dominant fuel for thermal electricity generation;

• gas consumption has increased rapidly, whereas oil consumption is continually decreasing;

• growth of other energy consumption has been fast, although there was a drop between 2009 and 2010.

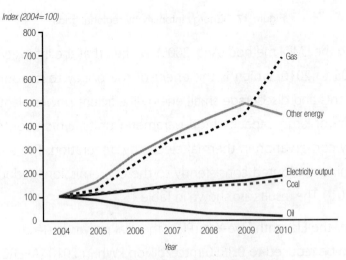

Figure 16   All regional grids, 2004—2010

2.3.1.3 Regional energy intensity and CO_2 emissions

Figure 17 shows the energy intensity of electricity by regional grids, and Tables 18 and 19 in this chapter's appendix offer further details. The results show that the energy intensity of most regional grids improved from 2004 to 2010. However, the trends showing improvement are distinct in the central, east, and south grids.

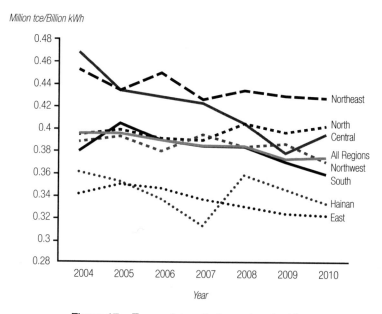

Figure 17   Energy intensity by regional grids

Using the LMDI method (Ang, 2005), we find that the intensity improved from 2005 to 2010, which is the effect of the policy to encourage large power plants and discourage small energy-inefficient power plants, and the promotion of large-capacity high-parameter units, which contributed to electricity conservation in thermal electricity generation. The effect of the energy mix contributed consistently to the CO_2 emissions reduction from 2004 to 2010. The results are shown in Table 15.

Under the Eleventh Five-Year Plan, thermal power generation efficiency was set to be reduced to 0.3550 mtce/billion kWh in 2010 (APERC, 2009). To accomplish this, the government encouraged the construction of large coal-fired units above 600 MW that would replace smaller and less efficient units.

Table 15   Complete decomposition of CO_2 emissions change (mtce), 2004—2010

	ΔC_{act}	ΔC_{str}	ΔC_{int}	ΔC_{mix}	ΔC_{emi}	ΔC_{total}
2004—2005	219.57	2.17	0.27	-11.38	-3.94	206.69
2005—2006	318.42	9.48	-40.56	-32.16	-10.36	244.83
2006—2007	317.72	1.48	-33.01	-27.85	-8.33	250.00
2007—2008	73.79	-0.76	3.95	-13.76	-3.76	59.46
2008—2009	183.82	5.67	-79.83	-23.72	-3.27	82.66
2009—2010	354.08	-4.73	10.78	-25.81	115.98	450.30
2004—2010	1,467.39	13.31	-138.40	-134.68	86.33	1,293.94
% in ΔC_{total}	113.40	1.03	-10.70	-10.41	6.67	100.00

*note: ΔC_x equal to CO_2 emissions change and the subscripts are the corresponding effects.

Indeed, smaller power plants built under past rural development programmes are a major cause of low efficiency in China's power generating sector. Table 16 shows there were 4,804 units with a generating capacity of less than 100 MW (77% in generating capacity) in 2006. On the other hand, large units of over 600 MW accounted for just 2.1% in terms of number of units and 18.4% in generating capacity.

Table 16   Thermal power generating units by capacity, (end of 2006)

Capacity of Generating units MW	Number of Units		Generating Capacity	
	Units	%	GW	%
> 600	132	2.1	82	18.4
100–600	1,307	20.9	281	62.8
100 >	4,804	77	84	18.8

Source: CEPYEC (2007)

As a further bid for a more efficient power supply, policies were also instigated for the development of advanced power generation facilities, such as large-capacity mine-mouth power plants, waste coal utilization power plants, large hydropower facilities, large capacity gas combined-cycle plants, gas turbine peak-shaving plants, water-saving power generation plants and nuclear power plants. Construction of conventional medium-sized and small units with a capacity of 300 MW or less (that are situated in high-voltage power grids) is restricted.

Table 17 shows the capacity of small thermal power units that were closed in the six grid regions in the first ten months of 2007. Altogether, small thermal power plants with a capacity totaling 10.39 GW were closed, greatly exceeding the national annual goal of 10 GW.

Table 17   Small thermal power plants closed in January—October 2007

Region	Capacity Closed GW	Total Capacity	
		GW	%
Central	3.07	92.58	3.32
Northeast	1.15	41.38	2.78
South	1.01	40.61	2.48
North	3.00	164.8	1.82
East	1.73	138.65	1.24
Northwest	0.43	35.62	1.2
Total	10.39	513.64	2.02

Source: CEPYEC (2007)

Consequently, the average thermal power station fuel consumption decreased from 0.3955 mtce/billion kWh in 2005 to 0.3740 mtce/billion kWh in 2010.

China has adopted the policy of accelerating the closure of thousands of small, inefficient coal- and oil-fired power plants (Zhang, 2010). Units facing closure include those below 50 MW, those below 100 MW and having been in operation for over twenty years, those below 200 MW and having reached the end of their design life, those with a coal consumption of 10% higher than the provincial average or 15% higher than the national average, and those that fail to meet environmental standards. The total combined capacity that needs to be decommissioned was set at 50 GW as a target during the period 2006—2010.

Closing small thermal power plants seemed to be very effective for the central grid, but not for the north grid, according to the intensity effects shown in Figure 18. From Table 17 we can observe that the central region needed to close a greater percentage of its capacity in 2007.

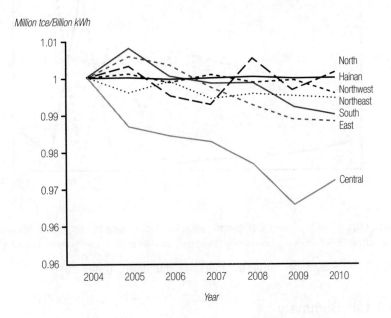

Figure 18   Intensity effects of different regional grids

We also note from Figure 18 that there were hockey-stick effects for the intensity effect in the central and north grids. It may be because by the end of the first half of 2009, the total capacity of decommissioned smaller and older units had increased to 54 GW, having met the 2010 target to decommission power plants with a total generating capacity of 50 GW one-and-a-half years ahead of schedule (Zhang, 2010). Figure 20 shows the results of this decommissioning smaller and older power unit policy.

Another possible reason for the hockey-stick effects may be that the energy intensity regional target of 2010 (energy consumption per GDP)was met one year ahead of schedule. Table 19 (in this chapter's appendix) shows the percentage reduction of energy intensity from the 2005 level. It can be noted that the central and north regions almost met the target in 2009.

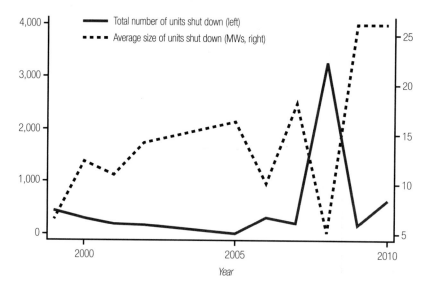

Source: Ma, C.B. and X.L. Zhao (2015) "Electricity Market Restructuring and Technology Mandates:Plant-Level Evidence for China's Changing Operational Efficiency from 1997 to 2010." Energy Economics 47: 227–37.

Figure 19   Small thermal units shut down, 1999—2010

2.3.1.4 Summary

We have analyzed the energy efficiency and reduction of CO_2 emissions of China's regional thermal electricity generation from 2004 to 2010 on a regional grid level. There are seven principal regional grids in China. By using LMDI analysis, we found that the intensity and energy mix have positive effects on the decrease of CO_2 emissions, but the structural and CO_2 emissions factor effects are insignificant. The accumulated intensity and energy mix effects account for 10.70% and 10.41% of the decrease in CO_2 emissions, respectively. Such improvements may be due to the implementation of the policy of encouraging large power plants and decommissioning small energy-inefficient power plants, and the promotion of large-capacity high-parameter units which have contributed to electricity conservation in thermal electricity generation. However, the regional results show that the north grid performed badly and there were hockey-stick effects in the intensity effect of the central and north grids. Hence, regional moving average targets are recommended. According to Dua et al. (2009), there was no evidence of efficiency gains in fuel input associated with the electricity reforms from 1995 to 2004. It is believed that the improved intensity effect from 2005 to 2010 originated from the policy aimed to encourage large power plants and discourage small energy-inefficient power plants, and the promotion of large-capacity high-parameter units which contributed to electricity conservation in thermal electricity generation.

2.3.2 The Transport Sector

Emissions from vehicular transport comprise greenhouse gas (GHG) emissions, including CO_2 and noxious emissions consisting of CO (carbon monoxide), HC (hydrocarbon), NO_x (nitrogen oxides), and PM (particulate matter). The transport sector, one of three high energy consuming sectors (i.e., industry, building, and transportation), faces challenges related to the preservation of resources and the environment. China is a developing country with a huge population and scarce resources. Therefore, moderating the relationships between transportation development, resource conservation, and environmental protection is very important to the Chinese government, along with finding ways to realize sustainable development of the environment in conjunction with cooperation with the transportation sector.

2.3.2.1 Environment–related policies

APERC (2008), provides us with the following background:

Transportation fuels account for a small fraction of energy used in China, but pollution from transport is increasingly important in many large Chinese cities, especially as vehicle ownership rises. In Beijing, vehicle emissions were responsible for 40% of PM10, 68% of NO2 and 77% of CO emissions. Recently, PM2.5 is considered as the most harmful pollutants which can be inhaled deeply into lungs, and some can even enter blood stream; they aggravate heart and lung diseases. Hence, PM2.5 reduction comes under the spot light. According to a study by Beijing Municipal Environmental Protection Bureau, vehicle emissions are responsible for 31.1% of PM2.5 in Beijing. To address transportation emissions, China has introduced higher standards for vehicle emissions over time.

Although Chinese vehicle emission standards are relatively stringent, the availability of higher quality fuels challenges implementation. If fuel quality falls below engine requirements, emissions will not meet standards. Low quality fuel also increases wear on advanced engines, reducing vehicle lifetimes and increasing maintenance costs.

The quality of motor fuel used in China is generally lower than that in developed economies, and the resulting vehicle exhaust is more polluting. Fuel quality standards, however, have progressed significantly over time. Higher standards are often implemented in key cities first before expanding to other areas. For example, leaded petrol was banned in eight cities in 1997 before being phased out completely by 2000, and Beijing is leading the way in the adoption of higher fuel and emission standards equivalent to those used in the EU.

A similar stepwise approach is being taken to reduce sulphur content in petrol and diesel over time. Despite these efforts, when new auto emission standards (equivalent to EURO III) were set to be in place for all of China starting 2007, the National Development and Reform Commission (National Development and Reform Commission) delayed implementation due to insufficient capacity of oil refineries to produce the necessary low-sulphur fuel. EURO IV-equivalent standards have being implemented in Beijing and Shanghai since 2008, and refineries are struggling once again to provide the higher quality fuels required.

The National Development and Reform Commission's decision to postpone broader implementation of the new standards may also have been influenced by smaller vehicle manufacturers who struggled to meet the higher technological specification. As this case illustrates, coordination between different industries (vehicle manufacturers and fuel producers) is vital to the successful implementation of cleaner technologies. Furthermore, this example emphasizes the need for strong domestic technology development when implementing environmental regulations in developing economies.

A further complication is that different transport modes in China are governed by different organizations. Road and water transport are governed by the Ministry of Transport (MOT), whereas railways are governed by the Ministry of Railways (MOR). Air transport is under the jurisdiction of the Civil Aviation Administration of China (CAA), and pipeline transport is governed by the China National Petroleum Corporation (CNPC), the China Petrochemical Corporation (SINOPEC Group), and the China National Offshore Oil Corporation (CNOOC). Despite these difficulties, in the Tenth and Eleventh Five-Year Plans (2001—2010) the central government did launch a series of policies regarding energy savings for environmental protection. These will be outlined below.

In 2004, the MOT issued fuel consumption limits for passenger vehicles."

215

The limits are divided into sixteen categories based on kerb mass and are subjected to two phases of implementation (July 1, 2007 and January 1, 2009) the first phase aimed to cut liters per 100 kilometers by up to 10% by 2008 and the second phase required vehicle fuel consumption to drop by another 10% from the first phase level. These limits apply to vehicles of kerb-mass less than 3,500 kg, less than nine seats, and a maximum design speed less than 50 km/h on petrol and diesel passenger cars.

In 2005, a *Notice about Encouraging the Development of Energy Conservation, Environmental Protection, and Small Displacement Vehicles* was issued. The notice encouraged:

- production of and investment in low-fuel consumption, low emission, small-displacement (engines), mini and high-power vehicles;

- implementation of national standard fuel consumption limits for operating vehicles;

- control of the development of high-fuel consumption vehicles; and

- improvement of technical standards of energy conservation and environmental protection of small-displacement vehicles.

In 2006, consumption tax was revised to place a higher tax burden on larger, energy-inefficient vehicles.

In the same year, the MOT issued *Guiding Suggestions on Building Economized Transportation*, and also *Guiding Suggestions to Implement "Decisions on Strengthening Energy Conservation by the State Council."* In 2007, MOT further issued *Suggestions about Further Strengthening Energy Conservation in the Transport Sector* and *Notice about Carrying out Energy Conservation Demonstration Activity in Transport Sector*. In the same year, the Chinese government revised the conservation law, which clarified the legal basis for the measures identified in the Eleventh Five-Year Plan and the government authority for energy efficiency in transportation. Also in the same year, the MOT issued *Guiding Suggestions on Energy Conservation and Emission Reduction in Ports*. Finally, in 2008, it enacted measures that enforced the conservation law in both road and water transport sectors.

Different policies have been implemented to deal with particular types of vehicles. For example, in 2007, fuel consumption limits for light commercial vehicles were introduced which are applicable to vehicles with a total mass of less than 3,500 kg and to light commercial vehicles with nine to twelve seats, including light trucks and buses (in force in February 1, 2008). In 2008, fuel consumption limits and measure method for operating passenger buses, and fuel consumption limits for operating trucks were issued. These enforcements are applicable to vehicles that operate on diesel and petrol as well as to passenger buses and trucks with a total mass greater than 3,500 kg. These are also applicable to operating trucks of 3,500 kg to 31,000 kg and dump trucks, and semi-trailer combination vehicles with a maximum total mass of 49,000 kg.

These fuel economy standards are more stringent than those in the U.S., Canada and Australia, but are less stringent than those in Europe and Japan.

Since 2007, China has followed European standards for emission requirements. In fact, the government has implemented the National Phase III (equivalent to Euro III standards) vehicle emission standards.

In 2008, the MOT issued *The Long and Mid-term Planning and Outline about Energy Conservation in Road and Water Transport*, choosing road, water transport, and ports as key fields. It also put forward overall goals and main tasks for 2015 and 2020. In 2009, the government issued *Notice about Demonstration and Promotion of Energy Efficient and Alternative Energy Vehicles*. It also initiated the programme "Ten Cities and Thousand Vehicles," which aimed at selecting at least ten Chinese cities and introducing more than 1,000 alternative energy vehicles in each of these cities within three years with support from a government subsidy. A total of twenty-five pilot cities have been selected to participate, and the number is likely to continue to rise since the promotion programme is still in the pilot phase at the time of writing.

In 2009, the government issued a *Notice about the Benefits to People of Energy Conserving Products Project*, which promoted energy conservation products, including energy conservation vehicles through government subsidies and other funds.

China has also propelled the electrification of railways to reduce the number of oil-based trains. The proportion has increased from 31.2% in 2005 to 46.2% in 2010, and the operating mileage of electrified railways in China was second in the world in 2011 (NBSC, 2011) and has been first since the proportion reached 52.4% in 2013 (financeifeng.com).

To investigate the effectiveness of these policies, we provide an overview of the energy efficiency of the transport sector overall and then in a regional context.

2.3.2.2 Overview of transport energy (2003—2009)

The energy efficiency of the transport sector can be defined as energy use by turnover, where turnover can be measured by passenger-km (PKM) and ton-km (TKM), Figures 20 and 21 show the changes in energy, PKM, and TKM, and energy mix. From Figure 20 the following can be noted:

- the growth of TKM is faster than that of PKM.

- the growth of energy use between 2003 and 2004 is the same as that of PKM. However, there is a sudden growth of energy use between 2004 and 2005. Between 2005 and 2009, the growth of energy use is comparable to that of TKM and faster than that of PKM.

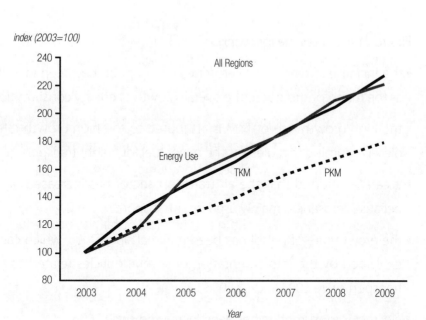

Figure 20   Index changes in energy use, PKM and TKM in China

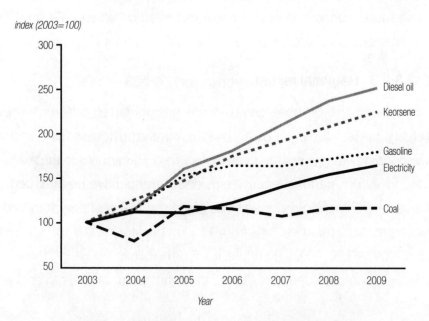

Figure 21   Index changes in energy consumption in China

219

Figure 21 indicates the following:

- the increase in diesel and kerosene consumption has been identified as the main contributor to the overall growth of energy consumption.

- the high growth rate of TKM is attributed to the high growth rate of diesel, assuming that diesel is the major fuel for freight transport.

- it can be inferred that the air transport sector has increased rapidly because kerosene is mainly used in air transport.

- the growth rate of petrol has been minimal since 2006, which can be explained by the implementation of several policies related to road transport since 2004 and/or 2006.

- electricity consumption has been increasing since 2006.

- a decrease in coal use was evident between 2003 and 2004. However, a sudden growth in coal use was observed between 2004 and 2005. Thereafter, coal use has remained roughly constant.

2.3.2.3 Regional results

Although the Chinese government has allocated different energy intensity targets locally, not all energy consumption sectors and the corresponding energy measures can be localized. This applies to the transport sector, for which national energy efficiency targets have been issued. For instance, the Chinese government has raised the fuel economy standard for new cars manufactured in China from 12.3 km per liter in 2002 to 15.3 km per liter in 2009 (APERC, 2009). Therefore, it is worthwhile investigating the energy consumption and efficiency of China's transport sector on the regional level, see Table 2.

A. Eastern region

Figure 22 shows that:

- the growth of TKM is faster than that of PKM;

- the growth of energy use is faster than that of PKM and TKM;

- the growth of the transport sector relies heavily on the use of more energy; and

- the growth of TKM is in line with that of energy consumption in 2003—2007, then decouples after 2007.

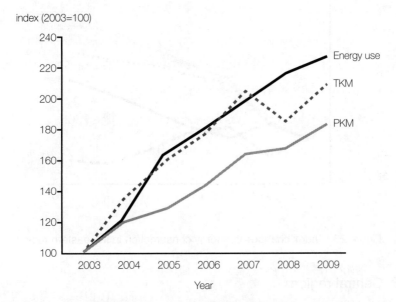

Figure 22   Index changes in energy use, PKM and TKM in the eastern region

Figure 23 shows that:

- the growth of kerosene and diesel use is the main contribution to the overall growth of energy consumption;

- since kerosene is mainly used in air transport, it can be inferred that the air transport sector is growing rapidly;

- the high growth rate of TKM results can be attributed to the high growth rate of diesel, assuming that diesel is the major fuel for freight transport; and

• there is an obvious change in 2004 and 2005. The growth rate of diesel
and petrol has become minimal since 2005, which can be explained
by the implementation of several policies related to road transport in
2004.

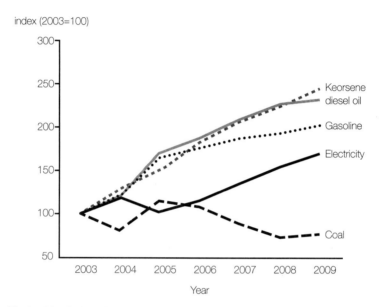

Figure 23   Index changes in energy consumption in the eastern region

B. Central region

Figure 24 shows that:

• the growth of TKM is the same as PKM in 2003—2007. Since 2007, the
growth of TKM has been faster than that of PKM;

• the growth of energy use is the same for PKM and TKM in 2003—2007.
Since 2007, it is interesting that TKM has grown much faster than
energy use.

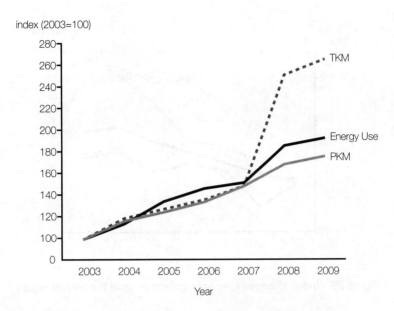

index (2003=100)

Figure 24   Index changes in energy use, PKM and TKM in the central region

Figure 25 shows that:

• similar to the eastern region, the growth of kerosene and diesel is the main contribution to the overall growth of energy consumption;

• since kerosene is mainly for air travel, it can be inferred that the air transport sector has increased rapidly;

• the high growth rate of TKM is attributed to the high growth rate of diesel, assuming that diesel is the major fuel for freight transport;

• the growth of petrol was minimal; in addition, since 2006, there has been almost no growth of petrol use; and

• Coal use has been increasing since 2004.

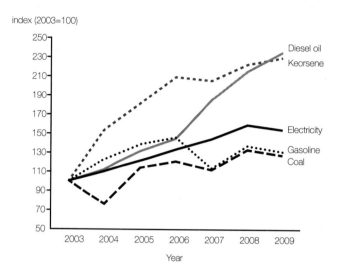

Figure 25   Index changes in energy consumption in the central region

C. Western region

Figure 26 shows that:

• the growth of PKM is slower than that of TKM; and

• the growth of energy consumption is as fast as that of TKM.

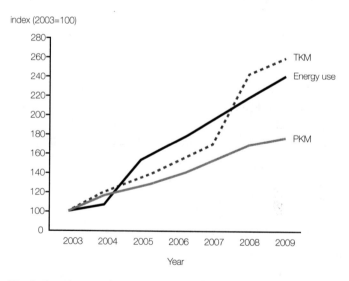

Figure 26   Index changes in energy use, PKM and TKM in the western region

Figure 27 shows that:

• the growth of diesel is the main contribution to the overall growth of energy consumption; and

• the high growth rate of TKM is attributed to the high growth rate of diesel, assuming that diesel is the major fuel for freight transport. There was an obvious switch to diesel in 2004 and the growth rate of diesel use has since become faster.

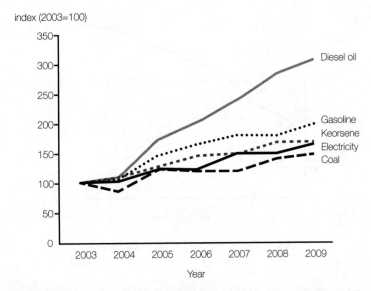

Figure 27   Index changes in energy consumption in the western region

2.3.2.4 Transport energy efficiency

To determine the aggregate energy efficiency defined as energy use per TKM, passenger-km must be converted to ton-km because we have PKM and TKM. Based on the conversion method used by China's government, the converted turnover of passenger and freight traffic is equal to the turnover of passenger traffic divided by a conversion coefficient, plus the turnover of freight traffic.

Figures 28 and 29 illustrate energy use and turnover by area. The energy use of the eastern area is twice that of the central and western areas. The reason may be that the eastern area has a higher growth rate and more direct foreign investments than the central and western areas overall. However, the turnover of the eastern area increased at a quicker rate than that of the Central and Western areas. Moreover, the turnover of the Eastern area decreased in 2008, which was caused by the global financial crisis that year, after a consistently increasing trend since 2003.

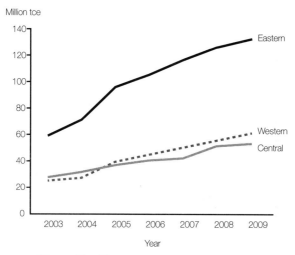

Figure 28   Transport energy use by area

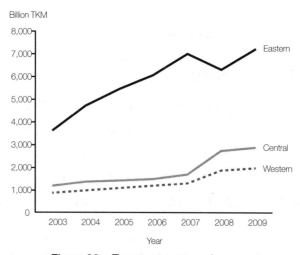

Figure 29   Transport turnover by area

The central area has a large population and is mainly agricultural, and the western area has comparatively low population density and is the least developed area. Despite these differences, the central and western areas are similar in terms of their energy use and turnover characteristics. However, the western area's transport sector has used more energy than the central area since 2005.

Figure 30 shows the results of energy efficiency by area for all regions. The eastern area continuously improves its energy efficiency, and is the main contributor to the improvement of overall energy efficiency. The central area's energy efficiency has clearly worsened since 2008.

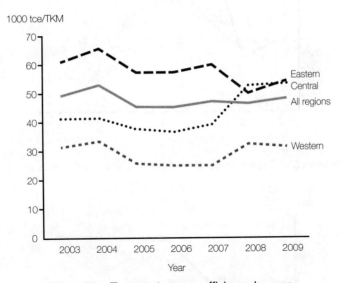

Figure 30   Transport energy efficiency by area

Using the LMDI method (Ang, 2005) to analyze the various effects of energy changes at the regional level, we can find the intensity effects and energy mix effects shown in Figures 31 and 32.

Figure 31 shows that the overall intensity has improved since 2005, which is consistent with the policy guidance in the Eleventh Five-Year Plan (2006—2010). A series of new policies in the transport sector were implemented to reverse the trend of energy intensity increase. These policies were more effective in the central and western areas.

Figure 33 demonstrates that the effects of energy-mix are insignificant. A similar result can also be observed in a decomposition analysis of CO_2 emissions. Hence, it is not necessary to conduct CO_2 emission decomposition analysis due to the redundancy of the observations.

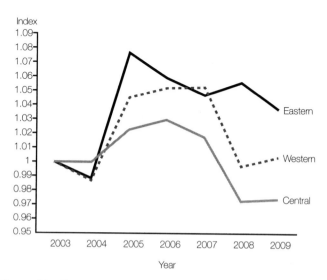

Figure 31　Transport sector—intensity effects of different areas

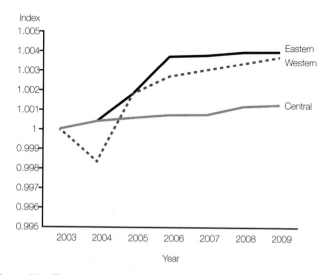

Figure 32　Transport sector—energy–mix effects of different areas

2.3.2.5 Summary

Despite the fact that the rate of increase of energy consumption and emissions has slowed in recent years, the total absolute quantity is still increasing. Improving energy efficiency and decreasing emissions in the transport sector require continued and greater efforts.

The results are consistent with the guidance policy stated in the Eleventh Five-Year Plan (2006—2010), in which a series of new policies were enacted in the transport sector. The eastern and central areas performed better than the western area based on the pure environmental performance index. The eastern area performed worse than the central and western areas, except in 2003 and 2005, and the central area performed better than the western area based on the mixed environmental performance index. In recent years, overall environmental performance of the central area has seen an increase, but those of the eastern and western areas are decreasing. Although the government has issued a series of environmental protection policies, environmental performance in the transport sector still leaves much room for improvement.

Appendix of Chapter

Table 18　Summary of energy consumption for regional thermal electricity generation (mtce)

Region	Energy	2004	2005	2006	2007	2008	2009	2010
North	Coal	199.63	235.27	264.41	299.81	320.03	326.92	367.23
	Oil	0.30	0.25	0.31	0.25	0.11	0.53	0.79
	Gas	5.70	7.59	11.53	18.92	24.19	28.56	45.33
	Other	2.03	2.67	4.80	7.18	7.68	9.17	4.15
Northeast	Coal	72.08	74.99	83.96	86.44	91.57	90.45	97.39
	Oil	0.30	0.25	0.22	0.18	0.22	0.11	0.16
	Gas	4.80	2.13	4.25	5.72	5.36	6.76	7.81
	Other	0.32	0.16	1.13	0.71	0.92	1.44	1.11

Continued

Region	Energy	2004	2005	2006	2007	2008	2009	2010
East	Coal	139.41	162.62	184.24	204.79	213.32	222.97	242.34
	Oil	6.06	4.98	2.57	1.75	1.23	0.83	1.17
	Gas	4.65	9.31	17.34	18.44	17.64	20.67	31.17
	Other	0.30	0.63	0.56	1.47	1.96	3.12	4.58
Central	Coal	125.12	129.99	146.18	163.39	154.86	156.72	175.30
	Oil	0.34	0.28	0.23	0.26	0.32	0.24	0.69
	Gas	0.68	1.41	4.49	7.14	7.33	10.67	22.17
	Other	0.55	0.40	1.35	1.76	2.34	2.42	4.15
Northwest	Coal	49.58	52.54	60.27	70.73	77.28	81.46	98.42
	Oil	0.06	0.06	0.06	0.07	0.06	0.04	0.04
	Gas	1.32	1.60	1.45	2.79	2.84	3.07	3.74
	Other	0.24	0.10	0.49	1.04	1.30	1.23	0.21
South	Coal	84.50	98.43	115.20	129.61	123.17	133.98	147.68
	Oil	14.69	13.39	10.32	7.19	5.23	3.01	1.54
	Gas	0.27	1.34	2.46	7.87	9.30	11.08	11.60
	Other	0.79	2.99	3.31	3.01	3.63	3.38	4.29
Hainan	Coal	1.35	1.64	1.83	2.42	2.77	2.89	3.37
	Oil	0.01	0.02	0.03	0.01	0.00	0.01	0.01
	Gas	0.70	0.87	1.00	0.73	0.82	0.82	1.01
	Other	0.00	0.00	0.00	0.00	0.24	0.20	0.23
Summary	Total	715.78	805.91	923.99	1,043.68	1,075.72	1,122.75	1,277.68
	% of other	0.59	0.86	1.26	1.45	1.68	1.87	1.47

Table 19   Energy intensity of electricity by region (mtce/billion kWh)

Region	Region	2004	2005	2006	2007	2008	2009	2010
North	Beijing	0.4245	0.3775	0.3762	0.3491	0.3269	0.3128	0.3121
	Tinjin	0.2987	0.3362	0.3374	0.3292	0.3428	0.3484	0.3504
	Hebei	0.3853	0.3925	0.3856	0.3866	0.4220	0.4127	0.4305
	Shanxi	0.3985	0.3823	0.3877	0.3980	0.4086	0.4066	0.3857
	Shandong	0.3860	0.4061	0.3736	0.3676	0.3626	0.3538	0.3842
	Inner Mongolia	0.4525	0.4432	0.4442	0.4323	0.4695	0.4467	0.4353

Continued

Region	Region	2004	2005	2006	2007	2008	2009	2010
Northeast	Liaoning	0.4448	0.4074	0.4209	0.4049	0.4023	0.4076	0.4265
	Jilin	0.5163	0.5212	0.5018	0.4875	0.5224	0.4877	0.4420
	Heilongjiang	0.4252	0.4197	0.4594	0.4184	0.4222	0.4243	0.4169
East	Shanghai	0.3626	0.3735	0.3714	0.3782	0.3627	0.3669	0.3549
	Jiangsu	0.3401	0.3471	0.3485	0.3295	0.3301	0.3222	0.3133
	Zhejiang	0.3390	0.3456	0.3359	0.3280	0.3180	0.3130	0.3093
	Anhui	0.3467	0.3771	0.3688	0.3622	0.3298	0.3279	0.3493
	Fujian	0.3159	0.3119	0.3059	0.3114	0.3218	0.3071	0.3152
Central	Jiangxi	0.4512	0.4382	0.4305	0.4282	0.4224	0.3991	0.4173
	Henan	0.4721	0.4286	0.3972	0.3976	0.3861	0.3705	0.3851
	Hubei	0.4229	0.4143	0.4175	0.4219	0.3937	0.3392	0.4302
	Hunan	0.4317	0.3315	0.3889	0.3942	0.3603	0.3289	0.3865
	Chongqing	0.4396	0.4040	0.4176	0.4197	0.4337	0.4257	0.3895
	Sichuan	0.5763	0.5982	0.5908	0.5517	0.5299	0.4664	0.3747
Northwest	Shaanxi	0.3971	0.4245	0.3968	0.4512	0.4065	0.4020	0.3886
	Gansu	0.3526	0.3395	0.3410	0.3403	0.3461	0.3444	0.3430
	Qinghai	0.3784	0.4778	0.4333	0.3739	0.3763	0.3610	0.3476
	Ningxia	0.3795	0.3758	0.3631	0.3679	0.3934	0.3893	0.3771
	Xinjiang	0.4340	0.4111	0.4025	0.4020	0.3750	0.4032	0.3631
South	Guangdong	0.3513	0.3606	0.3500	0.3451	0.3405	0.3319	0.3140
	Guangxi	0.4628	0.5172	0.5181	0.4473	0.4340	0.3856	0.3817
	Guizhou	0.3798	0.3935	0.3652	0.3781	0.3874	0.3662	0.3799
	Yunnan	0.5154	0.6080	0.5310	0.5319	0.5562	0.5107	0.5115
Hainan	Hainan	0.3610	0.3530	0.3367	0.3127	0.3581	0.3445	0.3328
All regions		0.3954	0.3955	0.3892	0.3836	0.3838	0.3728	0.3740

Table 20: Percentage reduction of regional energy intensity from 2005 level*

Region	Province	2006	2007	2008	2009	2010	Target in 2010**
Central	Chongqing	12.6	15.3	21.5	25.5	29.2	20
	Hubei	4.7	10.4	17.0	22.9	28.9	20

231

						Continued
Region	Province	2006	2007	2008	2009	2010	Target in 2010**

Region	Province	2006	2007	2008	2009	2010	Target in 2010**
Central	Hunan	6.4	11.5	18.6	22.5	27.4	20
	Jiangxi	7.4	12.5	17.8	19.7	24.7	20
	Sichuan	4.4	8.8	14.5	17.3	22.9	20
	Henan	3.7	8.1	12.9	16.6	20.9	20
East	Anhui	3.3	7.4	12.1	18.1	25.0	20
	Jiangsu	5.1	9.0	14.5	18.4	23.4	20
	Zhejiang	5.1	8.9	13.1	17.7	23.2	20
	Fujian	2.9	6.9	9.5	15.1	20.0	16
	Shanghai	5.4	10.1	10.8	15.7	17.6	20
Hainan	Hainan	2.7	2.2	6.3	8.1	14.9	12
North	Inner Mongolia	7.2	14.9	24.9	28.9	32.9	22
	Beijing	8.5	17.8	22.9	28.0	32.8	20
	Shanxi	3.3	9.4	19.6	20.9	29.7	22
	Tianjin	7.3	9.9	19.4	21.9	23.5	20
	Shandong	5.4	8.5	15.9	18.6	22.1	22
	Hebei	1.6	6.1	12.6	15.7	20.5	20
Northeast	Jilin	4.6	10.2	14.5	19.5	24.4	22
	Liaoning	4.1	7.2	14.7	17.6	23.3	20
	Heilongjiang	1.9	2.9	6.8	5.2	12.4	20
Northwest	Ningxia	5.0	14.0	25.3	29.7	36.4	20
	Shaanxi	13.5	17.2	24.1	25.9	31.3	20
	Gansu	6.6	10.5	13.6	16.1	22.4	20
	Qinghai	3.0	7.4	13.2	13.5	20.2	17
	Xinjiang	4.8	5.7	7.7	3.2	12.5	n.a.
South	Guizhou	5.8	10.5	18.7	22.0	26.4	20
	Guangxi	3.7	7.3	10.2	13.5	19.1	15
	Guangdong	4.6	7.9	11.3	15.2	18.1	16
	Yunnan	2.5	7.1	13.3	14.1	17.8	17

*   Regional GDP is in 2005 constant dollar; regional energy intensity is energy consumption per GDP.

**   Source: APERC (2009).

3

Effects of the Twelfth Five-Year Plan Energy Policy

3.1 Understanding the Background to the Twelfth Five-Year Plan Energy Policies

The Chinese government has set a general target in energy development, which can be roughly divided into the following stages: before 2030 development will focus on fossil energy with new and renewable energy as a secondary focus; from 2030 to 2050, fossil energy and new and renewable energy will have equal importance and be developed simultaneously; and after 2050, new and renewable energy will be the main energy source and fossil energy will be secondary.

In order to fulfil this ambitious target, the three strategies of optimization of the energy mix, improvement of energy efficiency and use of clean energy become key. If the energy policy of the Twelfth Five-Year Plan (2011—2015) is successful, it is expected that China's energy market and system will continue to be successful. This section presents the background and barriers to, and the guidelines and focus of these policies.

3.1.1 Background

By 2013, when the Twelfth Five-Year-Plan was officially launched, China's energy sector had developed greatly, especially after the endeavors of the

Eleventh Five-Year Plan, which laid a solid foundation for the government to do more. However, they faced both advantages and disadvantages.

3.1.2 Advantages

The energy self-sufficiency rate had been raised. Primary energy production was increased from 2.16 billion tce in 2005 to 2.97 billion tce in 2010 with an annual growth rate of 6.6%. China had strengthened its national oil reserve ability to 16.4 million cubic meters.

The energy mix had been optimized. New and renewable energy was expanded from 7.4% in 2005 to 9.4% in 2010, non-fossil fuels from 8.6% to 6.8% and natural gas from 2.6% to 4.4%. Energy intensity of per unit GDP had been decreased by 19.1%, while SO_2 and CO_2 decreased by 14.29% and 12.45%. New generating capacity of over 430 million kW was added and the overall generating capacity reached 950 million kW, with the largest grid scale in the world when Xinjiang and Hainan are included. Overseas equity oil had increased to 900 million tons with a total of 35 billion USD in mergers and acquisitions.

3.1.3 Disadvantages

As the main energy source of the country, for many years China's yield of coal, from thirteen large coal quarries, has been the largest in the world. On the one hand, this served national economic development well, but on the other, it also put great pressure on China to combat the environmental pollution and mine accidents.

The development of nuclear power accelerated significantly in China, with thirteen new nuclear projects, with a total capacity of 37.02 million kW, thirty-four generator units in total, approved by the government in Hongyan River (Liaoning), Ningde and Fuqing (Fujian), Yangjiang (Guangdong), Fangjiashan and Sanmen (Zhejiang), Haiyang (Shandong), Taishan

(Guangdong), Changjiang (Hainan) and Fangchenggang (Guangxi). Therefore there are now twenty-eight generator units of a capacity of 30.97 million kW being built, accounting for 40% of the world's nuclear power production. The Fukushima nuclear leakage aroused the public's worries about the safety of nuclear energy, and consequently protests occurred at the construction sites of the nuclear power stations.

From 2006 to 2010, the construction of hydropower plants and units increased rapidly, helping China's hydro installation exceed 200 million kilowatts: the number of newly-added units was nearly equal the number built in the previous ninety-five years. However, the construction of many small hydropower plants at the same time caused a number of ecological disasters, for example, a four-year drought in Yunnan province.

The wind power industry also developed rapidly: the cumulative lifting capacity of wind power in the whole country reached 31 million kW, but the monopoly ownership of the power grid has been a barrier to the electricity generated by the wind being used on the public grid. Hence some owners abandoned their plants in Inner Mongolia, Hebei, Jilin, and in other locations which resulted in a curtailment rate of around 20%~30% and a 10 billion yuan loss.

Solar power has also been advancing. A relatively complete industrial chain for PV batteries with an annual yield of 8 million kW was created. Nevertheless, less than 1% of world total solar energy consumption forced China to rely heavily on foreign markets, which has led to many trading conflicts.

3.1.4　Barriers

There remained some barriers for development of China's energy, as follows:

3.1.4.1 Conflict—energy growth and shortage of resources

China has been becoming the largest energy-consuming country in the world. However, its energy reserve per capita was very low, especially in petroleum and natural gas, of which the reserve is only 6% of the world average. During the Eleventh Five-Year Plan, the annual average growth rate of the national economy, which was 11.2%, was supported by an average increase of energy consumption of 6.6%. Although the elasticity of energy decreased from 1.04 to 0.59 during the Tenth Five-Year Plan, the need for energy is expected to increase greatly with national modernization. Energy security is a considerable challenge considering the short supply.

3.1.4.2 Conflict—coal–based energy mix and low–carbon development

In 2014, the annual consumption of coal exceeded 3 billion tons, accounting for 47% of the world's coal, 40% higher than the world level in the consumption of primary energy.

In the electricity industry, thermal power held its position as primary provider. The Chinese government established a development strategy of building a resource-saving and environment-friendly society, but it is a challenge to the existing mode of development based on resource-intensive and high-pollution coal industry. The conflict between the coal-based energy structure and low-carbon development will be in existence for a long time.

3.1.4.3 Conflict—intensive use of fossil energy and increased ecological demands

The petrochemical industry is the backbone of the national economy. Its products are widely used in many fields of industrial production, daily life and the science and technology behind national security, which has significant effects on industrial advances and economic growth. However, the long-term development of fossil energy causes severe effects on the ecology of the country, and has been the main constraint in constructing an environmentally-friendly society.

3.1.4.4 Conflict—domestic energy, supply and demand

China has a rich supply of energy in the west and scarce resources in the east, while the pattern of energy demand is the opposite. The future development of energy will focus more on the west, but the greatest demand still remains in the east and center. The problem of transporting energy from west to the east, crossing regions at a large scale over long distances, has been highlighted even more strongly.

3.1.4.5 Conflict—technological development and insufficient talent

Technological innovation has been becoming a critical force in energy development. In China, the technology used in energy has been poorly managed; there is insufficient senior talent and weak independent innovation, many key innovative technologies are limited by other existing technologies; and industries depend highly on foreign technologies. For these reasons, it has been hard for China to achieve the goal of becoming a technologically-advanced world energy power and leading the energy evolution.

3.1.5 Guidelines

To overcome these barriers, the Twelfth Five-Year-Plan policies had specific planning for energy development.

3.1.5.1 Optimization of fossil energy

A. Coal

On the one hand, the plan was to strengthen traditional coal production by accelerating the construction of new coal bases, such as Shaanbei, Huanglong, Shendong, Mengdong and Ningdong, promoting the old coal bases such as Jinbei, Jinzhong, Jindong and Yungui, and opening a coal base in Xinjiang.

On the other hand, non-traditional uses of coal, for example, the research and development of turning coal to natural gas, coal to liquid fuel and coal poly-generation, was to be undertaken in order to promote stable industrialization. The clean and efficient use of coal, by means of efficient and large-capacity coal combustion units, was also to be developed with cogeneration units in medium and large cities and industrial parks. Comprehensive generation plants such as large-sized coal-fired power plants were priorities.

B. Oil and gas

There were plans to promote the yield of oil and gas based on the development and use of non-conventional fuels like coal-bed and shale gas. The Tarim Basin, the Junggar Basin, the Songliao Basin, the Ordos Basin, the Bohai Bay Basin and the Sichuan Basin were to be merged into large-scale production areas. The exploration and development of oil and gas fields offshore was to be accelerated, and the exploitation and use of coal-bed gas in coal mines was to be further strengthened.

C. Pipelines

The domestic trunk pipeline network was to be completed. The strategic channel system for importing oil and gas in the northwest, northeast, southwest and offshore areas was to be built up, consisting of natural gas import pipelines, liquid natural gas receiving stations, the cross-area trunk gas pipeline network and distribution pipeline network as a whole. A gas supply pattern where natural gas, coal-bed gas and coal-made gas are coordinated was to be established. Stage two of the China-Kazakhstan raw oil pipe, part of the China-Myanmar oil and gas pipe, stage two of the Central Asia natural gas pipe, and lines three and four of the West-to-East Gas Pipeline Project were to be constructed. The total length of the oil and gas pipelines was planned to reach 150,000 km with the construction of gas warehousing. In addition, the energy reservation facilities such as the oil reservation system, the natural gas emergency holdings and coal reserve were planned.

3.1.5.2 Large–scale development of non–fossil energy

A. Solar power

The photovoltaic (PV) market in China was established during the Eleventh Five-Year Plan and local governments issued many financial stimulus schemes for solar batteries and PV buildings to drive the mutual promotion of the PV industry and the market. Meanwhile, the policies issued since 2009 such as subsidies on building integration photovoltaics and the Golden Sun Demonstration Project have opened an era of PV plants and building integration projects through a combination of private PV enterprises and national energy enterprises. This trend continued in the Twelfth Five-Year Plan. PV products are export-oriented and rely much on international markets, while China relies on imports of silicon materials and silicon ingots for the manufacturing of PV products. These two problems for the Chinese PV industry hinder its development. For that reason, maintaining the visionary nature of PV technologies and setting access standards for the industry have become a focus of future policies. Some provinces such as Tibet, Inner Mongolia, Gansu, Ningxia, Xinjiang and Yunnan have become focal points for development in this area and over 5 million kW of solar plants are planned for construction.

B. Wind power

In January 2010, the central government canceled the provision that the domestic rate of wind power equipment should be above 70% as stipulated in *Notice of the National Development and Reform Commission regarding the Requirements for Wind Power Construction and Management*, which was issued in 2005. The opening-up of domestic wind power markets and foreign-invested wind power equipment manufacturers were not to be limited by national policies. Foreign manufacturers were to be able to directly take part in the competition. Domestic wind power manufacturers were confronted with integration and increasing competition. Meanwhile, as China has unevenly-distributed wind resources, the development mode of constructing large bases and connecting to large grids, which focuses on grid connection with secondary distributed generation, was planned for development. As for technologies, large turbine manufacture and wind power grid connection become focal points of the R&D to optimize the control of wind power connected to the grid. For example, six land and two offshore large wind power plants were planned for construction during the Twelfth Five-Year Plan, with a generating capacity of over 70 million kW.

C. Nuclear industry

The government planned to promote the development of nuclear power in the coastal and central provinces with a target capacity of 40 million kW of nuclear power.

D. Hydropower

Construction of large hydropower plants was planned in major river areas such as Jinshajiang, Yalongjiang and Daduhe with a capacity of 120 million kW.

E. Biomass energy

Confronted with increasing costs of materials, the fundamental way to deal with high costs and limited materials is to produce wooden fibre biomass fuel ethanol at large scale. Projects on a local scale, such as cassava in Guangxi and Hainan, sweet sorghum in Shandong, Heilongjiang, Inner Mongolia and Xinjiang and jatropha in Sichuan and Yungui, were planned to lead the industrial development in individual areas. Moreover, projects and plans that can be used in application, such as the green power plan of biomass generation, and non-grain biomass transportation fuel application plans, will become important measures in promoting biomass energy.

3.1.6 Focus

Deep systemic reform of the energy system was the focus of Twelfth Five-Year Plan, mainly in the following four fields.

3.1.6.1 Energy pricing system

There has been great improvement in the energy pricing system, which has become more and more market-oriented. Coal pricing, for example, as the main energy source in China, was freed for the first time in 1993 and 1994, but the contracted thermal coal with government guiding prices remained in place for large energy consumers. In 2009, the contracted thermal coal price was also canceled and coal prices became fully marketized. At the same time, oil pricing has been gradually internationalized with the base price linked to Brent, Dubai and Cinta plus transportation tariffs, other taxes or costs. Natural gas pricing has been adjusted to be set by both government guidance and government setting according to different well levels. However, there are still three big problems existing in China's energy pricing system. First, no real competition has formed in the market except for coal, not only upstream but also downstream; second, the energy price cannot really reflect the costs including the waste of resources and pollution of the environment; third, there is no specific classification of energy types.

A. National energy company

The de-administration of national energy companies has been a tough challenge for the State Council of China. The challenge of how to make use of the advantages of national energy companies, e.g., their greater efficiency, safeguarding national energy security and rapid response to central government's strategic needs, but coordinate them with the medium and small energy enterprises in the market and to end their monopoly of the market, became the emphasis of reform during the Twelfth Five-Year-Plan.

B. Role of government

We discussed in the introduction the visible hand and the invisible hand. Governments, no matter whether central or regional authorities, are all the visible hand. It is hard to keep a balance between the central government and regional government, government and enterprises, and also the government and society. Considering the long history of the planned economy, now is the right time for the Chinese government to learn to distinguish the things that need to be governed from the ones that do not after more than thirty years of implementation of the Open and Reform Policy. The role of government should be transformed as much as possible from a governor to an enabler.

C. Reurbanization

Reurbanization is a buzz word repeated often since the new government of Xi and Li which wants to liberate the peasants from the country and deal with the issues of land ownership in order to raise domestic demand and take advantage of the huge low-cost labor force as much as possible. It undoubtedly pushes the energy demand also. How to effectively transform the means of energy consumption and energy production to adapt to urban growth is a great challenge along with reurbanization.

D. Going–Out Policy

Given that China cannot manage to strike a balance between its energy demand and supply, using overseas resources to compensate for the internal shortage of demand was another focus of China's Twelfth Five-Year Plan in terms of energy development. Trying to transform from "Energy Big Country" to "Energy Big Power" is China's aggressive objective. The following measures were planned:

- speed up going-out: to expand the volume of foreign investment, upgrade the ability of overseas resources exploitation, and increase the export of energy engineering services and equipment;

- raise energy trading level: to optimize China's foreign energy trading structure, steadily increase oil and gas imports, actively enhance coal, uranium and electricity imports, while controlling exports;

• improve the situation of imported energy technology: to guide foreign investment to the national new energy industries, encourage hi-tech inventions through absorption of the so-called "bring-in" technology with Chinese management and talent.

3.2 Energy Mix, Energy Intensity and Environmental Effects

3.2.1 Introduction

The Twelfth Five-Year Plan for Energy Development was announced on January 1, 2013, setting out key development goals for the energy industry in order to enhance energy security, with a strong emphasis on clean energy and energy efficiency. Key development goals in the Twelfth Five-Year Plan are shown below:

• energy intensity (energy consumption per unit of GDP): reduce energy intensity by 16% compared with 2010 levels;

• total energy consumption: 4 billion tons of standard coal by 2015, of which domestic supply shall take up 3.66 billion tons of standard coal;

• total electricity consumption: 6.15 trillion kilowatt-hours by 2015;

• overall energy efficiency: 38% increase by 2015;

• optimization of energy structure: the proportion of non-fossil energy consumption was planned to be increased to 11.4% of primary energy consumption by 2015, with natural gas accounting for 7.5%; and

• construction of national energy bases: the five major energy production areas, namely Shanxi Province, the Ordos Basin, eastern Inner Mongolia, Southwest China, and Xinjiang, were expected to realize an overall energy production capacity of 2.66 billion tons of standard coal in 2015, accounting for more than 70% of the country's total capacity.

Besides the above general goals, particular policies apply to the various energy sectors, as presented in the following sections.

3.2.2 Policies for Coal

3.2.2.1 Supply and security

As mentioned above, there has been a large demand-supply imbalance between western and eastern China, which has resulted in high costs of long-distance coal transportation, more demand for railway capacity and road traffic congestion caused by coal transportation. Hence, the Twelfth Five-Year Plan explicitly defined the future development of coal stocks. China planned to build up its national coal emergency stock in coastal and inland ports, in central China and in the northwest, and establish and improve the operation and management system to guarantee sufficient stock.

- Another policy to be pursued was the closure of inefficient small coal mines, accompanied by:

- large-scale coal production bases in Shannxi, Inner Mongolia, Ningixa, Shanxi, Yunnan and Kweichow provinces;

- new coal production centres in the western Xinjiang Autonomous Region to supplement production capacity;

- fourteen coal bases contributing 2.8 billion tons per year;

- better resource utilization by harnessing the coal-bed methane extraction; and

- coal and environmental protection.

3.2.2.2 Production caps

The Twelfth Five-Year Plan capped coal production at 4 billion tons per annum. Moreover, China introduced regulatory controls to limit environmental degradation, tax evasion, and mine accidents. The aim was to reduce the number of coal enterprises from about 11,000 to 4,000. It was expected that about ten big coal companies would account for nearly 60% of all China's coal production by 2015.

3.2.2.3 Utilization of clean coal energy

The proportion of coal washing was expected to be increased. New coal mines were to be constructed with coal-washing equipment built-in to increase the usage of washed coal. Existing coal mines were to speed up their construction and reformation. The rate of screened raw coal is planned to reach over 70% by 2017. It has been forbidden to import high-ash and high-sulphur coal of low quality. New measures of managing coal quality were to be introduced. The import of petroleum coke with high sulphur was to be constrained. Building clean coal distribution centers was highly encouraged in villages in northern China so as to promote the usage of clean coal.

3.2.2.4 To enhance overall improvement and reduce emission of multi–pollutants

Coal-fired boilers were to be improved. Construction projects like central heating supply, coal-to-gas, and coal-to-electric were sped up. By 2017, aside from the essential ones, any coal-fired boilers evaporating ten tons of steam per hour and below are to be eliminated in cities of prefectural level or above. It has been forbidden to build any new coal-fired boilers of less than twenty tons of steam per hour. In other regions, it is not permitted to build any coal-fired boilers below ten tons of steam per hour. In areas that pipelines of heat and gas do not reach, electricity, new energy and clean coal were to be adopted, and the use of high-efficiency and energy saving boilers were promoted. Individual coal-fired boilers were to be gradually replaced by gas engine cogenerators systems in areas with industries like chemical engineering, papermaking, printing, tanning, pharmaceuticals, etc.

3.2.2.5 Desulphuration, denitration, and dedusting in key industries

Desulphuration was installed for sinter machines and pellet production equipment in coal-fired plants and steel enterprises, for catalytic cracking in petroleum refineries and for non-ferrous metals plants. Desulphuration was applied to coal-fired boilers of over twenty tons of steam per hour. All coal-fired units were equipped with desulphuration facilities except circulating fluidized bed boilers. Low-nitrogen combustion and desulphuration were employed in new dry-process cement kilns. Upgrades and renovations were required for the existing dedusting facilities in coal-fired boilers and industrial kilns.

3.2.2.6 Coal market efficiency

China allows electricity producers and wholesale end-users such as industrial consumers to negotiate with each other directly. Coal markets were to be reformed further, including the development of a coal exchange market and futures market.

3.2.3 Policies for Oil

3.2.3.1 Supply and security

There was no explicit policy on the security of oil supply in the Twelfth Five-Year Plan. However, China had been trying to increase the security of its oil supply by encouraging Chinese companies to become involved in upstream investment activities abroad in cooperation with international or local companies, and by speeding up the development of its large strategic petroleum reserve (SPR), raising proven oil reserves by over 6.5 billion tons.

China protects its own oil companies by not allowing foreign oil companies to operate in China. However, international oil companies can have access to offshore oil prospecting, like in the Bohai Bay area, mainly through production sharing agreements. Currently, there are five oil production centers; in the Tarim Basin, the Junggar Basin, the Songliao Basin, the Ordos Basin, the Bohai Bay Basin and the Sichuan Basin. Offshore and deep-water oilfields exploration and exploitation are encouraged, and long-distance oil transport pipelines were commissioned in 2015 (to increase the crude oil pipeline network length by 8,400 km and processed oil pipeline length by 21,000 km).

In 2011, the Ministry of Commerce issued guidance on the development of oil circulation industries during the Twelfth Five-Year Plan period. Its goal was to further improve the oil distribution system and expand the scale of oil circulation enterprises. It proposed to establish the local reserve of diesel oil, improve the exit mechanism, and actively promote the promulgation of regulations on the management of oil markets for the first time.

Moreover, China aimed to stabilize oil production near 200 million tons and raise oil processing capacity to 620 million tons and processed oil production to 330 million tons.

3.2.3.2 Market efficiency

It was announced in March 2013 that prices of oil products would be adjusted every ten working days to better reflect changes in the global oil market.

3.2.4 Policies for Natural Gas

3.2.4.1 Supply and security

Natural gas is mainly used as domestic fuel and industry fuel in China due to its high calorific value, low cost and low pollution. Natural gas is also used as a raw material in the chemical industry for producing chemical products like synthetic ammonia and methanol. Recently, gas consumption has grown rapidly in the manufacturing industry, electric power industry and transportation industry. China's natural gas supply mainly comes from domestic production, imported by pipeline and LNG. The aim of the Twelfth FYP was to increase input capacity of LNG terminals by over 50 million tons, and this goal was almost met, capacity reached 49.8 million tons by the end of 2015. In 2012, the output volume and import volume of natural gas was 107.7 billion cubic meters and 42.5 billion cubic meters respectively[1].

① http://www.cs.com.cn/sylm/jsbd/201301/t20130128_3839899.html

In the Twelfth Five-Year Plan for Energy Development, China planned to increase the share of gas in the primary energy consumption from 4.6% in 2010 to 7.5% by 2015. In 2015, the share of gas was 5.9%. It also aimed for production of 6.5 billion cubic meters (bcm) of shale gas by 2015, which is equivalent to 2%~3% of projected Chinese gas production in 2015.

Long-distance gas transport pipelines were planned to be commissioned, including the third and fourth routes of the West-to-East Gas Pipeline Project with a total length reaching 150,000 km by 2015. However, these have still not been commissioned in 2016. Large strategic gas reserves are also scheduled to ensure the security of supply.

In 2010, the West-East Natural Gas Transmission Pipeline was approved. It connects the West-East Natural Gas Transmission Pipeline, the Second Shanxi-Beijing Natural Gas Pipeline, Zhongxian-Wuhan Gas Transmission Pipeline and Sebei-Xining-Lanzhou Gas Pipeline, so that the diversity of sources for natural gas and supply reliability in north, east, central and northwest China can be achieved.

In 2012, the National Development and Reform Commission (NDRC) issued the *Notice on Printing and Distributing the Twelfth Five-Year Plan for*

Natural Gas. Its aim was to expand the scale of the use of natural gas and to promote development of natural gas industry. The NDRC studied and formulated together with relevant departments the Twelfth Five-Year Plan for Natural Gas. The plan focused on natural gas infrastructure, and considered the exploration and development of upstream resources and the utilization in downstream markets to be of equal importance. The plan covered the development of coal-bed gas, shale gas and coal gas. The plan is an important basis to guide the healthy development of China's natural gas industry.

The Development Plan for National Shale Gas (2011—2015) was issued in 2012. This plan defined the main task during the Twelfth Five-Year Plan period as overcoming barriers to key technology in exploration and development so as to lay the foundation for large-scale development of shale gas during the Thirteenth Five-Year Plan. It is worth remarking that for shale gas development, the geological conditions are complex and pose great technical and investment challenges.

3.2.4.2 Environmental protection

In order to accelerate clean energy utilization and substitution, the supply of natural gas, coal-made natural gas and coal-bed methane needed to be increased. Natural gas pipelines with an additional capacity of over 150 billion cubic meters were planned to cover the Jing-Jin-Ji, Yangtze River Delta and Pearl River Delta regions by 2015. So far, three phases with a capacity of 77 billion cubic meters have been completed. To optimize the use of natural gas, priority was given to the replacement of coal for domestic heating. Efficient utilization projects like natural gas distributed energy source (DES) were encouraged, and natural gas chemical projects were constrained. Plans were to systematically develop natural gas peak shaving plants and there were to be no new construction projects of natural gas power plants.

Urban restricted zones for high polluting fuels were to be expanded and gradually extended to suburbs. Through measures including compensation, peak/off-peak tariffs, seasonal tariffs, progressive tariffs and peak-load tariffs, we believe that China will gradually reinforce the use of natural gas to replace coal in line with the renovation of villages in cities, rural-urban continuum and shanty areas.

3.2.5 Policies for Electricity

China streamlined its energy regulations in March 2013. The Twelfth Five-Year Plan called for the key power regulator, the State Electricity Regulatory Commission, to be merged with the National Energy Administration, reducing overlapping duties in energy reform, investment and project approval.

3.2.5.1 Supply and security

In the Twelfth Five-Year Plan, China planned to increase the non-fossil fuel share of generation of electricity from 8% in 2009 to 11.4% by 2015 and to 15% by 2020. That is, by the end of 2015, China planned to have—and succeeded in having—a total power generation capacity from non-fossil fuels of 464 GW, being 30% of the total power generation capacity.

During the Twelfth Five-Year Plan period, new power generation installations with renewable energy sources were planned to reach 175 GW, including:

- hydro: 62 GW;

- pumped-storage: 12 GW;

- wind: 70 GW;

- solar: 20 GW;

- biomass: 11 GW.

The goal was for renewable energy sources to reach more than 20% of total generated energy by 2015.

China's total power generation capacity was expected to increase from 970 GW in 2010 to around 1490 GW in 2015. A prediction of the breakdown of the use of fossil-fuel energy and alternative energy sources by 2015 are as follows:

- coal-fired thermal power: 960 GW;

- natural gas thermal power: 40 GW;

- nuclear power: 40 GW;

- hydroelectric power: 260 GW;

- pumped-storage: 30 GW;

- wind power: 100 GW;

- solar power: 21 GW;

- biomass: 13 GW;

- others: 10 GW.

Table 21 shows the summary of energy mix in power generation in 2010 and 2015.

A. Closure of inefficient power plants

Since the closure of inefficient power and industrial facilities helped contribute to the targeted decline in energy intensity during the Eleventh Five-Year Plan, with a reported 72.1 GW of old thermal power plants forced to close down, it was planned that additional old and inefficient power plants would be forced to close down in the Twelfth Five-Year Plan period.

B. Gas–to–power (26.42 GW—40 GW)

Natural gas generators can start fast and adjust easily for peak shaving

Table 21: Summary of energy mix in power generation

| Energy type | Unit | 2010* | 2015 | In the 12th Five-Year Plan Period | | | In 2010 | |
				New Installation	% increase	% by energy type	% by energy type	Expected trillion kWh/%
Natural gas	GW	26.42	56	29.58	112%	3.76%	2.72%	
Coal-fired	GW	646.6	960	313.40	48%	64.43%	66.66%	
Nuclear**	GW	10.82	40	29.18	270%	2.68%	1.12%	
Hydro**	GW	198.21	260	61.79	31%	17.45%	20.43%	0.837/13.6%
Pumped storage**	GW	17.84	30	12.16	68%	2.01%	1.84%	
Wind**	GW	29.57	100	70.43	238%	6.71%	3.05%	0.19/3.1%
Solar**	GW	0.86	21	20.14	2342%	1.41%	0.09%	
Biomass**	GW	1.7	13	11.30	665%	0.87%	0.18%	
Others	GW	36.92	10	0.00	0	0.67%	3.81%	
Total	GW	970	1490	520.00	53.6%	100%	100%	
Electricity consumption	trillion kWh	4.2	6.15	1.95	46			

*   Source: China Electricity Council, National Grid Energy Research Institute.
** Total non-fossil 464GW (30% of total GW) by 2015.

and can reduce GHG emissions, compared with coal power. However, natural gas resources in China are limited, and supply capacity is inadequate. Moreover, the price of natural gas is highly affected by the market price of oil. Hence, natural gas generation in China should be located mainly in the eastern region to cover peak demand for power and develop cogeneration units. The installed capacity of gas-fired power was only 26.42 GW in 2010, and was required to reach the target of 40 GW in 2015.

C. Coal–to–power (646.6 GW—960 GW)

Under the Twelfth Five-Year Plan, China focused on decarbonizing its power sector by building new coal-powered plants, which are more efficient and burn less coal to produce the same amount of energy as the old ones.

D. Hydro (62 GW—260 GW)

By 2010, China had 48,500 hydropower generating stations. The provinces which have the best water resources for hydropower (Sichuan, Yunnan, Guizhou, Hubei, Hunan, Guangxi) are located in the west of China while, as explained above, the provinces which are top electricity consumers (Henan, Hebei, Shandong, Jiangsu, Zhejiang, Guangdong) are located in the east of China.

E. Solar (1 GW—21 GW)

China decided to reduce the cost for energy fed inside the national grid resulting in lower expenses for solar-energy developers. This was aided by a projected quadrupling the installed capacity of solar power to a value that exceeded the 2 GW generated in 2011. However, China's solar PV market is 95% export-oriented due to its low-cost production. However, the domestic PV market lacks the technological know-how to produce poly-silicon raw material as well as PV equipment-manufacturing expertise. As China plans to develop the domestic PV market, these two areas will especially require significant R&D efforts[1].

[1] http://newenergy.giec.cas.cn/tyn/gfdt/201108/t20110808_220911.html

F. Wind power (30 GW—100 GW)

The installed capacity of wind power connected to the grid in China was to reach 100 GW by 2015. As mentioned in section 2.1, eight wind power plants were constructed, six on land and two offshore. The annual energy output was to reach 190 billion kWh by 2015.

G. Biomass (to 13 GW)

The Twelfth FYP planned to increase biomass-generation capacity to 13 million kW with 3 million kW coming from organic urban waste.

3.2.5.2 Grid infrastructure

According to statistics published in the *China Securities Journal*, since April 2012 the National Development and Reform Commission has approved construction of ultra-high-voltage power transmission lines and supporting distribution networks with a total dynamic investment of 7.661 billion yuan. Ultra-high-voltage lines can transfer more electricity over longer distances compared with conventional lines, with a transmission capacity of around 1,000 kilovolts (kV) compared with around 500 KV for conventional power lines. It is expected that the network of ultra-high-voltage transmission lines will start transporting electric power from both coal-red and renewable-based electricity generation hubs in the northern and western rural regions to the densely populated demand centers, which are concentrated in the eastern and southern provinces. According to the proposed programme, new transmissions were expected to account for 20% of energy exported from western areas.

Moreover, over 200,000 km of +330 KV power grids were expected. In addition, smart grids, smart meters and infrastructure for recharging electric cars were to be developed in conjunction with the strategic plan of power development.

3.2.5.3 Feed–in tariff of renewable energy

In 2011, the National Development and Reform Commission and the State Electricity Regulatory Commission issued the *Notice on the Feed-in Tariff and Quota Trading Scheme of Renewable Energy from January to September in 2010*, making clear the items and amount of the subsidies for electricity price and the quota trading and settlement of the electricity price.

3.2.5.4 Energy efficiency

In 2011, the Ministry of Industry and Information Technology issued guidance on the management of the power demand side in industrial areas for implementing the basic national policy of saving resources and protecting the environment. This entailed the orderly advancement of the management of the power demand side in industrial areas, optimizing the industrial structure of electricity use, adjusting the methods of electricity use, improving the efficiency of industrial energy, and promoting sustainable development of the industry and the national economy.

3.2.5.5 Market efficiency

China implemented a tiered electricity pricing system in July 2012.

In 2011, the National Development and Reform Commission issued the *Notice on Improving Solar Photovoltaic Electricity Prices Policy*, stating that before and after July 1, 2011, the approved photovoltaic power generation projects electricity price are 1.15 yuan per kWh and 1 yuan per kWh, respectively. This marks the real start of the domestic market for the photovoltaic industry.

Later, in 2013, the National Development and Reform Commission issued the *Notice of the General Office of the National Development and Reform Commission on Further Reducing Electricity Tariffs for Producing and Circulation of Agricultural Products*.

3.2.6 Policies for End-Use Efficiency

The Twelfth Five-Year Plan included indicative caps on total energy consumption and on power consumption for 2015. There were also mandatory targets to reduce the energy intensity of the economy by 16% compared with 2005, including the Top 10,000 program that set energy savings targets for 2015 for the largest industrial consumers. The energy efficiency standard for a number of energy-intensive industries, like cement production, oil refineries and chemical industries, were required to improve their energy efficiency by at least 10%.

3.2.6.1 Transport sector

A. Infrastructure

Investment in China's transport infrastructure was about 6.2 trillion yuan for the duration of the Twelfth Five-Year Plan, mainly used in highway construction. Hence, the scale of the economy's highway network was expected to expand. The total road network was expected to reach 4.5 million kilometers, and the total length of high-speed dual carriageways was expected to reach 108,000 kilometers. This highway network was planned to connect more than 90% of the towns and cities with populations of over 200,000 people.

B. Reducing private vehicle use

To slow down the growth of private vehicle use, China invested in urban mass-transit rail systems and high-speed rail services. Automobile ownership was to be appropriately managed in accordance with urban development and plans. In megacities like Beijing, Shanghai and Guangzhou, strict restrictions were to be imposed on the number of vehicles.

C. Improving vehicle efficiency

A fuel consumption testing and management mechanism was

introduced in China in March 2011. Under this mechanism, a list of vehicle models that satisfied the fuel consumption standards in 2011 was published. The average fuel economy of passenger vehicles will be 4.5 L/100 kilometers by 2020, the same as European standards.

D.Improving quality of fuel

The upgrade and renovation of petroleum refineries were to be accelerated. By the end of 2013, petrol of National IV Standard was expected to be provided countrywide; by the end of 2014, diesel of National IV Standard was expected to be supplied all over the country; by the end of 2015, petrol and diesel of National V Standard were expected to prevail in key cities in the Jing-Jin-Ji, YRD (Yangtze River Delta) and PRD (Pearl River Delta) areas, and be available for supply nationwide by the end of 2017. The state was expected to strengthen its supervision and inspection of oil quality and stringently crack down on illegal production and sales of non-standard vehicle fuels.

E. Eliminating yellow label vehicles and old cars

The central government set forbidden zones and provided financial compensation to gradually phase out yellow-label vehicles and old cars. Yellow-label vehicles are defined as gasoline vehicles which do not meet China's emission standards. By 2015, yellow-label vehicles registered before the end of 2005 were expected to be taken off the roads, including 5 million yellow-label vehicles in the Jing-Jin-Ji, YRD and PRD regions. By 2017, almost all yellow-label vehicles will be eliminated.

F. Enhancing environmental protection

Joint efforts made by departments relating to environmental protection, industry and information, quality control, and industry and commerce were to be put into environmental protection supervision on car manufacture. Any illegal production or sales of vehicles not meeting environmental standards were to be prosecuted. In annual vehicle examinations, no passing stickers were to be issued for vehicles failing to meet environmental requirements, and those vehicles were not to be used. The construction of urea additive supply for diesel vehicles was to be sped up. Shortening the time limit for mandatory scrapping of old buses and taxis, encouraging yearly replacements of effective exhaust purification devices, and carrying out pollution control for ships and any machinery not using roads are other policies which should have been considered.

G. Speeding up the upgrade of low–speed vehicles

It was also believed that China should set higher environmental protection requirements for low-speed vehicles (three-wheelers, low-speed trucks) in order to reduce pollution emissions and quicken the upgrade and alteration of relevant industries and product technology. From 2017, new low-speed vehicles should share the same energy conservation and emission standards with light trucks.

H. Promoting alternative energy vehicles

Public transport, environmental sanitation and government organizations were to take the initiative to use new, alternative energy vehicles. In the Development Plan for Energy Saving and New Energy Automobile Industry (2012—2020), the focus was on electric-powered vehicles (EVs and FCVs) and plug-in hybrid vehicles (PHVs) to enhance China's competitiveness in the domestic automobile industry and thus to reduce carbon emissions. Individuals were to be given free vehicle license plates and financial subsidies for purchasing new energy cars. Furthermore, there were attempts to kick-start the deployment of electric vehicles through government purchasing programmes aimed especially at public buses and taxis: up to 1,000 buses for each of the pilot cities were to receive a 450,000 yuan subsidy and up to 55,000 yuan for taxis.

An alliance of the largest state-owned companies was set up to accelerate the development of electric vehicles in China, and it was expected that the investment could be up to 100 billion yuan. The production and sales of EVs, FCVs and PHVs were expected to total 500,000 units by 2015, and more than 5 million units by 2020. Subsidies and tax exemptions were provided for EVs, FCVs and PHVs. More than 2,000 charging stations with 400,000 quick chargers for EVs were expected by 2015. In Beijing, Shanghai and Guangzhou, etc., buses with new energy or clean fuel were to represent over 60% among the new or upgraded buses every year. In particular, the Twelfth Five-Year Plan set a target of 30% reduction for fuel consumption and carbon emissions of new vehicles.

3.2.6.2 Buildings

The government established energy-efficient design standards for both residential buildings and public buildings, and a code for acceptance inspections of energy-efficient building construction. For instance, in 2012, the Ministry of Finance and the Ministry of Housing and Urban-Rural Development issued the *Notice on Improving Policies for the Application of Renewable Energy Buildings and Adjusting Management Methods for the Allocation of Funds*. The aim was to actively promote solar and other new energy products with access to households and public facilities, to further enlarge the application policy effects of renewable energy buildings, and to improve security, normalization and effectiveness on the use of fiscal funds.

Further, in 2013, the Ministry of Housing and Urban-Rural Development issued the *Notice on Action Plan for Green Buildings* to thoroughly implement the scientific concept of development, effectively change the mode of urban and rural construction and construction development, improve resource utilization efficiency, achieve binding targets on energy conservation and emission reduction, actively respond to global climate change, build a resource-saving and environment-friendly society, improve the level of ecological civilization and improve people's quality of life.

3.2.6.3 End–use products

By the end of October 2011, China had an energy-efficiency labeling program covering twenty-five product classes. To enhance this program, in 2012 the Ministry of Finance and the Ministry of Housing and Urban-Rural Development issued the *Notice on Improving Policies for the Application of Renewable Energy Buildings and Adjusting Management Methods for the Allocation of Funds.* The purpose of this measure was to actively promote solar and other new energy products through access to them by households and public facilities, to further enlarge the application policy effects of renewable energy buildings, and to improve security, normalization and effectiveness on the use of fiscal funds.

3.2.6.4 Industrial sector

In 2012, the General Office of the Ministry of Industry and Information Technology issued a notice regarding energy efficiency benchmarking indicators of key energy-consuming products (processes) of steel and other industries and the list of enterprises in 2011. This notice was to implement the spirit of the State Council's Comprehensive Work Plan for Energy-saving and Emission-reduction during the Twelfth Five Year Plan. The notice defined energy efficiency benchmark indicators for sixteen kinds of key energy-consuming products of iron and steel, nonferrous metals, building materials, light industry, textile and other industries and related enterprises in 2011.

3.2.7 Environmental Protection

In the Twelfth Five-Year Plan, China included plans to put a price on carbon and has separately announced plans to introduce city and provincial level pilot carbon emissions trading schemes in the near future.

China has a national target of reducing carbon intensity by 40-45% by 2020. The Twelfth Five-Year Plan contained a mandatory target of reducing carbon intensity by 17% compared with 2005, and a 10% reduction target for other pollutions, e.g. COD, SO_2.

In 2013, China launched a further five-year plan to improve its heavily polluted climate. The objectives of this environmental improvement plan are:

- air quality to be improved nationwide, and for there to be fewer days with heavy pollution;

- air quality will be noticeably improved in Jing-Jin-Ji (Beijing, Tianjing and Hebei Province), YRD (Yangtze River Delta), and PRD (Pearl River Delta);

- in another five years or longer, bad weather resulting from heavy pollution will be eliminated, and air quality will be remarkably improved nationwide.

Specific targets by 2017:

- by 2017, the decrease of PM10 concentration in cities of prefectural level or above will be at least 10% compared with 2012, and the number of good quality air days will be rising;

- PM10 concentration will decline by 25%, 20% and 15% in the area of Jing-Jin-Ji, YRD, and PRD, respectively;

- the annual mean concentration of PM 2.5 in Beijing will be within 60 $\mu g/m^3$.

4

China's Energy Evolution and Revolution

4.1 The Hard Road of Reforming the Power and Natural Gas Sectors

In April 2015, the Chinese government issued three announcements: the first one concerned the non-residential NG ceiling city gateprice cut (15%);[1] the second one related to the power tariff cut (~4%),[2] and the third one was about the huge coal-fired power project (Rmb50bn, ±1100kV UHV transmission line spanning 3500km, 66M MWh).[3]

Will China keep using a centralized plan for its power and natural gas market? Has China been reforming these two markets since 1978? This chapter summarizes the reforming progress based on the information collected in May 2015.

---

[1] The NDRC announced that it would adjust PRC non-residential NG ceiling citygate prices on April 1, 2015. These comprise the prices of incremental volume to cut $Rmb0.44/m^3$ (15%) whereas those of existing volume to rise up to $Rmb0.04/m^3$ (1%)

[2] Power tariff cut effective on April 20, 2015—National Development and Reform Commission (NDRC) announced on its website that they would cut on-grid coal-fired tariff average by around RMB0.02/kWh (~ 4%) due to lowered unit coal cost under coal-price power-tariff linking mechanism. Meanwhile, retail commercial & industrial power tariffs are cut average Rmb0.018/kWh (about 2.5%) at the same time to lower operating expense of various corporates to boost the economy.

[3] The Zhundong coal-fired power project, an important part of the "Xinjiang Power Going Out," commenced construction. This project consists of an Rmb50bn investment supporting coal-fired power plants and a ±1100kV UHV transmission line from Zhundong, Xinjiang to eastern China spanning 3500km. It is estimated to generate 66M MWh, convert 33 m tonnes of coal, and realize revenue of RMB3bn pa.

4.1.1   Brief Background

Energy pricing reform in China has taken place against a backdrop of both rapid industrialization and a broader economic system transformation (that is, from a planned to market economy). Such overlap significantly complicates the reform process (APERC, 2008). Certain characteristics of the Chinese energy system have a persistent baseline influence on energy price, namely:

- diversity in the endowment and variety of energy resources geographically;

- diversity in regional development, divergence across energy industries; and

- variation in government policy across time.

For example, the case of natural gas development in China illustrates the influence of diversity in the endowment of energy resources.

In China, central government energy pricing policy seeks to reflect a wide range of economic, social and political goals while local governments generally seek to boost local economic development as much as possible while implementing central government policies. Meanwhile, industry associations seek to align governmental and industrial benefits and individual enterprises seek to increase market share and profits so as to ensure financial viability.

However, current energy price distortions reflect the inadequate nature of the pricing system. For instance, coal pricing has not traditionally, but is now beginning to, include external costs (such as those for environmental protection) and other implicit expenses (such as those for depreciation and safety).

4.1.2   Pricing Policies in the Power Sector

Pricing reform has been ongoing in the power sector over the past two decades and continues today.

Before 1985, the Chinese government uniformly constructed power projects and managed power prices. This mandatory-price system set the end user sales price rather than providing on-grid power tariffs. However, due to the rapid growth of the Chinese economy and slow development of the power industry, there was a serious power deficiency.

Thus, in 1985, China implemented a policy of power plant construction through capital raising along with a system of multiple power prices, so as to encourage broader investment in the generation sector:

- firstly, power prices were adjusted according to the loan and interest conditions of capital raised for construction;

- secondly, power prices were linked to fuel and transportation tariffs to reflect changing costs;

- thirdly, a fee of CNY 0.02 per kilowatt-hour was established to fund local power construction.

Despite such strong promotion of power industry development, this policy nevertheless led to a disorderly price system incorporating new prices for new power plants, old prices for old power plants, and different prices for different power plants and even different power generation units. Over time, it also led to intentional increases in power price, escalating power construction costs and haphazard power plant construction.

From 1997, China began to implement operational period power pricing, shifting from a capital cost-plus based system to one based on the average cost of the "social-advanced level." At this time, China also standardized the rates of return on capital investment for power construction.

In 2002, power generation enterprises were separated from power network enterprises. Under this reform, independent power generators established on-grid power prices for the power network, which in turn set the power sales price for end users. Except for on-grid prices determined through government-hosted bidding and new energy power generation projects, a uniform on-grid power price benchmark was adopted for new generators operating in the same area, and was gradually expanded to power generation companies using the existing pricing system.

As of 2008, there is no corresponding pricing mechanism on power transmission and distribution. Instead, the power transmission and distribution price is mainly reflected through the difference between the power sales price and the on-grid power price set by the government.

Moreover, there are significant differences in the power sales price and on-grid power price among different regions. End-user prices are stratified by category. The Chinese government sets different price standards for different use types, including: residential living, non-residential lighting, commercial, general industry, large industry, agricultural production, and agricultural drainage and irrigation in poor counties. Power prices for agriculture and residential use are protected by relevant policies; for example, residential prices can be increased only through public hearing.

Large industrial users with high-energy consumption have benefited in the past from preferential government-set power prices so as to stimulate economic growth, but this preferential policy has been canceled in favor of a differential power price in recent years.

4.1.2.1 Coal–power pricing issue

There have been great improvements in the energy pricing system, which has become more and more market-oriented. Coal pricing, for example, as the main energy source in China, was freed for the first time in 1993 and 1994, but the contracted thermal coal with the government-guiding price remained for large energy consumers. Control of coal prices have been loosened in China while power price remains controlled, making it difficult to implement a coal-power price linking mechanism. After the first such linking attempt in May 2005, Chinese power prices increased on average by 0.0252 yuan per kilowatt-hour; after the second adjustment in May 2006, power sales price increased slightly, but increasing coal contract prices for power plants have outpaced such adjustments; the third attempt has been delayed due to high inflation. The relationship between coal and power pricing has become increasingly prominent, so as to influence the supply and demand of power.

In 2009, the contracted thermal coal price was also canceled and coal prices became fully marketized.

Deep systemic reform of the energy system was the focus of the Twelfth Five-Year Plan, mainly around the following four fields (Xu and Chung, 2014): energy pricing system, national energy company and role of government, reurbanization, and Going-Out Policy.

However, there are still three big problems. First, no real competition has formed in the market except for coal, not only upstream but also downstream; second, the energy price cannot really reflect the costs including the waste of resources and pollution of the environment; third, there is no pricing mechanism for power transmission and distribution, to the detriment of development and structural optimization in the economy's power network.

The current end-user power price mechanism is inefficient. Different power sales prices for different types of use distorts cost structures, and thus power price does not accurately reflect and regulate the balance of supply and demand in the power sector.

4.1.2.2 Market efficiency

China implemented a tiered electricity pricing system in July 2012.

In 2011, the National Development and Reform Commission issued the *Notice on Improving Solar Photovoltaic Electricity Prices' Policy*, stating that before and after July 1, the approved photovoltaic power generation projects electricity price are 1.15 yuan per kWh and 1 yuan per kWh, respectively. This marks the real start of the domestic market for the photovoltaic industry.

Later, in 2013, the National Development and Reform Commission issued the *Notice of the General Office of the National Development and Reform Commission on Further Reducing Electricity Tariffs for Producing and Circulation of Agricultural Products*.

However, all these notices cannot ease the phenomenon that solar and wind power cannot sell through the power grid companies who become monopoly players in selling power to the end-users since 2002. Hence, a structural shift is expected.

4.1.2.3 Document no. 9, issued March 15, 2015

This document (*Opinions Regarding Expanding the Reform of the Power Sector*), increasing reform of the power market was issued on March 15. Since this policy document was co-signed by the Central Committee of the Communist Party and the State Council, it is considered as a follow-up to the last major power sector reform document—State Council Decree no. 5—released in 2002, and the importance of the reform has been raised to a higher level. This policy document provides a broad road map for reforming the power industry using almost 50% coal-fired technology.

The document recognizes that the reform should focus on reducing emissions, promoting renewables, and boosting energy efficiency while power security and safety must meet the rapidly-growing demand for electricity services.

The document also outlines five basic principles which power-sector policy should follow:

- the need for security and safety;

- making use of market mechanisms;

- stabilizing tariffs of non-industrial sectors, like residential and agricultural consumers;

- energy saving, emissions reductions, and increased use of renewable and distributed generation; and

- better governance and regulation, including better planning and strengthened capacity in terms of regulatory agencies and approaches.

Along with the above principles, the Chinese government would like to introduce a wholesale marketplace to the power market. This would unlock trading between generators and large electricity consumers. It also, hopefully, opens the door for micro-grid and distributed energy business models. Hence, we would like to highlight several key policies below:

A. Grid operator reform

By setting transmission and distribution prices based on cost and reasonable profit basis, the revenue model for China's grid operators would be changed like the one that is already operating in Shenzhen (*Notice for Transmission and Distribution Rate Reform Pilot in Shenzhen* October 23, 2014) and West Inner Mongolia. The grid operator will not set the power sales price for end users, like the one in 2002. This should switch the grid operators to a revenue-cap regulatory regime, which may open up greater opportunities for these companies to support energy efficiency and distribute renewables, depending on implementation details. The new policy extends the regulatory approach used in the recent Shenzhen grid company pilot to cover the entire country. It should be noted that the issue date of the Shenzhen grid company pilot scheme was October 23, 2014 and the first evaluation period is from the January 1, 2015 to the end of 2017. Hence, this Document no. 9 should not be considered as the results of the Shenzhen scheme. Instead, it should be understood that China's central government is expediting the reform progress and aims to have more regions initiate this reform.

B. Multiple electricity retailers

The government wants to allow multiple retailers including industrial/ high-technology development parks, social capital investment companies, distributed generation end-users (and/or energy service companies, good news for all renewables), water and gas utilities, and generators to compete in the retail market.

C. Retail competition

It allows large users to bypass the grid companies and negotiate prices directly with generators. The document requires that both demand-side and supply-side parties be screened, with participation limited to those demonstrating good performance in terms of energy efficiency and compliance with environmental regulations.

D. The market for larger users

A list of larger users, retailers, and generators will be developed according to their performance in energy saving and emissions reduction. Any players in the list can join the power market and negotiate the power prices. Any players who cannot satisfy the preset performance standard or belong to industries which are becoming obsolete cannot join the market.

E. No market for certain end–users

No market for: residential consumers, agricultural consumers, and important social service providers.

4.1.2.4 General comments on the above key policies

In 2002, the first step was the decoupling of grid operators and generators. After more than a decade, China took the second step to introduce the wholesale power marketplace in this Document no. 9. Obviously, this document outlines the second step of power market deregulation in the near future while the document is couched in very general terms. The Chinese government is expected to develop and issue more detailed supporting regulations in the near future. There will be much work to do in fleshing out the details and moving ahead with implementation. We would like to address some of them from our observation:

- A long road to achieve market deregulation: In the document, the tariff for residential consumers, agricultural consumers, and some important social service providers will be determined by the Chinese government. No hint is provided as to when and how the above consumers can join the marketplace.

- Who and how to set the preset performance standard?

- What to do if the companies do not achieve the preset standard? It is mentioned that if the companies' performance cannot achieve the preset standard, they are not allowed to be in the power marketplace. Will these companies keep using the old generation technologies and generate more non-green GDP?

- The power demand and supply from the new industrial users and generators under the new market mechanism will not be included in China's centralized plan as mentioned in D-13 of Document no. 9. Who makes the decision on the use of new generators with different fuel types? Such decisions affect the energy mix and emissions reductions simultaneously.

- While improving inter-provincial, cross-regional power trading mechanisms, will the regional governments become a player in the power marketplace which has not be mentioned in the document? If yes, how will the preset standard apply to the local government?

- Power planning should take full account of environmental carrying capacity. The document stresses the need to revamp the environmental responsibility of power sector planning. Should we totally rely upon the preset standard for the environmental carrying capacity?

- Foreign Investment Opportunities: A final decision on whether the power distribution and sales business will be opened up for foreign investment will be based on the "negative list" that is under preparation, Wang Qiang, a senior official in the department of economic system reform under the NDRC [1], told *China Daily*. A negative list refers to specific areas where foreign capital is restricted. Foreign capital infusion is allowed in all the fields that are not on the negative list and the same also does not need approval from the government. Currently China uses a catalog for the guidance of foreign investment industries. Policymakers have said that the government will actively work to explore the management model for a negative list. The NDRC reform plan envisages that China will further optimize its energy mix and improve the share of renewable energy in electricity generation. China had the world's largest installed electricity generating capacity of 1.36 billion kilowatts in 2014.

[1] *China Daily*, 2015
Reforms will power change across electricity industry
By LAN LAN (*China Daily*)
Updated: 2015-03-26 08:01
http://usa.chinadaily.com.cn/business/2015-03/26/content_19912857.htm

4.1.3 Pricing Policies in the Natural Gas Sector

According to APERC (2008), the natural gas sector follows a parallel pricing system: an old price applies to projects that were completed before 1995 while a new price applies to projects completed in 1995 or later. This system, the result of a 1997 reform referred to as "new price for new line," established an end-user price based on a cost-plus approach.

Transmission of natural gas from well-head to users includes:

- exploration;

- exploitation and purification of gas field;

- transportation of gas via long-distance pipelines; and

- gasification and distribution of urban gas.

The price of natural gas is composed of three corresponding components:

- the well-head cost and purification fee charged by the gas field (including project cost, various taxes including resource tax, a value-added tax, add-on taxes such as the municipal construction fee and education cost fee, income tax, and profits);

- the pipeline transportation tariff charged by long-distance transportation pipeline companies (determined according to consumption region, pipeline diameter, transport distance, taxes such as business tax, customs tax, income tax and profits); and

- the local distribution tariff charged by local authorities.

At present, these three components are largely managed by local governments and enterprises in consultation with the central government (particularly NDRC). The ex-plant price (well-head price plus purification fee) is set by the NDRC, the pipeline transportation tariff is set through the approval of the NDRC for the suggested fee submitted by local price control bureaus, and the local distribution tariff is set directly by provincial price control bureaus based on a cost-plus approach.

The well-head price itself is divided into three categories: a within–quota price, which is for the volume of gas sold within the allocated quota; an out-quota price; and a contract price which is freely negotiated between producers and consumers.

In 2005, the NDRC issued the *Notice on Reforming Pricing Mechanism & Recent Proper Improvement of the Ex-plant Price of Natural Gas*. This served to combine residential, commercial and small industrial users who receive gas through an urban natural gas pipeline network into a single category. Gas price categories were then simplified into gas for chemical fertilizer production, directly supplied industrial gas, and urban gas. Furthermore, ex-plant prices of natural gas were divided into two categories based upon ex-plant gas production conditions and end user affordability. Category one gas includes existing natural gas production in oil/gas fields sold at planned or near-planned prices, and all other planned gas production, including all gas in the Sichuan-Chongqing, Changqing, Qinghai, and Xinjiang oilfields (excluding natural gas in the West-to-East Gas Pipeline Project) and current planned natural gas in the Dagang, Liaohe and Zhongyuan oilfields. Category two gas includes all other natural gas.

In short, natural gas pricing has been adjusted and set by both government guidance and government setting according to different well levels. In particular, the NDRC aims to link China's NG prices with market prices of its substitutes because a rising proportion of China's NG supply comes from imports (32% in 2014), hence it is important to reflect market prices. The conversion of existing and incremental volume prices would render a fair operating environment. The ultimate goal of NG price reform is to fully liberalize NG feedstock prices under market mechanisms; this would mean more frequent city-gate price changes in response to its substitute price changes. The government will continue to supervise NG transmission and distribution tariffs.

4.2 China's Energy Revolution

Stick to the guidelines of conservation first, diversified development based on domestic resources and environmental protection. Strengthen reciprocal international cooperation, adjust and optimize energy structure, and build a safe, stable, economical and clean modern energy industry system. Such was the header of Chapter 11, "Accelerate the Reform of Energy Production and Utilization Mode" of the *National People's Congress (NPC)'s Twelfth Five-Year Plan 2011—2015*. Recently, Chinese President Xi Jinping has been making frequent public appearances where he gives out information regarding the future Thirteenth Five-Year Plan 2016—2020 plan, notably saying that The nation needs to find new ways to produce and consume fuels to ensure its long-term energy security. Considering the latest development in China's energy situation, the previous plan's lines and actual results, this section will attempt to predict the future elements that might be encountered in the plan and to assess if there will indeed be a revolution and what it means for China's energy policy.

4.2.1 The Evolution of China's Long-term Energy Structure

The sheer size of the Chinese population means it requires the stimulation of high-rate economic growth. It is difficult to turn around the comparatively low level, intensive energy consumption industries. The pressure of ensuring the demand for energy security keeps increasing, there is serious environmental pollution, and prospects for emission reductions look grim, especially after the heavy smog situation in 2013. International efforts to control climate change have increasingly pressured China to reduce carbon emissions. In the face of the intensive competition for global energy resources, China has to accelerate its adjustment in energy consumption and production structure. The medium to long-term adjustment of China's energy development will certainly and strongly affect the international energy market and the political and economic situation, especially in the Asia Pacific region.

To ensure China's energy security, the overall plan is to:

- gradually suppress the usage of the so-called "dirty energy resources" like coal;

- rapidly develop clean and new energy, especially gaseous resources which mainly include conventional natural gas, unconventional coal-bed gas, combustible ice, shale gas, gas of non-biological origin; and processed methane, coal gas, liquefied petroleum gas, artificial gas and hydrogen;

- develop nuclear energy projects in a timely manner;

- vigorously develop foreign energy resources.

We have summarized the results of the energy outlook from different research groups in China below and in Table 22.

Table 22: Result summary of the studies by CEG, CAE and SCDRC

Energy		2014	CEG (2035)	CAE (2050)	SCDRC (2020)
Fossil	Coal	66-67%	48%	35-40%	2.5-3.3 (billion tons)
	Oil	22%	14%		
	Natural gas	5%	14%		
Non-fossil	Nuclear	7%	7%	> 15%	
	Hydro	1%	9%		
	Bioenergy	~1%	3%		
	Others		5%		

4.2.1.1 SCDRC

The report *China Energy Comprehensive Development Strategy and Policy Research* from the State Council's Development Research Center analyzed three scenarios for energy demand and development. It stated that with the accurate energy strategy and related policies, by 2020 the demand of primary energy would be 2.5 to 3.3 billion tons standard coal; the mean value is 2.9 billion tons standard coal. The structural demand for energy will undergo important changes. The ratio of increased energy utilization over the total energy consumption for the Transport Department and buildings will rise to 57%~75% in 2020 from less than 35% in 2000.

4.2.1.2 ESR

The Energy Strategy Research group of the Chinese Academy of Sciences has completed a report entitled *Research on National Medium and Long-Term Strategic Technology Development for Energy Year 2050*, mapping out a roadmap from 2010 to 2050. It stated that the target for strategy development should be more forward-looking to ensure a smoother transition from fossil energy to sustainable energy. Based on figures from 2005, the increase of consumption of fossil energy should not be more than 50%; energy consumption as a unit of GDP should equal that of medium developed countries; non-hydropower renewable energy should be more than 25% of total primary energy.

4.2.1.3 CAE

The Chinese Academy of Engineering launched a research project on strategic development of Chinese medium and long-term (2030, 2050) energy in 2008. It stated that the strategy for sustainable energy development in China is the "scientific, green and low carbon strategy": a reasonable quantity of safe coal production should be controlled within 3.5 billion tons standard coal. The ratio of coal consumption by 2050 should decrease to 40%, or even lower at 35% of total energy consumption; and the aggregate consumption of nuclear and renewable energy should be above 15% of total consumption.

4.2.1.4 CEG

The Chinese Energy Group of the Chinese Academy of Social Sciences had the following forecasts on the ratios of total consumption in the Chinese energy structure by 2035: coal 48%; oil 14%; natural gas 14%; nuclear energy 7%; hydropower 9%; bioenergy 3%; and other energy 5%.

As previously stated, the medium to long-term adjustment of the

Chinese energy structure will have a huge effect on the international energy market and political and economic developments.

4.2.2 Five Requirements of China's Energy Revolution Raised by Xi Jinping

In the sixth meeting of the Leading Group for Financial and Economic Affairs held on June 13, 2014, Chinese President Xi Jinping led the study on China's national energy security strategy, and issued a rallying statement to promote "China's energy revolution."

Xi's speech pointed out that, "China has made great achievements in the energy development, but it is still confronted with many challenges, e.g., huge pressure of energy demand, a lot of restrictions on energy supply, serious damages made by energy production and consumption to ecological environment, the generally backward level of energy technology, and so on. We shall, from the strategic perspective of national development and security, size up the situation and take the opportunity to find a road conforming to the general trend of energy."

The speech has clearly described the general background of China's energy revolution, which can be used to define the 3E approach to energy security, i.e., energy, economy and environment. China's national strategy of energy security attempts to initiate an energy revolution with the premise of finding a balance between energy, economy and environment, and aims to solve the problems in low-carbon development such as the energy bottleneck in economic development, underdeveloped technology in the energy industry, and low compatibility between energy development and the natural environment.

Xi has raised five requirements concerning the promotion of energy production and consumption revolution in China:

- The first requirement focuses on energy consumption. It is necessary to adhere to the priority of energy-saving, namely to "promote the energy consumption revolution, and restrain irrational energy consumption. Firmly control the total volume of energy consumption, effectively implement the priority of energy-saving, adhere to the energy-saving principle throughout the whole process and all areas of economical and social development, firmly readjust the industrial structure, attach great importance to energy saving in urbanization, set up frugal consumption concept, and speed up the formation of energy-saving society."

- The second requirement focuses on energy supply. It is necessary to persist in pluralistic development and environment protection within China, namely, "promote energy supply revolution, and set up a pluralistic supply system. Ensure the domestic supply security by pluralism, vigorously promote clean and efficient utilization of coal, focus on the development of non-coal energy, and shape an energy supply system driven by multiple energy types including coal, oil, gas, nuclear, new energy and renewable energy, and simultaneously strengthen the construction of energy transmission and distribution network and storage facilities."

- The third requirement focuses on the comprehensive development of energy itself. It is necessary to adhere to reliance on science and technology, namely, "promote the energy technology revolution, and promote industrial upgrading. On the basis of the national conditions of China, keep in step with the new trend of international energy technology revolution, follow the orientation of green and low-carbon economy, promote technical innovation, industrial innovation and business model innovation as per classification, tightly combine with the high-new technologies in other domains, and make energy technology and its related industries become a new point of growth for upgrading of Chinese industries."

- The fourth requirement is to adhere to the energy system revolution by generally adopting market principles, namely, "promote the energy system revolution, and open up the fast lane for energy development. Unswervingly propel the reform, restore the commodity attribute of energy, establish effectively competitive market structure and market system, form an energy pricing mechanism mainly determined by the market, change the mode of governmental supervision on energy, and establish and improve the energy law system."

- The fifth requirement focuses on energy security. It is important to strengthen international cooperation and realize energy security "on the premise of mainly footing in China's homeland, strengthen international cooperation in all aspects involved in the energy production and consumption revolution, and make effective use of international resources."

4.2.3 Remarks on China's Energy Revolution Regarding Demand, Energy Mix, and Marketization

4.2.3.1 Demand

Xi Jinping stated that an energy revolution was needed in order to ensure that China's demands are met. This is quite understandable when China has been the world's primary energy consumer since 2011 with an impressive primary consumption of 101.781 quadrillion Btu, a figure that has been steadily increasing over the past decades. This figure is expected to keep on increasing as China's GDP grew by approximately 6.9% in 2015 and is expected to grow by 6.7% in 2016. Indeed, several economists have established a causal link between GDP growth and energy consumption as "A high level of economic growth leads to high level of energy demand and vice versa." Furthermore, when we analyze the country's data in terms of China's massive population, we observe that according to data from 2011, China's consumption per capita was of 1.69 tonnes of oil equivalent (TOE) per person, which is barely under the world average of 1.79 TOE and approximately 40% of the 4.27 TOE average for the Organization for Economic Co-operation and Development (OECD) member countries. It is therefore predicted that China's already large energy consumption will keep on rising in the next years as the country pursues its course as a developing country heading towards developed country status. Considering this situation, conservation and optimization of the energy structure will be recurrent needs and will certainly remain part of the future plan.

4.2.3.2 The energy mix

In order to meet this vast and increasing demand, China's energy mix still relies primarily on fossil fuels. The latest figures show that coal is still the major source of primary energy as it accounts for 66% of China's total energy consumption. Coal has been the favored energy source as Beijing has traditionally preferred domestic energy products to imported ones. Coal is indeed locally produced and abundant as it is currently estimated that China holds the world's third largest proven reserve of coal amounting to 114.5 billions of tons (BT). As it has been used to fuel China's industrialization, coal consumption in China has risen to 4 BT per year, making it equal with the combined production from the rest of the world in 2014[1]. This has come with great environmental costs as coal is currently estimated to be responsible for 70% of China's emissions of CO_2, 90% of the SO_2 emissions, 70% of dust emissions and 67% of the NOx emissions. China's electricity production is therefore highly

[1] EIA,. (2015). *International Energy Statistics*. Eia.gov. Retrieved 24 July 2015, from http://www.eia.gov/beta/international/data/browser/#/?pa=8&tl_id=1--A&c=ruvvvvvfvtvvvv1vvvvvvfvvvvvvfvvvsu20evvvvvvvvvvvvvvuvg&ct=0&f=A&cy=2013&sta rt=1980&end=2013

dependent on a non-renewable fossil fuel, the consumption of which leaves a deep ecological footprint. Nevertheless, coal's benefit in being locally produced means that it will remain as the dominant electricity source but not without certain conditions.

As the last plan demanded an optimized utilization of coal, massive efforts have been put together to reach this goal. Indeed, while China's coal was usually mined in the west and transported in the east to be transformed, the current trend is to build more plants in the west along with the infrastructure to transport the resulting gas toward the electricity production and consumption centers. Furthermore, it has been announced that smaller and inefficient coal plants that do not meet environmental standards will be shut down and replaced by larger and more efficient plants. In this spirit, plants that had an aggregated 3.3 GW capacity were closed in 2014 to be replaced by gas plants powered by gasified coal from western China. Also, technical advances in terms of carbon footprint reduction technologies have been made. This especially concerns the desulphurization process which helps to reduce a great number of pollutants from entering the atmosphere during the coal combustion process, as well as carbon capture technologies which allow for the storage of CO_2 emissions rather than releasing them into the atmosphere. We can therefore see that a great number of incentives are being developed in order to optimize the coal-powered generation of electricity both in terms of efficiency and environmental impact. Considering the still prominent place of coal in China's energy mix, the trend of optimization of coal utilization that was already in place in the last plan should continue into the next five year plan.

Other fossil fuels, which include petroleum and other liquids as well as natural gas constitute 22% and 5% respectively of China's energy mix. These do not share coal's characteristic of being essentially locally produced. Indeed, China used to be a net exporter of oil but as production did not keep up over the years, China has become a net importer and is today the world's largest importer of oil, importing an average of 6.1 million barrels per day in 2014. Furthermore, China has concluded deals in order to increase its imports of natural gas with Turkmenistan, its current prominent provider (88% of China's natural gas imports were from Turkmenistan in 2013), as well as with Myanmar and with Russia. Under this current situation, China now a has foreign dependency rate of 64% as far as oil is concerned and of 32% as far as natural gas is concerned. As these two energy sources are those for which China is a net importer, they are responsible for China's 11% energy foreign energy dependency rate. Nevertheless, as these resources are not currently sufficiently harvestable in China, making deals with foreign nations in order to supply them securely was considered by the government as necessary to ensure China's energy security during the last FYP, and these import deals should therefore also be expected to continue under the next FYP.

Even if international collaboration is used to obtain oil and gas, there is also a large interest in technologies that will eventually allow China to harvest these resources locally. As the 2011—2015 plan gave high priority to offshore oil harvesting, the production of offshore oil has risen to 20% of China's output. Also, China is said to possess a shale oil and gas reserve approximately equivalent to that of the U.S. However, extracting shale products requires extensive technical knowledge that China does not possess at the moment. Nevertheless, Chinese state-owned companies have been making investments in Australia, Canada and the United States in order to acquire technological knowledge as far as shale gas and oil extraction is concerned.

For instance, the state owned CNOOC purchased the Canadian company, Nexen, which is heavily involved in shale gas and oil projects for $15.1 billion (plus $2.8 billion in Nexen's net debt) in 2013. The previous FYP only briefly mentioned shale gas and oil but gave no precise targets. Considering China's will to utilize its own resources and the acquired technologies, offshore oil mining will certainly remain a part of the plan and it is highly possible that shale will play a much larger part in the future plan.

Considering the different inconveniences associated with fossil fuels, diversification seem to be one of the ideal ways to go. Other sources, which have not been discussed earlier, also contribute in a minor scale to the overall energy mix. Hydroelectricity, nuclear power and renewable energies such as solar and wind account respectively for nearly 8%, 1% and 1% of the total energy consumption. Investments have already been notable in a certain number of these fields. Indeed, China's net installed nuclear capacity was more than 23 GW as of April 2015, as ten reactors with more than 10 GW have been added since the beginning of 2013. Furthermore, by April 2015, Chinese companies were constructing an additional 23 GW of capacity, more than one-third of the global nuclear power capacity currently being built. Hydropower is also on the increase; since the completion of the three gorges dam in 2012, China has become the world's largest hydroelectricity producer with a generation of 894 GW. There are hopes to bolster its already strong 280 GW hydroelectric capacity to 350 GW by 2020. However, despite its low emission when producing energy, hydroelectricity is known to cause massive environmental damage during dam construction, which can cause unrest among the affected population. Massive investments are also under way as far as wind production and solar power production are concerned. China is indeed hoping to increase its wind and solar capacities of 96 GW and 15 GW respectively in 2013 to 200 GW and 100 GW in 2020. China is said to have made the world's largest investment in renewable energy in 2014, 89 billion USD. These massive investments seem logical as these energy sources are produced in China, are renewable and are leaving very little carbon footprint. The diversification and the usage of clean technology can have already been emphasized in the last plan and China's will to diversify and to reduce its carbon foot print will also have a bearing on the next plan.

4.2.3.3 Marketization

As most of the previous elements mentioned earlier already appeared in the previous five-year plan, market pricing is the newcomer. Xi Jinping has been saying at many government levels that the future of China resides in its industrial renewal. In the past, many inefficient and heavy industries have relied on energy subsidies in order to continue production. However, as the internal demand for heavy industry goods is declining in China and abroad, China is entering a phase where it wants to balance consumption and production in a more economically efficient way. In order to put an end to the subsidized fuel price meant to protect those energy intensive industries form inflation, the liberalization of the energy sector seems like the logical way to go. It can therefore be assumed that Xi will indeed go forward with his "push for market-based pricing for energy" agenda from "stage-regulated pricing system." Should it appear clearly in the next plan, this new element might indeed be an important part in China's energy revolution. For example, the future market of the oil sector has been established in Shanghai in 2014. The natural gas pipeline industries and the power grid companies have become a set of detached businesses from the existing vertical integration in energy sectors. These detached businesses are owned and operated independently.

4.3 Conclusion

As has been observed throughout this section, Xi Jinping's energy revolution will incorporate a large number of elements that have been put in place by his predecessors. Indeed, most ideas that had been expressed in the previous five year plan will be taken into consideration and perhaps accentuated in the future plan. It should, however, be noted that some innovations might be added such as the beginning of shale gas exploitation and the liberalization of the energy sector. As shale gas has been considered as the initiator of the north American energy revolution and such a liberalization will bring considerable changes to the way Chinese energy companies have been operating in the past, it is possible that China will indeed make its energy revolution a reality in the next plan despite its resemblance to the last one. It is therefore to be hoped that these policies will be put in place carefully in order to fulfill China's demands in a sustainable manner in the long run.

5

The Evolution of China's Foreign Energy Policy

5.1 The National Energy Security Situation and the Effect on Foreign Energy Policy

The first section of this chapter focuses on how energy policies have changed with the transformation of the security emphasis since the Reform and Opening Up Policy was launched in 1987. Looking at the history of Chinese energy industry development, we may conclude that Chinese energy security has gone through a transition from energy self-sufficiency to energy dependence, and has switched focus from traditional energy sources to renewable energy, thereby changing China's international energy cooperation model.

Before the Reform and Opening Up Policy, the Chinese energy industry had long been self-sufficient due to limited demand and the high yield of the Daqing oilfield, with a low volume of international trade. However, the situation changed as demand increased, and so under the Eighth Five-Year Plan China became a net importer of oil in 1996 and thus began the adjustment of Chinese energy policy. From then on, Chinese energy security gradually came to align with the classic interpretation of energy security—a stable energy supply at an affordable price.

Given the inadequate domestic supply, ensuring foreign energy supply was a key component of Chinese energy security. This was to be attained in two ways. One was to acquire equity oil by cooperation in overseas projects, while the other was to purchase directly from international oil markets. These two measures constitute the Going Out strategy which has formed the core of Chinese foreign energy policy. As early as December 1993, the then President Jiang Zemin, at the Central Committee's Leading Group for Financial and Economic Affairs, proposed the utilization of overseas oil and natural gas to supplement domestic supply, which unlocked the overseas development of Chinese energy companies. Thus traditional energy self-sufficiency gave way to supply-centered energy security, making China more dependent on external markets.

During the Going Out process, the three main Chinese energy companies—China National Petroleum Corporation (CNPC), China Petroleum & Chemical Corporation (Sinopec) and China National Offshore Oil Corporation (CNOOC)—have been participating actively in a growing number of overseas energy projects located in various places. As to the import volume of direct deal oil, China's foreign oil dependence rate is growing sharply, as displayed by Figure 33.

As for equity oil, in the twenty years between 1993 and 2013 CNPC have increased their number of partners from two to over 100 with more than seventy overseas projects, mostly located in North Africa, the Middle East, Central Asia and Canada. These collaborative projects contain oil-gas explorations in the upstream, oil refining and transmit operating in the middle reaches, and sales in the lower reaches. CNPC has become an upstream, middle-stream and downstream integrated energy company through the Going Out Policy. The overseas business of Sinopec is mainly in the Middle East and Central Asia. The operating value involved in the new contracts signed between 2003 and 2007 grew from 1.8 billion dollars to

19.3 billion with a growth rate of 81%. As the third-largest energy company in China, CNOOC has been engaged in collaborative projects for oil and gas exploration at sea, with several top-ranked multinational corporations such as Shell, ConocoPhillips, American International Group and so on, monopolizing the international energy cooperation at sea condoned by the central government since the 1980s.

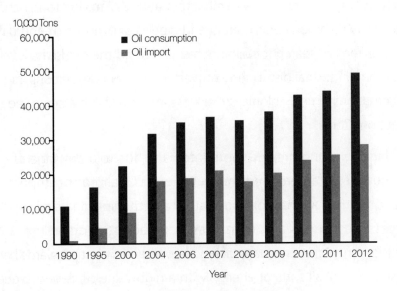

Figure 33   Oil import situation, 1990—2012

The changing Chinese energy security situation has also affected Chinese foreign energy policy, its shape and its implementation. We divide the process into two stages.

5.1.1 Oil-Centered Energy Supply Security

Compared with the extensive coal reserves, oil and natural gas are scarce in China, especially when measured per capita of population, provoking concern for the Chinese government. Thus, for the three largest companies, the key objective of their going out is the exploration of oil and natural gas around the world. For example, between 1997 and 2007, the China

National Petroleum Corporation formulated five oil and natural gas strategic investment zones in Africa, Central Asia and Russia, South Africa, the Middle East and the Asia Pacific region with projects in the Muglad Basin in Sudan, the acquisition of Akejiubin company in Kazakhstan, and exploitation in the Caracoles oilfield and Intercampo oilfield in Venezuela. At the end of 2007, the China National Petroleum Corporation had overseas business in more than twenty-nine countries, with oil output at 89.392 million tons, natural gas output at 17.06 billion cubic meters, and pipelines of more than 6,100 meters. China's extensive search for oil and gas all around the world, has disturbed the existing industrial distribution of Western energy corporations and stirred up accusations of new colonialism and resentment about a perceived energy threat from China.

Under growing pressure both internally, due to a shortage of oil, and from outside, as a perceived threat, China has realized the importance of enhancing international communication and multiplying its energy supply sources. The result is that China has made adjustments to the policy of energy security in recent years, taking an evolutionary path towards balanced development of all sorts of energy, with a high value on renewable energy, through improving market conditions, technological communication and experience sharing with developed and developing countries. President Hu Jintao addressed the G8 summit on July 17, 2006, elaborating the new energy security vision according to the Chinese understanding which includes energy conservation, diversification of energy usage, environmental protection, and mutually beneficial cooperation with other countries to build a stable, economical and clean energy supply system for the world. This new vision of energy security has had a strong impact on China's foreign energy policy and practices.

5.1.2 Energy Security Emphasizing Environmental Protection

In 1998, the energy efficiency voluntary agreement system was established in China. Environmental protection became one of the most important objectives of the Tenth Five-Year Plan period. However, there were no concrete measures to realize this objective as rapid economic growth has increased energy demands. It was not until the Eleventh Five-Year Plan that higher value was placed on the relationship between energy security and environmental protection. The *Medium and Long Term Plan of Energy Conservation*, published in 2004, pointed out ten measures to conserve energy, including giving priority to energy conservation, setting up industrial regulations, taxation policies, price policies and investment policies to promote awareness, increase the percentage of electricity from renewable energy and so on. *The Renewable Energy Law* was passed in 2005 to provide a series of directions for private enterprises entering the renewable energy industry. Later, in 2008, the law was amended to include the role of buildings and transportation in energy conservation. In 2007, the *Medium and Long Term Plan of Renewable Energy* was issued to offer a plan to develop renewable energy, it includes the national construction plan for energy, and the medium and long term plan for nuclear power (2005—2020), to name but a few. The Twelfth Five-Year Plan set a target for non-fossil fuel to represent 11.4% of primary use by 2015, which was surpassed, as fossil fuels came to represent 12%.

Remarks

To sum up, the transformation of Chinese energy security is mainly shown through two aspects, i.e., openness and diversification. Openness denotes that the economic orientation in the Chinese energy industry has turned from self-sufficiency to active participation in international energy trade and energy exploration. Diversification denotes that oil-centered energy security has been replaced by the policy of developing a variety of energy types. At the same time, energy supply security is being outweighed by energy demand security.

5.2 Changes in Foreign Energy Policy

China's foreign energy policy initially referred to a series of diplomatic activities involving gaining energy interests, which can also be called energy diplomacy, with the Going Out Policy at its core. China's official talks with stakeholders in the Middle East, Central Asia, Russia and Africa laid the foundations for China's international energy cooperation. Gradually, the main players and the policy measures have changed from energy diplomacy alone to foreign energy policy.

Referring to energy diplomacy, to take Sino-Saudi Arabian relations as an example, high-level visits have been extremely frequent since diplomatic relations were established. High-ranking Chinese officials who visited Saudi Arabia include Foreign Minister Qian Qichen (1990), Prime Minister Li Peng (1991), Prime Minister Li Lanqing (1993), Member of State Council Luo Gan (1995), Defence Minister Chi Haotian (1996), President Jiang Zemin (1999), Member of State Council Wu Yi (2002), and President Hu Jintao (2006). In addition, high-ranking Saudi Arabian officials including representatives from the Diplomatic, Financial, Commercial, Energy, Law, Agricultural, Telecommunication, Education and Health Departments have paid visits to China. Among the fruits of this have been the *Protocol on Cooperation in Oil, Natural Gas and Mineral Areas* and four other documents that were signed when Crown Prince Abdallah first came to China in 2006.

As for relationships with neighboring Russia and Central Asia, China has cooperated in both energy exploration and pipeline construction. The Agreement on Inspecting Investment of Sino-Kazakhstan Pipeline Construction and Framework Agreement on Cooperation in Oil and Natural Gas were signed by China and Kazakhstan in June 2003 and May 2004, based on which CNPC and Petro Kazakhstan Incorporated signed the Fundamental Principles on Atasu-Alashankou Oil Pipeline Construction. In April 2006, the General Working Agreement on Natural Gas Line and Related Sales was signed by China and Turkmenistan, followed by a sharing contract signed in July 2007 in Beijing. There is an even longer tradition of Sino-Russian energy cooperation; as long ago as 1996 China and Russia signed the Inter-Governmental Agreement on Common Exploitation of Energy. Later President Jiang Zemin visited Russia in July 2001, signing the Working Agreement on the Feasibility of a Sino-Russian Pipeline. In the same year Prime Minister Zhu Rongji and Russia's Premier Kasyanov officially signed the General Working Agreement on the Feasibility of a Sino-Russian Pipeline. In addition, President Hu Jintao visited Sudan in 2007 and Special Representative Liu Gui has made frequent visits to Sudan to deal with the Darfur crisis together with local government.

With the progress of the Going-Out Policy, China's foreign energy policy has evolved into two modes of international cooperation.

5.2.1　From Government-oriented to Corporation-oriented

With Chinese energy security inclining towards diversification, China's mode of cooperation is deviating from the previous government-oriented one. As long ago as the 1970s and 1980s, China had communications with Europe and the U.S. regarding renewable energy and related technology, with intergovernmental cooperation being the main stream of communication. However, this mode was inadequate for China, which was lagging behind and required energy corporations to take the lead by learning advanced technology and management from developed countries. The Clean Development Mechanism (CDM), one of the three flexible fulfilment mechanisms under the Kyoto Protocol is one of the best methods of advancing renewable energy. Under this mechanism project-based cooperation is funded by developed countries and implemented in developing countries. Certified emissions reductions (CERs) produced by these projects are used to help developed countries realize their commitments under the Kyoto Protocol while also helping the sustainable development of developing countries.

As for the approval process, a project should be approved initially by the related departments in developing countries; in China it is the National Development and Reform Commission (NDRC). It is then submitted to the Clean Development Mechanism Execution Board in the U.N. for further approval. Regarding the implementation of the Clean Development Mechanism, governments are only the approvers while energy corporations are the practitioners. Some of the large-scale projects, out of the 122 Clean Development Mechanism projects initiated from September 2010 to January 2012, are listed in Table 23.

The first batch of Clean Development Mechanism projects for emission reductions were approved by the Execution Board on July 3, 2006 (Table 24). By January 2013, China had gained 2,980 projects; this represents 52.1% of the total of Clean Development Mechanism projects worldwide (Figure 34), with China ranking first globally in percentage growth rate.

5.2.2 From Bilateral to Multilateral

As mentioned above, the government-led cooperation highlights the realistic energy views especially with regard to geopolitics. In recent years, particularly after Hu Jintao proposed China's new energy security vision at the G8 summit in 2006, emphasizing renewable energy development and multilateral cooperation, Chinese multilateral energy cooperation has received widespread attention. After all, by participating actively in international organizations to share information, China can better maintain its energy security under the common world energy security safeguard system. Taking several dominant global and regional organizations for example, we can see China's participation in international energy mechanisms in the twenty-first century (Table 25).

Table 23   Examples of CDM Projects in China

Project title	Types of Emission Reduction	Project Owner	Foreign Partner	Approximate Annual Emission Reduction (tCO2e)
Hydropower station of 135 MW in WenQuan, Xinjiang Province	New energy and renewable energy	Hydroelectric Development Limited Corporation in Xinjiang under China Guodian Corporation	Eco Asset Management Corporation	632,614
Second phase project of wind farm in Jilin province	New energy and renewable energy	Wind Power Limited Corporation in Zhenlai	United Carbon Credits Limited	101,774
Second phase project of wind farm	New energy and renewable energy	Wind Power Limited Corporation under China Guangdong Nuclear Power Company	Carbon Asset Management Corporation	110,737
Fukuan biodiesel project in Hebei province	New energy and renewable energy	Fukuan Biolipid Limited Corporation in Hebei	ICF-International Clean Fund LLC Lewes,Mendrisio Branch	212,224
Wind farm project in Kiamusze	New energy and renewable energy	Wind Power Development Limited Corporation under China Guodian Corporation	Vitol SA	117,789
Recovery of waste heat at 27 MW	Energy conservation and energy efficiency	East Hope Cement Limited Corporation in Chongqing	Masefield Carbon Resources SA	154,178
Jiangsu Dafeng wind power project	New energy and renewable energy	China Power Dafeng Wind Power Co. Ltd.	Japan energy-saving investment company	314,050
Tongliao Jianhua No. 2300MW wind farm project	New energy and renewable energy	East Union New Energy Co., Ltd.	Russian Natural Gas Industry Marketing and Trade Corporation Ltd.	633,268
Huadian Sichuan Muli river at Lizhou Hydropower Station Project	New energy and renewable energy	Sichuan China Bakelite Li River Hydropower Development Co.,Ltd.	Arreon Carbon Trading Limited	1,110,980

Source: http://www.cdmpipeline.org/cdm-projects-region.htm

Table 24 Details of projects approved by CDM Execution Board

Emission Reduction Types	Approximate Annual Emission Reduction (tCO2e)	Percentage of Total Emission Reduction	Project number	Percentage of total projects
New energy and renewable energy	10,410,193.4	10.91	86	72.88
HFC-23 disintegration	58,813,446	61.66	10	8.47
Energy conservation and energy efficiency	5,673,085	5.95	8	6.78
Recycle of methane	4,307,347	4.52	8	6.78
Disintegration of N2O	14,726,343	15.44	3	2.54
Alternative fuel	1,300,233	1.36	2	1.69
Garbage burning	150,158	0.16	1	0.85
Forestation and reforestation	0	0	0	0
Others	0	0	0	0
Total Emission Reductions	95,380,805.4	100	118	100
Data from July 3, 2006 to June 12, 2009				

Source: http://cdm.ccchina.gov.cn/web/item_data.asp?ColumnId=63

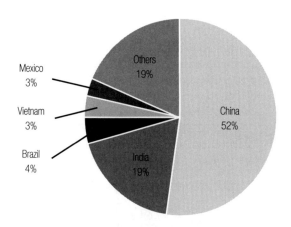

Source: www.Chinawe.org/news_933.shtml, January 8, 2013

Figure 34 Clean Development Mechanism projects approved by the Execution Board in various countries (June 2013)

Table 25   China's participation in multilateral energy organizations

Asia-Pacific Economic Cooperation (APEC)

Since the foundation of APEC in 1989, energy issues have always been crucial in ministerial meetings. Since entry in 1993, China has been actively participating in energy ministerial meetings, the Energy Working Group and the Asia-Pacific Energy Research Centre. In November 2004, Hu Jintao suggested that energy discussion should be strengthened to enhance energy efficiency, to deal with poverty and to develop renewable energy. The Fukui Declaration was passed in the ninth energy ministerial meeting in 2010 to execute demonstration projects of low carbon cities, nominating Yujiabao Financial District as the first demonstration area in Binhai New Area, Tianjin Province. China sought greater cooperation with other APEC countries during 2014, the APEC China year.

Association of South East Asian Nations (ASEAN)

Given common regional energy security, multilateral energy cooperation is becoming more prominent. On June 9, 2004 the 22nd ASEAN energy ministerial meeting and the first ASEAN plus South Korea, China and Japan energy ministerial meeting suggested energy supply and cooperation should be reinforced, providing a new channel for Sino-ASEAN energy coordination. As the China-ASEAN Free Trade Area was launched on January 1, 2010, energy cooperation will definitely be expanded. In September 2010, the China-ASEAN seminar on technology of new energy and renewable energy was held in Chengdu, in which experts discussed the great potential for cooperation in new and renewable energy.

Gulf Cooperation Council (GCC)

GCC contains the United Arab Emirates, Oman, Bahrain, Qatar, Kuwait and Saudi Arabia, constituting the main exporting base of oil. Although China has frequent bilateral contacts with every member of the GCC, it has not yet had multilateral cooperation with this organization. Since FTA negotiations were launched in July 2004, consensus has been reached in many fields. When President Hu Jintao met Secretary-General Atia of GCC in February 2009, he pointed out that FTA offered long-term benefits and related agreements should be signed as soon as possible.

International Energy Agency (IEA)

Albeit not a member of the International Energy Agency, China has had contact with it since 1996, when the executive director of the International Energy Agency visited China to agree a Memorandum of Policy Understanding on Energy Cooperation. Hence intermittent communication has occurred, allowing for thre being a chapter on China in the annual report. China participates in the International Energy Agency's ministerial meetings, seminars and so on. General cooperation describes the Sino-International Energy Agency relationship. Not until October 15, 2009 did the International Energy Agency decide to sign China's partnership with the International Energy Agency and to open closer policy coordination.

Source: China International Energy Cooperation 2012/2013, CIEESS

Remarks

China is now inclined to choose a multilateral cooperation mode in energy organization, with more and more enterprises both national and private as the leading players, seeking to exert more influence. Such inclination is not only founded in renewable energy cooperation but also in traditional energy cooperation such as that with the GCC.

5.3 Twenty-year Review of China's Foreign Energy Policy Implementation

Since 1993, China has become a net importer of refined oil and, since 1996, a net importer of crude oil. In the early 1990s, in order to implement the central government's policy of "full use of both resources and both markets both at home and abroad," China began to implement the Going Out strategy and actively conduct international energy cooperation. If 1993 was the first year of China's international energy cooperation, 2012 marked the twentieth year of China's foreign energy policy implementation, and 2013 the first year after the convening of the 18th National Congress of the CPC. Therefore, 2013 was a transitional year regarding the future of China's international energy cooperation. This section reviews China's international energy cooperation over the past two decades, with discussion of the results, the policy reasons for the results, and the positive and negative effects of international cooperation.

5.3.1 Results

With two decades of exploration and development, China's international energy cooperation has achieved remarkable results and entered a stage of rapid development. These results are presented below.

First, energy diplomacy has achieved significant results. Through high-level government visits and various summits, China has signed inter-governmental energy cooperation agreements with many countries around the world, and energy framework cooperation agreements with several national organizations, which have laid a solid foundation for China to carry out bilateral and multilateral international energy cooperation.

China has implemented more than 100 international oil and gas cooperation projects in thirty-three countries around the world. It has designated five major international oil and gas cooperation regions: the Africa region based on projects in Sudan; the Middle East region based on projects in Oman and Syria; the Central Asia and Russia region based on projects in Kazakhstan; the Americas region based on projects in Venezuela and Ecuador, and the Asia-Pacific region based on projects in Indonesia. Thus China has been carrying out international cooperation in oil and gas resources globally. In 2012, the production in overseas oil and gas interests of Chinese oil and gas companies exceeded 100.15 million tons of oil equivalents.

China has established a foreign energy trading system. The initial establishment of the energy import and export trading system was mainly based on oil, liquefied natural gas (LNG), natural gas, coal and uranium. These are transported mainly with tankers and supplemented with pipelines and railways, and traded in a variety of ways such as stocks, futures and long-term purchase agreements in the international market[1]. Chinese energy companies have greatly improved their own international competitiveness. After twenty years of development, Chinese national energy corporations have not only mastered the operation model for international energy cooperation projects, but also accumulated rich experience in capital operation, contract negotiation, etc. They have continuously improved their effectiveness in overseas investment, with growing strength and international influence. In 2012, both CNOOC and CNPC entered Canada, which is a concrete manifestation of their strength.

① CIEESS report, 2013
The China International Energy Cooperation Report 2012/2013, Center for International Energy and Environment Strategy Studies of Renmin University (CIEESS), Energy Outlook Magazine and the China Council for the Promotion of International Trade (CCPIT)

China's international energy cooperation has experienced great changes in terms of channels, contents, mechanisms and partners. Overall, these changes show the following three features discussed below.

5.3.1.1 Types of energy

The types of energy cooperation continue to diversify. China's international energy cooperation was mainly in oil and natural gas initially, and has gradually extended to various fields including natural uranium, coal, electric power, wind energy, bio-fuels, energy conservation, energy technology and equipment, etc.

5.3.1.2 Actors in international energy cooperation

Both state and non-state actors such as the international governmental and non-governmental organizations are taking part in international energy cooperation. China has established bilateral energy cooperation mechanisms with nearly forty countries, such as the Sino-U.S. energy policy dialogue, the Sino-U.S. oil and gas forum, the Sino-Russian energy negotiation mechanism, the Sino-Kazakh energy subcommittee, the Sino-Japan energy minister dialogue, and the Sino-Indonesia energy forum, etc. Partner countries have been gradually extended from the initial neighboring countries and the Middle East to vast areas of Central Asia, Africa, the Americas, Oceania, covering the world's major energy-producing and consuming countries, and the pathway countries.

5.3.1.3 Ways of cooperation

More innovative ways of cooperation are being discovered. On the one hand, this innovation appears as "the constant intervention of the financial elements," namely taking advantage of China's foreign exchange reserves to implement a package for cooperation on energy and finance within international energy cooperation, such as a variety of oil-for-loans agreements in recent years. On the other hand, it represents "the participation of non-state-owned enterprises, with the growing number of cooperation bodies," that is, forming a multi-level, multi-country, multi-ownership cooperation body that is mainly based on state-owned companies, with the participation of non-state-owned companies from the resource-producing countries and the investing countries.

5.3.2 Policy Background

The main reason for the rapid development of international cooperation in China's energy sector is the fact that China's concept of energy security has fundamentally changed. In other words, China has undergone a fundamental change in the policy basis for formulating the foreign energy policy from a realist perspective to a liberal perspective. This shift is reflected in official government policies on energy security and the economic activities of energy enterprises, but also the changes of direction allowing China to participate in international energy cooperation. The change in the concept of energy security led to a series of multilateral trends in energy cooperation, prompting energy companies to gradually enter the markets, which played the main role in breaking down the form of energy cooperation that was characterized as "government being first to pave the way for the enterprise."

The discovery of the Daqing oilfield in 1959 was a turning-point in the Chinese oil industry and in the history of China's energy development, achieving oil self-sufficiency and a small volume of exports for a time. However, with the sustained economic development in the 1990s, China's oil demands began to climb. In 1993, China became a net importer of oil, and consequently, dependence on foreign oil has increased year by year. China's oil industry is now inextricably linked with the international oil market. At the same time, China's coal-dominated energy consumption structure increases carbon emissions, and under enormous international pressure, China is actively carrying out various measures to reduce emissions. In the development process, China's energy security concept is changing from the initial concept of energy independence to the concept of energy interdependence, from a focus on security of energy supply to the security of energy demand. This represents a corresponding change in the way in which China participates in international energy cooperation, reflecting the redirection from a realist concept of energy security to a liberal concept of energy security.

Since the period of reform and opening up, the evolution of China's energy security concept may be divided into two stages. The first stage was the beginning of the reform and opening up (from 1978), developing from energy self-sufficiency towards international energy cooperation. The second stage was during the Eleventh Five-Year Plan (2005—2010), when it changed from an oil-and-gas-based energy supply security concept to an energy security concept of balanced development of multiple energy sources. In 2006, Hu Jintao proposed a new energy security concept at the G8 summit in St Petersburg. So far, China's energy security concept has shifted from isolated national security of self-supply, going through the 4A energy security concept that meets the four requirements of adequate supply, affordable price, accessible transportation and admissible environment, gradually shifting to the 3E+S energy security concept that combines the concerns on energy, economy, environment, and social security, paying more attention to the energy security concept with common development of a variety of energy resources. After the 18th National Congress of the CPC, the concept of energy security has also been increasingly connected with the ecological civilization of society as a whole, focusing on sustainable development.

With the constant evolution of the concept of energy security, China began to actively participate in multilateral international energy cooperation in the early twenty-first century. In the twenty-first century, with the greater opening up to the outside world and the profound changes of the world energy situation, China's participation in multilateral and bilateral cooperation shows a rapid growth trend. So far, China has established a relationship of exchange and cooperation with the world's major energy-producing countries, as well as consuming countries and the International Energy Agency. Currently, China is an official member of the International Energy Forum (IEF), the World Energy Council (WEC), the Energy Working Group of the Asia-Pacific Economic Cooperation (APEC), the Central Asia Regional Cooperation Energy Coordination Committee, and other multilateral energy cooperation mechanisms. Moreover, China is an observer of the Energy Charter, with close cooperation with the International Energy Agency. China has also established the normal mechanisms of cooperation with the Gulf Cooperation Council, the Organization of Petroleum Exporting Countries, the European Union and other regional organizations.

5.3.3 International Effects

Since the early 1990s, China has experienced more than twenty years of international energy cooperation practices. The vast majority of the effects from this have been positive, but there are also some problems.

5.3.3.1 Positive effects

China's international energy cooperation and development helps it to establish the image of a responsible big country. For twenty years, China has been transforming from the initial exchanges and dialogues to hosting a number of meetings and taking a number of initiatives, from the lack of information communication to the establishment of smooth energy data information exchange with major global organizations, and from a follower of the international energy system to a member that can influence and participate in the formulation of international rule. China's international energy cooperation is not just the going out of Chinese companies with ongoing mergers and acquisitions and expansion in the oil and gas sectors on the downstream, midstream and upstream, it also contains the burgeoning influence of Chinese innovation in energy development concepts, the integration of negotiation mechanisms, and the resolution of international energy issues, etc. For example, China has put forward a series of new initiatives in a variety of regional multilateral cooperation mechanisms, practised a series of new initiatives, and produced a wide-range of positive effects on the world. When Chinese enterprises implement the Going Out Policy, they actively help those countries with a shortage of energy infrastructure in the construction of a variety of energy supporting and auxiliary facilities. For example, a refinery was established in Chad to improve the lives of the local people, which reflects the social responsibility of Chinese enterprises.

Moreover, China's international energy cooperation and development has changed geopolitical ecology to a certain extent. Take energy relations as an example, China's international energy cooperation strengthens the intergovernmental and non-governmental exchange with organizations in major countries and regions worldwide, promotes mutual understanding, and eases or even defuses potential geopolitical crises. Take the APEC as another example, the situation of the Asia-Pacific region was at its most tense in 2012, while the rapid progress of China's multilateral and bilateral energy cooperation weakened the conflict in the region and continued to support a bright future for cooperation.

The year 2012, as an election year in China, marked the beginning of a new political cycle. Regarding relations among major powers, the traditional force of the U.S. and other developed Western countries continues to be challenged by the rising status and influence of emerging countries. It has become increasingly preferable to participate in multilateral diplomacy and international mechanisms, since no country or mechanism can lead the international order alone. China's rising status and the implementation of the "rebalancing" strategy of the U.S. makes the Asia-Pacific region central to global politics. In the context of the international regime structure changes, China is facing the situation of rising factors of conflict on its peripheries. The Asia-Pacific region is the most important testing ground for whether China and its neighboring countries can establish mechanisms of normal state-to-state relations to control conflicts through a break-in period. Multilateral energy cooperation in the Asia-Pacific region is carried out smoothly and successfully, which not only provides important opportunities to build a situation in the region which is beneficial for all, but also provides a solid material foundation to build a harmonious and prosperous new Asia-Pacific order.

Finally, China's international energy cooperation and development has reshaped international relations. International energy cooperation relies on energy products—the first attribute of the energy sector is a commodity that readily meets common business interests. Therefore, cooperation focusing on this special commodity, energy, is less likely to be disturbed and influenced by ideology and post-Cold-War mentality. In this case, international relations established on the basis of international cooperation in energy will be above the differences in culture, political systems and economic development between countries. It will be fully developed by the net axis of energy-resource-exporting countries, energy-consuming countries and energy-pathway countries. Through two decades of practise, one of the greatest results is the fact that the world order of international relations has become more stable due to China's participation in energy exploration, production, transportation and consumption.

5.3.3.2 Negative effects

There are also problems, and how to resolve these problems is the focus of Chinese foreign energy strategists. The most critical point is the potential political risk of the Going Out Policy for Chinese enterprises, because going out will be subject to the impact of global and regional as well as geopolitical economics. More going out means increased interdependence, which also means that China's fortunes are subject to growing risks. In such circumstances, China's international energy cooperation may have a negative effect on China's foreign relations; the normal bilateral relations will be labelled "energy," and it increases the suspicion of partner countries over China's "resource plundering." In Myanmar, Kazakhstan, Russia, Latin America and other resource-rich countries, the voice of opposition to Chinese enterprises, from the private sector to the government, is in an endless stream. Besides, it has become more difficult for other nations in the world to take the initiative to accept China, after the initial honeymoon period, due to China's huge economy, huge population and huge energy demands.

5.3.4 Policy Suggestions and Outlook

The shift from a negative impact to a positive impact requires a higher level of system design on the basis of the success in the last two decades. Specifically we offer the three proposals below.

5.3.4.1 Enhance mutual trust for the correct understanding of China's energy security policy

In the face of China's huge and continuously expanding demand for energy, many countries have expressed concern and anxiety. As the world's largest energy consumer, China's behavior in using normal energy diplomacy to meet its own energy needs has often been criticized, which is not conducive to China playing its role in global and international regional energy cooperation. Therefore, China needs to do more public relations, to explain itself and promise to adhere to the principle of mutual benefits, with the effective implementation of a stable external energy policy.

5.3.4.2 Coordination between various countries with caution and sensitivity

The properties of energy make the world's major countries, no matter whether resource-exporting countries, consuming countries, or pathway countries, extremely sensitive to the issue of energy security, in order to guarantee their own energy security, which sometimes naturally leads to fierce competition among them. In addition, China has territorial disputes with individual neighboring countries, the core interests of territorial integrity coupled with strategic properties of oil and gas resources make the issue more sensitive. This complex and sensitive state of international relations restricts, to some extent, China's role in the global and intra-regional energy cooperation.

5.3.4.3 Encourage commercial and industrial enterprises and non–governmental forces to participate in global and regional multilateral and bilateral energy cooperation

The participation of industrial and commercial enterprises and non-governmental forces can dilute to a certain extent the political sensitivity of the cooperation. The enterprises are also the ultimate perpetrators for most of the energy cooperation plans or initiatives, and the regional cooperation mechanisms and government level cooperation agreements have to rely on enterprises and institutions to be implemented. Therefore, encouraging the participation of enterprises and even non-governmental forces is an important measure to carry out China's energy international cooperation smoothly.

5.3.4.4 Conclusion

After 2013, China's international energy cooperation is faced with greater opportunities and challenges. From the perspective of opportunities: With the increasingly fierce global discussion on the issue of climate change, a new industrial revolution has emerged, which will completely change the world economy and people's way of life. The basis of the new industrial revolution is an energy revolution. This energy revolution marks the change of human production and utilization of energy varieties, such as shale gas from 2009, with the development from conventional oil and gas to unconventional oil and gas. It also changes the manner in which humans produce and use energy, such as the use of distribution energy. This energy revolution will greatly broaden the areas of international cooperation.

From the perspective of challenges: As the concept of energy security changes from the old demands to new, from pure energy to a higher level of the so-called 3E+S energy security which combines the economy, environment and social safety in the aftermath of the Fukushima catastrophe, China's foreign energy policy bears not only heavy responsibility to safeguard the traditional Chinese energy security, but also the norms of traditional energy security spillover to other national security needs. There are also some problems with China's foreign energy policy implementation. The administrative examination and approval procedures are burdensome, and cooperation and coordination mechanisms have yet to be improved. International energy cooperation funds need to be better supported by national fiscal and financial policies. China needs to establish cooperation risk protection and emergency response mechanisms; it needs to establish and improve the external energy trading system in order to avoid energy price volatility (Table 26).

Table 26 Main challenges met by China's "Going Out Policy"

National Policy	How to treat the role of state-owned enterprises in the Going Out strategy: With their government background, state-owned enterprises can obtain powerful political and financial support when they make overseas investments, however, they will also suffer discriminatory treatment in several nations which have resources. In performing the Going Out strategy, how to reduce the difficulties due to the background of state-owned enterprises has been a topic that deserves attention.
	How to coordinate the conflict of interests among enterprises during the process of Going Out: China still implements severe restrictive measures in terms of resource imports, which means private enterprises face more difficulties compared with state-owned enterprises. Meanwhile, in the history of implementation of Going Out by Chinese energy enterprises, competition between Chinese enterprises in overseas markets has brought negative effects and losses to a certain degree for China. For future development, coordination and avoiding the conflict of interests for enterprises of various natures is an urgent task facing China during the process of the Going Out strategy.
	How to evaluate technology integration and innovation issues: One important objective for the going out of Chinese enterprises is to obtain high-end resource exploitation and utilization technology. During the process of implementing the Going Out strategy, has the objective been achieved effectively? What difficulties exist in terms of obtaining technology? What are the technical advantages and disadvantages for Chinese enterprises in the field of resource exploitation?
Continuity and Security of Going Out Policy	How to coordinate the relationship between continuous overseas expansion and prudent operation: The overseas expansion of Chinese enterprises has been quite vigorous in recent years, which has made several Chinese enterprises rapidly become important participants in the international energy market. In the meantime, the burdens for the enterprises are also increasing, particularly in terms of debt. In accordance with the performance of stock prices for the three major oil and gas companies of China, the profitability of these enterprises is doubted. Against this background, are large-scale overseas mergers and expansion a long-term policy? How to guarantee and promote the profitability of enterprises in a continuous way? Have Chinese enterprises taken relevant issues into account and figured out corresponding business plans?
	How to solve the cultural diversity issues in operations caused by overseas expansion: The target countries for Chinese overseas expansion have been shifted to developed countries from third-world countries with underdeveloped economies and unstable political situations. The business management styles and systems of countries such as Canada and the USA are quite different from those of Chinese enterprises. Because Chinese enterprises gradually accept the development models of international consortiums, the coordination of various cultures among different enterprises is unavoidable. Chinese enterprises retain their own unique features when implementing the Going Out strategy, such as maintaining a relatively high proportion of Chinese staff in the target country. Have Chinese enterprises formulated corresponding measures in dealing with cultural diversity?
	How to deal with the issues with local governments and people arising out of overseas expansions: Chinese enterprises will face more and more actual problems of dealing with social relations during the going out process. Due to the connection of energy resources with national economic security, local governments and people are quite sensitive about the utilization of domestic energy resources by foreign enterprises. During the process, Chinese enterprises shall consider not only the economic costs of the projects, but also the local political and social costs they incur. Do Chinese enterprises have certain experience and measures in dealing with these issues?

Continued

International Energy Governance	Participating in global energy governance and improvement of domestic energy structure: As a major consumer of energy resources, China is playing an increasingly important role in deciding the outcome of international energy issues, and the voice asking for China to participate in global energy governance is also getting louder. When participating in the global energy governance China will adapt to the requirements of its own energy strategy. Therefore, the methods of improving the energy utilization structure of the country have a significant impact on the effectiveness of China's participation in energy governance, which also plays a guiding role for Chinese enterprises to implement the Going Out strategy in the future. What are the objectives and measures of the Chinese government for improving energy structure? Against the backdrop of constant improvement of the unconventional natural gas and new energy utilization technology, how can the objectives and measures be realized? How to solve the issues of energy pricing: The Going Out process for Chinese enterprises is basically simultaneous with the continuous rise of international oil prices. The purchase of oil with high prices has been denounced by Chinese industries. As the largest oil and gas importer of the world in the future, it is reasonable for China to demand the energy pricing power, while there are two major difficulties. Firstly, China has no domestic oil type that can circulate freely within relevant areas; secondly, it is quite hard for China to establish the benchmark for the international market with its status of being a major importer of oil and gas; and Japan is a typical example in this regard. Against such a background, does the Chinese government have detailed planning to solve the international energy pricing issue to make it more accurately reflect the supply and demand for the world as a whole and to conform better to Chinese interests?
Bilateral Energy Relations	The impact of the energy independence of the U.S.: The effective development of unconventional oil and gas resources in the U.S. makes the energy independence of that country possible. Global industries and academic circles attach great importance to any event that may initiate a global energy revolution. The Centre for International Energy Strategy Studies of Renmin University of China has held international academic conferences on this topic. How does China regard the energy independence of the U.S.? What impact will the energy independence of the U.S. have on China? With respect to Sino-Russian energy cooperation: The Sino-Russian energy cooperation has made considerable progress in recent years. Major breakthroughs have been achieved in the field of petroleum, and the establishment of the Sino-Russian crude oil pipeline is of significant strategic and economic importance. However, Chinese enterprises still have enormous difficulties in terms of accessing the upstream of Russia for development and cooperation of natural gas. How can we comprehend the history and current situation of the Sino-Russian energy cooperation? What are the factors that affect the Sino-Russian energy cooperation? What is the future of the Sino-Russian energy cooperation?
Implementation of Going Out Policy	How to treat the rising status of energy resources in Chinese diplomacy: In recent years, one feature of Chinese diplomacy is the increasingly important role of energy resources. One significant topic for discussion for summit diplomacy is undoubtedly cooperation in the field of energy. State-owned enterprises have become major policy implementers in energy diplomacy. The "bundle up" conduct of governments and enterprises has been an important system for China to participate in overseas energy markets. How to treat this system, how to define the diplomacy interests of the nation and that of enterprises, as well as how to coordinate and unite the two kinds of interests, are relevant questions. How to treat the role of finance for energy enterprises in the Going Out strategy: After the financial crisis, Chinese enterprises utilized the system of "loans for resources" to accomplish a series of large acquisitions.

310

5.4 China's Foreign Energy Policy by Region

As pointed out earlier, China has not yet completely established its foreign energy policy. However, as the Chinese economy is investment-oriented and fast growing, energy is a necessity for safeguarding economic sustainability. The People's Republic of China found its first large oil well at Daqing Heilongjiang province in 1959. It was not until 1993 that China started to feel energy insecurity: from that year China became an oil products importer and the net importer of oil in 1996. Oil supply security has inevitably become the greatest stumbling block for Chinese development.

However, this turned out to more of a perception than a reality. In the past two decades, Chinese oil companies have been developing their strategic arrangement (or layout) of oil quest, more or less, with the help of the Chinese government, in order to meet the needs of 1.3 billion people. To some extent, the rudiments of China's foreign energy policy have been manifested through the policy of Going Out, which was initiated at the end of the 1990s just after China became a net importer of oil.

In the Middle East, Africa, America, Europe, Asia-Pacific and Central Asia and Russia, China has met with the opportunities and challenges of energy collaboration. The long-term outlook is that China's energy foreign relations will be strengthened not weakened, with clear strategic targets, practical guidelines, efficient policies, more stakeholders and diversified implementation, but will also be more tolerant to the benefits of partners.

So far, energy diplomacy is the core of China foreign energy policy and going out is the key means for policy implementation. China has been making the best of its influence as the largest developing country in the world and the emerging country with speediest development. It has been taking full advantage of its comparative advantages in terms of funding, technology, manufactured goods and labor force. China has been actively involved in some regional organizations such as the Shanghai Cooperation

Organization (SCO), the Forum on China-Africa Cooperation and ASEAN 10+1 to develop cooperative energy relationships with countries possessing energy resources.

5.4.1 Central Asia and Russia

Among the regions with resource-rich countries, Central Asia and Russia have been China's preference. This is not only because these countries are neighbors and developing countries, the same as China, but also because they are China's diplomatic priority, and Russia especially is also China's main strategic partner.

5.4.1.1 Opportunities

Since the breakdown of the former Soviet Union, a comparatively favorable relationship has laid the foundations for the energy relationship. Developing the energy relationship with Central Asian countries and Russia is also of importance to meet collaborative partners' needs both in politics and economics. One of the largest markets for energy consumption and one of the largest energy resources in the world, are inevitably drawn together. By using energy as the commodity, and energy pipelines as the chain, a booming economy can help stabilize the region's security and social safety, which is the key objective of President Xi Jinping's New Silk Road Economic Belt.

5.4.1.2 Challenges

The geostrategic competition among world powers and among the major energy importers of the world for the energy resources around the Caspian Sea is increasingly fierce. Multinational corporations from Western countries, compared with Chinese corporations, which control a large number of high-quality oil fields, can exert more influence on the region. The possibility of political power instability in Central Asian countries, and social conflicts deep-rooted in the regions caused by the differences among ethnic groups and religious sects, constitute various geopolitical risks to China's "something-done" foreign policy philosophy in the region.

5.4.1.3 Policy Choice

In order to take full advantage of SCO, China will propel the shift of multilateral energy cooperation mechanisms in SCO, e.g. the establishment of the SCO energy club, and activate the idea of the New Silk Road with five points as its policy core: communication of policy measures, connection of transportation (road, railway and airway), smoothness of trade, circulation of currency and appreciation of people across the countries of the region. In addition, the Sino-Russia gas pipeline, co-utilization of uranium, construction of a transnational electric power network and coal E&P collaboration will be the highlights of Chinese foreign energy policy in the region.

5.4.2 Africa

For quite some time, China has been regarded Africa as a major source of oil imports. In fact, North Africa is listed in second place only after the Middle East for China's oil imports. China's policy of nonintervention in internal affairs' in Africa has won great praise in African countries. The establishment and highly efficient operation of the Forum on China-Africa Cooperation provided an important platform for China's engagement in Sino-Africa energy relations. The oil development by China in Africa has made significant progress; on one hand obtaining energy through trading, on the other hand producing equity oil through taking over African local companies, either directly or as a joint acquisition with other transnational energy companies.

5.4.2.1 Opportunities

There are numerous newly proved rich oil and gas reserves, which are waiting for exploration and production. African economies show strong tendencies of growing, with the rate around 5% in 2012, sub-Saharan Africa even surpassed 5%, a striking contrast to other areas of the world. According to KPMG statistics, African GDP will reach 2.6 trillion USD in 2020, the infrastructure is being upgraded and foreign direct investment is being increased. Positive transformations both in politics and economics will bring great investment potential: the African political and economic situation has been gradually improving, with the accumulation of capital earned through exports. The development of resource industries, finance, energy and communications and other non-resource type industries is also notable. Africa has been playing a more and more important role in the global energy regime, as it has become a variable, re-balancing the energy structure between the Middle East—the old supply center of traditional fuels, and North America—the new supplier of non-traditional fuels, and between OPEC and non-OPEC nations.

5.4.2.2 Challenges

Though China has succeeded in cooperation in coal, oil and gas and NRE such as solar power with African countries, there are some uncertainties. Cultural diversity in languages and business practises are the main barriers for both parties to overcome. The political turmoil in some African countries will last for a long time. African economies are unsteady and most of them are underdeveloped with a shortage of capital and technology and underdeveloped infrastructure. All these disadvantages may increase investment costs. Compared with some countries that entered into Africa earlier, China has no competitive advantage.

5.4.2.3 Policy Choice

China should enter the downstream refining and chemical fields in a mutually beneficial and proper manner to participate in more infrastructure construction in Africa.

5.4.3 The Middle East

The Gulf region has the richest accumulation of oil and gas. It is of significant strategic value for Chinese energy security to strengthen the oil and gas cooperation with Gulf region countries, which is supposed to be "the priority of emphasis" (Figure 35).

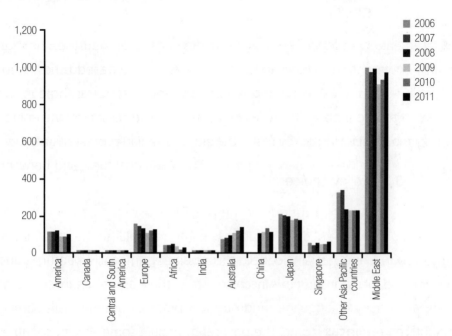

Figure 35   Importers of Middle Eastern oil

5.4.3.1 Opportunities

For almost twenty years, the region has been the largest supplier of oil and gas to China. China's energy cooperation is mainly with Kuwait, Saudi Arabia, Iraq, Iran, Qatar, Oman, Angola and the UAE, whose energy relationships with China have been stable and continuous since the Iraq War. In 2012, Kuwait surpassed Qatar to be the largest supplier of LNG to China. Iran signed an agreement to raise its oil exports to China by 0.5 mbl per day though it cannot get the income from China directly because of economic sanctions by the U.S. China increased its oil imports from Saudi

Arabia to 1.17 mbl per day in 2013. China has already established a long-term comprehensive strategic cooperation mechanism with the UAE, deepening the E&P, involving storage infrastructure construction, multi-level collaboration on oil and gas refineries, and trying to realize the liquidation with both countries' national currencies in energy trading.

5.4.3.2 Challenges

The energy independence of North America is reshaping U.S. foreign policy towards the region. The Middle East has entered into a neo-geopolitical game with conflict between its various states. Existing conflicts between ethnic groups and religious sects were exacerbated by the Arab Spring, the rebalancing policy of the U.S. and the Iranian nuclear crisis.

5.4.3.3 Policy choice

China should be cautious of the possible cost of expanding energy cooperation with the Middle East in case conflicts similar to the Iraq War and Libyan civil war erupt again. To avoid this possibility, anti-crisis measures must be arranged for the institutions involved.

5.4.4 The Americas

The oil reserves in some Latin American countries and North America (specifically Canada) are abundant. In recent years, China has progressed a lot in working with Latin American countries such as Brazil, Ecuador and especially Venezuela to import large amounts of oil. Latin America has also become China's third largest oil supplier. With the successful take-over of shale gas fields in Canada by China National Offshore Oil Corporation and China National Petroleum Corporation by the end of 2012, Canada has become one of the few developed countries to open its upstream resources for Chinese companies' foreign direct investment, though the results have brought controversy over whether there may be other material for China to extract in Canadian soil. The U.S. plays a very important role in the foreign policies of Mexico, Canada and Latin America. Therefore, it is necessary to diagnose the energy relationship between the U.S. and China.

5.4.4.1 Opportunities

It is more than thirty years since the first U.S. representative, James Schlesinger, visited Beijing in 1978. Sino-U.S. energy cooperation has passed through four stages: exploration, stagnation, solidarity and development and deepening and institutionalization. The speed of developing non-traditional energy such as tight oil and gas, shale oil and gas, etc. has been accelerated. With the icebreaker that was the trading of natural gas between China and the U.S. and the transferring of clean energy technology, the two countries' cooperation is on the fast track to adjusting the energy mix, developing clean energy, safeguarding oil security and improving energy efficiency.

5.4.4.2 Challenges

Both countries are the world's largest energy producers and consumers with the same interests and responsibilities, while meeting the same challenges. However, the objectives for cooperation between Beijing and Washington are not always the same because of the diversity of political and economic systems and different stages of social development. For example, the U.S. has three objectives: energy security, ecological sustainability and business benefits. Washington wants Beijing to open its upstream resources but Beijing hopes Washington will supply nuclear and deep-sea drilling technology. However, the two partners have realized sufficient mutual trust.

5.4.4.3 Policy Choice

So far, there are dozens of inter-governmental and inter-departmental collaborative agreements signed between China and the U.S. These include two bilateral mechanisms of OGIP, the U.S.-China Policy Dialogue and

Renewable Energy Industry Forum, three multilateral mechanisms of GNEP, the International Advanced Biofuels Forum, five energy ministers from China, India, Japan, South Korea and the US Convention were established and the U.S.-China Clean Energy Research Center and one platform of enterprise cooperation (ECP) were set up. But how to implement the cooperative bilateral policies through the institutionalization and paralleling of government and enterprise joint endeavors is the key point.

5.4.5 Asia-Pacific

The Asia-Pacific region refers to Southeast Asia and South Asian countries. The main consideration for China in this energy relationship is that these countries are connected with China by land or adjacent with each other by sea. All are members of the Association of Southeast Asian Nations (ASEAN).

5.4.5.1 Opportunities

The "10+1" cooperation with ASEAN is significant for the diplomacy between China and neighboring countries. The positive expansion of energy cooperation with Southeast Asian countries and South Asian countries is conductive to relieving the dispute over the sovereignty of the South China Sea. The Sino-Myanmar oil and gas pipeline is a demonstrative example of China's foreign energy policy in the region. The project was successfully completed in November 2013 and is expected to realize the intended target of transporting 20 million tons of oil annually. The energy resource reserves in the region are relatively abundant, and the oil-producing fields are adjacent to the eastern region of China which is the main economic developed region with huge energy consumption and open to the ASEAN economies. In addition, the land transportation to mainland China is more convenient and safer than by sea.

5.4.5.2 Challenges

Some countries in the region are resistant to China. Disputes over the sovereignty of islands in the South China Sea as well as disputes of rights and interests with China in terms of the oil and gas development on the South China Sea always exist.

5.4.5.3 Policy choice

It is necessary to make a key point of developing cooperative relationships with energy resource-rich countries in the region due to China's consideration of requirements of diplomatic strategy and geographical conditions. The coal and uranium reserves are also abundant in Australia, a country which is enthusiastic about developing energy cooperation with China and which has already laid a good base for further cooperation.

5.4.6 The European Union

China and the E.U. are cooperative and also competitive in energy. In the field of stabilizing international markets and new energy research and development they are cooperative partners, but in the quest for Russian and Caspian oil and gas they are rivals.

5.4.6.1 Opportunities

The long-term cooperation between China and the E.U. has a relatively stable pattern. Being the frontrunner in clean energy production technology such as CCS, most E.U. members have the comparative advantage. The E.U. has a significant impact on the formulation of international energy rules, as many E.U. member states are members of the International Energy Agency and some of them are members of the G8, and are quite active in international energy governance organizations. The E.U. has a unified economy and market with a common energy strategy, which also attractive to Chinese enterprises.

5.4.6.2 Challenges

Since the financial crisis in 2008, the E.U. has become more protectionist regarding trade with China. The E.U. has not only exerted high and punitive tariffs on Chinese PV products but also tried an aviation carbon tax levy. Their tough stance on climate change issues makes the E.U. and China incompatible, which has damaged bilateral energy cooperation.

5.4.6.3 Policy choice

In traditional energy cooperation with the E.U., China prefers using the way of share buy-outs and joint projects, while in technology the bilateral cooperation is usually in the form of high-level dialogues or forums.

5.5 Remarks

If we analyze the 4As of energy from the six regions discussed above, we can understand why China chooses Central Asia and Russia as its foreign energy policy priority. For availability; the reserves in Central Asia and Russia are huge. For accessibility, as oil and gas can be transported to China directly by pipeline, railway or through power grid and shipping, e.g., LNG from Russia to China, which is safe and efficient. For affordability; China has the flexibility to choose different methods of cooperation with its neighbors—barter, loan or advance payment—and settlement in RMB or rouble rather than always in dollars, which is more economical. For acceptability; based on the close ethnic relations, energy resources from the region are relatively easier for Chinese to accept. If there were no Turkmenistan gas, Beijing's winter air quality might be worse than in the time before the fuel source shifted from coal to gas. Based on the above development trend, we believe that the former regional structure for oil imports, as Figure 36 shows, will be changing gradually.

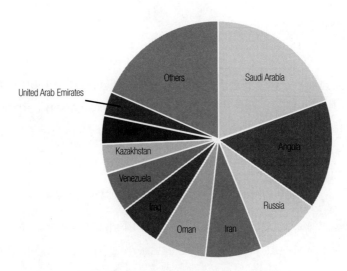

Figure 36   China's oil imports by region

China may also pay attention to developing its energy relationships with developed countries even though they are also energy consumers like China, to jointly maintain the stability of global energy markets. Developed countries as energy consuming countries have comparatively advanced technology for energy exploration and mining, energy conservation and cost reduction, new energy development and environmental protection as well as modern business management experience.

6

Energy Cooperation under the Belt and Road Initiative

6.1 Major Changes in the Global Oil Market and its Implications for China

Oil prices have been dropping sharply since the end of 2014, for which reason 2015 can be considered a year out of the ordinary, even more so for China. This extrordinariness is mainly reflected in the third greatest transformation in energy history from fossil resources i.e. conventional oil and gas, coal to new and renewable resources. Added to this was the drop in oil prices from November 2014 to reach a new low point in 2015.

This transformation from fossil energy to non-fossil energy, begun by the Northern American shale gas revolution, compared with the former two transformations (from timber to coal and from coal to oil), will take a longer time. However, similarly to the former two energy transformations, it will fundamentally reshape the global energy structure. Almost all countries have to make policy choices in this process, and launch an energy revolution/transition strategy following the new energy orientation.

Coal is still China's main source of energy. The initiation of the energy revolution will be based on the current global energy situation and the need for adjustment.

6.1.1 Views of Notables in China on Low Oil Prices [①]

① The notables or "big shots" of energy got together in the Center for International Energy and Environment Strategy Studies of Renmin University of China which is one of the ten research consultancy bases of the National Energy Administration (NEA), China on January 11, 2015, moderated by the director of the Center Professor Qinhua Xu, to analyze the reasons for this particular oil price drop, its impact on the global energy situation, and China's strategic countermeasures. The symposium was a fierce collision between ideas onenergy and international politics, international relations, domestic energy and international energy and how China's energy can be internationalized.

Zhang Kang, an associate director of the Sinopec Advisory Committee: From the end of the last century to the beginning of this century, the global situation of oil-gas supply and demand has undergone a fundamental change. The situation of supply and demand has changed from there being a balance to significant excess supply; under the background of continuous unrest and warfare in the world oil depot, there has been surplus production, and the strategic reserves of surplus refining capacity have increased substantially. From the beginning of this century, unconventional oil-gas resources, in particular, shale oil and gas, have grown rapidly. This has impacted the price of conventional oil and resulted in a price slump. We are experiencing a change in energy structure, from fossil energy to non-fossil energy. In my opinion, they are of equal importance in the twenty-first century, but not non-fossil energy is replacing fossil energy. Throughout history, the world has gone through alternating periods of war and peace, and this has been reflected in the fluctuation of oil prices. In general, a world oil background where the supply and demand is more relaxed and prices fluctuate only moderately is favorable for China's development. I think that such a price correction is a more favorable environment for China's development, and we should take advantage of this to carry out China's energy revolution.

Wang Haiyun, a general, and a senior adviser in the China Institute for International Strategic Studies: It is wrong to deem oil price fluctuation as a normal performance only affiliated with market-based resource allocation.

The reasons for a drop in oil prices include international capital speculation and magnification by geopolitics. It is said that geopolitical factors are no longer relevant, I don't agree; it's also said that geopolitical factors are typical of a Cold War mentality, I don't think this either. We should not disregard geopolitical factors. If we neglect these and believe they are irrelevant, we will suffer a great deal. I think it is especially necessary to remind our domestic research community of this. As for the U.S. suppressing Russia, won't this harm U.S. transnational oil companies also? It is a question of prioritizing short term or long term goals. In spite of this, the low oil price era is still some time off. For the next thirty years, oil will still be a strategically important energy; the expansion of oil consumption is a long-term process. It will even take longer to transition from the coal era to the oil era and then to the clean energy or new energy era. Furthermore, from a military point of view, at present oil is very far away from being substituted on a large scale. Therefore, the market will make corrections and it will rebound soon.

Li Junfeng, the director of the National Center for Strategic Research and International Cooperation on Climate Change: We cannot ignore the political factors for low oil prices, but this is not a conspiracy theory. The depreciation of the rouble in Russia should not be solely attributed to the economic sanctions imposed by the U.S.; the excessive dependence of Russia's economy on oil, and its poor anti-strike capability are the primary causes. Through promotion of hybrid cars, countries such as the U.S. and Japan can reduce 40% of oil consumption. Consequently, the oil consumption of countries such as China and India that lag behind in the development of energy-saving technology will become the greatest factor in raising oil prices. Domestic oil companies cannot make predictions about the global market according to their own production capacity. Nowadays, global development issues have to be taken into consideration when estimating long-term demand. During the course of globalization, there are two major factors restricting oil development. The first factor is emission reduction, which used to be a bogus statement, but now it has become substantial. The second factor is the geopolitical situation. We should not underestimate the geopolitical contest among leading powers, oil is a commodity, and its nature should not be ignored.

Han Xiaoping, the Chief Information Officer of cnenergy.org: The fundamental problem with oil prices is the problem of the old and new revolutions. The old revolution is that of shale oil and gas, and the new is the revolution of energy-saving technology. The reason why OPEC countries such as Saudi Arabia maintain oil production is that they have recovered the cost long before, even though the price at present is lower than sixty, they will keep on producing, otherwise, their market shares will be lost. The United States is the initiator of the shale oil and gas revolution, so it will not quit. Nor will Russia. This country may cause some uncertainty at some point as history is repeated over and over again. The financial crisis in 1929 was greatly similar to the crisis in 2008; a cause of both was the underlying problem of structural transformation. The crisis in 1929 was caused by the transformation from coal to oil, which finally resulted in the Great Depression. This is similar to the more recent situation. The discovery of the East Texas oilfield led to a steep fall in global oil prices, and this further promoted the structural transition. Subsequently, the coal-based energy structure was further forced out by the needs of the internal-combustion engine.

Yang Yuanhua, a senior reporter in the Xinhua News Agency: Development, adjustment, instability, distortion and chaos are the keywords in the development of the oil-gas market. Opinions in China tend to follow western mainstream media, which is very dangerous. Finance should not be ignored in the analysis of the oil market, it is the core of modern economic development, and it is finance that determines future global development. Geopolitical factors are complicated, we should analyze low oil prices and what is conspiracy, and not lump them together as a conspiracy theory. Now we analyze according to the laws of supply and demand, the competition rules, and the law of value. These three apply at different times, sometimes one or another is dominant. Therefore, when we analyze the present problem, we should not attach too much emphasis to supply and demand, but take more factors into consideration.

Chen Weidong, the chief economist of CNOOC Energy Economics Institute: The shale oil-gas revolution in the U.S. has changed the current energy structure. During the current price drop, OPEC persisted in not cutting prices or production, and attempted to maintain the market; what problems does this reveal? It indicates that they have realized the energy transformation is underway, and low oil prices or the low rise of oil prices might be the most effective and the most lasting protection for oil producing countries. High oil prices will propel development of renewable energy, and we have also seen some signs of alternative oil technology. On the one hand, the exchange rate of the U.S. dollar to gold is decisive for oil prices. According to the data, one barrel of oil equals 1.5g gold, which has not changed much. We have experienced three ups and downs in oil prices, respectively in 1986, 1998 and 2008, in which we have not seen any sign that oil can be replaced. But during the recent drop in oil prices, we have seen the sign of oil substitutes, or some products that will greatly reduce oil consumption, which have come about through technical advancements. A technical advancement is not something supplied to the market after mining and processing of natural resources, it is an explosion of knowledge. On the other hand, without the phenomenon of China, there would have been no reentry of coal into the market, and no slowdown of natural gas. China has made a substantial impact on global energy trends and the global energy structure. We don't have to discuss the oil price, or argue about geopolitics, or how China's energy strategy should progress. I think we should have a group of people paying attention to the issues of energy transformation and civilization evolution, and pondering what China should do at this point.

Shi Ze, the director of the Energy Security and Diplomatic Center, China Institute of International Studies: We should study the impact of the Belt and

Road Policy on energy. The policy is the starting point for promoting energy cooperation. The framework covers aspects such as energy security, the soft environment of energy, and the construction of an energy cooperation system.

Zeng Xingqiu, the former chief geologist of Sinochem Group: China's energy revolution takes the following four factors into consideration: first, low-carbon development has become a global aim, and the transfer from low density to high density is also irreversible. Second, fossil energy such as oil, gas and coal still occupy a high proportion of primary energy sources, and we will suffer if we ignore this issue. Third, technical development is the key to realizing development in developing countries. New technology will bring a new stage, new technology will bring new development, and new technology will determine a country's competitiveness. China needs to make long-term plans on this issue. Fourth, reform is a global trend. Governmental reform and enterprise development should take advantage of the window of low oil prices, and make a firm decision to explore potential and implement reform and explore the potential. Reform means that we have to thoroughly remould ourselves, restructure our enterprise architecture, and start over again from the ideological and institutional aspects, in particular, the ideological aspect. Nothing can be changed if ideas do not change. What ideas are the most important? There are two ideas. The first is to respect and believe in the market. The second is to clearly recognize the legal system, laws and disciplines.

6.1.2   The Implications for China's Foreign Energy Policy

The great change in the global oil market may reshape China foreign energy policy in a number of ways.

6.1.2.1   Reshaping ideas regarding foreign energy policy

As we have seen, the current drop in oil prices is different from the previous slumps in 1986 and 2008. This drop is occurring during a period of energy transformation, and a scramble for market share for conventional and unconventional oil-gas (shale/tight oil-gas) resources on the basis of the supply and demand fundamentals. The total yield of conventional oil-gas and unconventional oil-gas is higher than the consumption volume, and the economy is still weak, especially as the weak prospect of developing economies (including China) is affecting the world economy, so the downward pressure is further magnified. It should be said that the success of the unconventional oil-gas revolution in North America is the major initiator of this current drop in oil prices, and this is lifting the curtain on a new energy era.

The low oil prices are actually a new normal, that is prices gradually moving closer to a rational oil price after the oil price foam is extruded. To adapt to the new normal low oil price is to respect the economic law of the international energy market. For China, to establish a new system for international energy cooperation under the new normal of low oil price, it is necessary to promote international energy cooperation more in line with the spirit of international energy's economic market law.

6.1.2.2 Pushing China to get a clear understanding of its status and role in the global energy order

The low price of oil foreshows the coming of a so-called "great energy era", which has increased China's weight in the international energy market. The great energy era is a period when coal and conventional oil-gas resources will not outshine others any longer, and unconventional oil-gas and new energy such as tight oil-gas, shale oil-gas and coal-bed gas will develop prosperously. The technologies of nuclear energy and various types of renewable energy such as solar energy, wind energy and tidal energy will become increasingly mature; from the point of view of energy development regions, less focus will be put on exploration and development of continental oil-gas, and efforts in the exploration and development of offshore oil and gas will be increased; from the point of view of the relationship between energy and the natural environment, energy development will be more restricted by factors such as climate change.

In the great energy era, energy power will be reconstructed, oil power will no longer be the core of energy power, and concepts such as energy supply power, energy demand power, energy technology power, energy finance power and corresponding low carbon power will be introduced. Various regions/economies in the world will be dominant within a certain domain in the global structure of energy power owing to their respective advantages in energy power. Energy supply power means that an energy source country possesses absolute supply power of energy resources in the world energy market, e.g., Saudi Arabia. Countries with energy resources and energy producing countries, taking advantage of their energy supply power, stay at the tip of the pyramid in the global structure of energy power. Energy demand power refers to a country that possesses strong market power regarding the demand for energy resources owing to its huge energy consumption volume, e.g., China. Energy technology power refers to a country in this third industrial revolution that possesses advanced technologies and is influential to the world's future development, e.g., Germany. Energy finance power refers to a power which, due to its having a developed financial system and influence on the global finance markets exerts a greater power in affecting energy prices than would be expected, e.g., the United States. Low carbon power refers to a country which has relative power in the low-carbon economic order because of the calculation method of carbon content in energy products and its discourse power in carbon politics, e.g., E.U. countries.

The core of global energy demands has gradually moved from developed countries to developing countries, in particular emerging nations and the regions in the Asia Pacific and the Middle East. China has become the largest energy consumer and crude oil importer in the world; its tremendous consumptive power and huge market make it influential to energy prices, and it is also reshaping its foreign energy relationships.

6.1.2.3 Improving China's position in foreign energy policy

China's increase or decrease in oil consumption and the speed of growth of China's economy have a certain impact on the fluctuation of the global oil market especially oil prices. The current drop in oil prices also suggests two points. First, the modern petroleum industry has been functioning for more than 100 years, and the mechanism has become sophisticated; any government or country trying to manipulate international oil markets can only take advantage of some instruments such as financial capital on certain specific occasions (e.g., geopolitical conflicts), and in the world's political and economic order, the manipulation of oil price will inevitably end up as a double-edged sword, with an incomplete victory. Secondly, China, due to its tremendous volume of consumption, has obtained more power in the energy market. Historically, the country with the largest volume of energy consumption became a hegemonic power, for instance, the Netherlands and Spain in the timber era, the United Kingdom in the coal era, and the U.S. in the petroleum era. It is certainly worth considering how China can transform its market power into state power in the sense of international politics through international energy cooperation in order to increase China's discourse power with respect to global resources.

Therefore, China may be improving its position in foreign energy policy. On the premise of ensuring domestic development, China will strengthen international investment and make effective use of international resources in various aspects involving energy production and consumption. In the meantime, how to transform market power into state power in the sense of international politics may be the biggest goal and task China is facing at present.

6.1.2.4 Reallocating the strategic focus of the foreign energy policy

Since 1993 when China became a net importer of oil products, the focus of China's foreign energy policy has been to become more of a global player. Through arrangements with the major energy producing countries throughout the world, China has gradually set up five blocks for upstream exploration and development, and has constructed an international network of oil-gas pipelines on land. Due to the major changes occurring in the global energy situation, the strategic focus of China's foreign energy policy might be re-allocated.

First, a new focus may be to lay stress on "bringing in" at the same time as persisting in global involvement, importing new technologies, capital and talents etc.; second, it may be necessary to adjust the strategic focus of international energy cooperation from procurement of raw materials such as oil, natural gas and coal as before, to speeding up the transfer of technologies concerning new energy, clean energy and low-carbon energy, fostering of management experience, construction of an energy financial market and growing the pool of talent by means of international cooperation.

In summary, the coming of the low oil price era, as far as China is concerned, is a strategic opportunity to launch an energy production and consumption revolution. China will try it best to adapt to the changes in the global energy situation, make adjustments to its foreign energy policy and strengthen international cooperation in various aspects to internationalize its energy more effectively. The year 2015 was a critical year for the adjustment of China's energy policy regarding the creation of a greener GDP, it was also the first year after President Xi advocated an energy revolution, and the year China promised the world that they would reach their emission targets.

6.2 China-Russia Oil and Natural Gas Cooperation: the Geopolitical Impact

On May 21, 2015, after about ten years of negotiation, China signed a thirty-year natural gas supply contract with Russia. According to the contract, starting from the year 2018, Russia will export gas to China through the Sino-Russia gas pipeline. The volume of gas exported will increase annually up to the level of 38 billion of cubic meters with a total value of 400 billion dollars (2500 billion yuan). Before the gas agreement, China agreed in April 2009 to lend 10 billion dollars to the Russian oil pipeline monopoly Transneft and another 15 billion to state-run oil major Rosneft in exchange for 300 million tons of Russian oil to be transported over twenty years. About 15 million tons of crude oil will be sent to China every year upon the completion of the pipeline, which occurred in September of 2010. We will examine the oil and gas cooperation between China and Russia: why did the unsuccessful cooperation suddenly become successful, who is the winner of the cooperation, how can the cooperation last and what is its geopolitical impact.

6.2.1 The Economic Evaluation (Bilateral Cooperation)

In May 2015, the oil imported from Russia to China increased by 20%, reaching a height of 3.92 million tons, which means 927,000 barrels per day. At the same time, the oil imported from Saudi Arabia decreased by 42% to 392,000 barrels. For the first time, Russia became China's largest importer, replacing Saudi Arabia. Before the year 2009, the total amount of oil imported to China was only around 25 million tons and was transported mainly by railway, the sudden increase in import volume shows that the energy cooperation between China and Russia has been growing rapidly.

The change in the bilateral cooperation is not only shown in the trading amount, but also in the trading pattern, such as the new loan arrangement.

In addition, the method of transportation has been pluralized to include pipelines, rail, trucks and shipping. Chinese energy enterprises are invited to invest in the upstream of the Russian energy industry. There must be some key factors driving China and Russia, as they, in particular Russia were not so keen for closer cooperation before. Let us do some economic evaluation firstly to see what sort of economic benefits Russia and China may gain through the energy cooperation.

According to BP data, by the end of 2013, the proven oil reserve of Russia was 12.7 billion tons, occupying 5.5% of the world's reserve. Oil production increased by 1.3% year on year to 531 million tons. The proven reserve of gas is 3130 billion cubic meters, occupying 16.8% of the world, while the gas production increased by 2.4% to 0.605 billion cubic meters. It is clear that Russia is a country affluent in energy resources and one of the top oil and gas producers and exporters.

For Russia, energy security means enough of a foreign market of consumers for it to sell oil and gas for capital, as we know that almost 30% of Russia's budget is from its sale of oil and gas. There are two core points in Russia's current energy security: one is to own an international oil and gas market; another is to move its export emphasis to Asia, which is the largest energy consuming area with major oil and gas consumers such as China, India, Japan and South Korea. In recent years, Russia has been suffering from the decreased need in the European market. For example, the ratio of Russian gas in the E.U.'s gas consumption fell down to 31.9% in 2012 from 45% in 2003, which is really a big jump. Under the circumstances, Russian oil and gas began to pay more attention to exporting eastwards.

Therefore, in 2014, Russia issued its new energy strategy 2035, outlining Russia's new strategic target for 2035, which is to upgrade the competitiveness of Russia's energy companies, to increase its export sources and energy products, to raise its product quality, and to maintain Russia's market share in the world energy market. One point to be highlighted is that the new strategy emphasized that the Asia Pacific market will be the most promising one for Russia. Russia will enlarge its energy export share to the Asia Pacific region by at least 28%, while the oil and oil products will be 23% and crude oil and gas will be 32% and 31% respectively. For the first time, Russia realized and admitted publicly that China is the most important country for Russia to promote an energy relationship with.

Trading oil and gas with Russia is also of priority to Chinese energy diplomacy and foreign energy policies. China's strong economic growth in recent years has led to a very significant increase in its oil consumption. This rise in consumption and in oil imports is the result of several factors, including rapid GDP growth, the energy-intensive industrial sector, a sharp increase in the number of vehicles, and the need to reduce the relative weight in energy consumption of inefficient and extremely polluting coal. China is already actively seeking oil beyond its borders. In particular, China intends to diversify its supply sources, importing more oil from Russia, Central Asia, North Africa and Latin America, and trying to secure transport lanes for its crude imports.

In 2014, China's oil foreign dependence rate reached 60.6%, exceeding the international warning line of 50%. The gas foreign dependence rate reached 40%. The imbalance in the demand and supply of oil and gas poses a challenge for Chinese energy security. Under pressure to reduce the GHG emission, the Twelfth Five-Year Plan raised the importance of developing clean energy which will propel the consumption of natural gas. The IEA expect that the annual increased need for natural gas would be around 7.8%. Unlike the situation with Russia's energy security, China's focus is on the security of energy supply, i.e. the 4As (the availability of the resources, the accessibility, the affordability and the acceptability) and the security of the transportation of energy, e.g. the land oil and gas pipelines and the overseas shipment.

The solutions to the gap between the national supply and demand are in the following ways: first conserve energy, and raise efficiency; second, focus on self-dependence, enlarging the exploration of national resources; third is with technological research and development, promoting the new and renewable energy; fourth is through the full use of international oil and gas resources.

Through the above analysis, we find that the large exporter Russia meets the energy needs of the large importer China, which is the key driving force to the success of oil and gas cooperation between the two countries. However, despite having imported enough gas for its consumption for the next ten years (pipelined gas from Central Asia, mainly Turkmenistan, through the Central Asia-China gas pipeline, the LNG from Middle East region, mainly Qatar, and from Indonesia and Australia), China still signed the contract for a comparatively high price under the low oil price situation. Therefore, there must be other factors affecting the cooperation.

6.2.2 The Trigger for Cooperation (Economic and Political)

Through the description of both Russia and China's energy development, we still cannot fully understand why Russia has become so active in the energy cooperation with China and also put this cooperation under the framework of the Belt and Road Initiative. Though we know that because the E.U. nations have reached their oil and gas consumption peak and because of the NRE (new and renewable energy) and other alternative resources with greater energy efficiency, there will be a gradual decrease in their oil and gas needs, nevertheless, the E.U. is still the largest market for Russia's oil and gas. So, the decreased need is not the only trigger for the energy cooperation between Russia and China.

It is interesting that the major progress in the Sino-Russian energy cooperation after ten years of unsuccessful negotiations occurred during the financial crisis. And there was further progress when international oil prices started dropping. Since the Ukraine crisis, the Putin government seemed to be more intent to push the two countries' full-scale cooperation and this culminated in Russia joining China's Belt and Road Initiative. Even though the two governments cooperated a long time ago, undoubtedly it was the crises—the financial crisis, oil price crisis and the Ukraine crisis—which pushed the Putin government.

As the Table 27 shows, there are three stages in the long-tern vision for Sino-Russian cooperation. The first stage, from 1994 to 2003, was when two dignitaries tried to open the bilateral energy collaboration and set up a coordinating committee. The original projects included nuclear energy and the oil pipeline. The second stage from 2003 to 2009 was the launching time. The governments opened the discussion of natural gas trading. The countries established the vice premier level energy negotiation mechanism. Besides, an absolute new cooperation pattern, "loan for oil" was invented by the two countries' state-owned companies: China National Development Bank, Russian oil companies and their oil transportation company. China provided $25 billion in loans to Russia who will feed back oil supply to repay the loan. The third stage is from 2009 to present, when the cooperation enters implementation: the Sino-Russian crude oil pipeline was completed. In May 2015, during the visit of the Chinese president Xi Jinping to Moscow, the two governments agreed on the Sino-Russian gas cooperation project memorandum, ending the ten years of natural gas supply negotiations between the two countries. The fourth stage is the era of full-scale and comprehensive energy cooperation between China and Russia. Russia's target energy market is moving towards to the Eastern Asian region, and China started its Belt and Road Initiative in 2013, so the cooperation is expanding from oil and gas to nuclear, from middle-stream and down-stream to upstream, from energy field itself to the oil service and equipment, from conventional energy to unconventional and new and renewable energy, from resources to technology. It should also be clarified that from 2015, the cooperation was not limited to energy but advanced to a more strategic level, in which energy begins to play the role of a tool, though energy cooperation is still the key in the bilateral trade.

Table 27　Sino–Russia oil and gas cooperation timeline

Date	Key figure or event	Vital document	Achievement or significance
I The first stage (1994—2003) exploration			
1996.4	Boris Yeltsin (Russian President)	Agreement on joint development and cooperation in the field of energy	Opens the China—Russia energy cooperation process
1996.12	Li Peng (Chinese Premier)	Agreement on joint development and cooperation in the field of energy	Establishes a China-Russia energy cooperation committee
1999.10	Tianwan Nuclear Power Plant started		
2001.9	The premiers of China and Russia	Feasibility study of Sino-Russian oil pipeline	Opens Anda oil pipeline project
II The second stage (2003—2009) launch of cooperation			
2003.5	China and Russia's natural gas companies	General agreement on the basic principles and common understanding of the long-term purchase and sale contract of crude oil pipeline between China and Russia	Opens cooperation in the field of natural gas
2006.3		Memorandum of understanding on supply of natural gas from Russia to China	Substantial progress in the field of natural gas
2008	Hu Jintao and Medvedev		The establishment of vice premier level energy negotiations
2008	Wang Qishan and Igor Ivanovich Sechin	China National Petroleum Corporation and the Russian character road transport company of Skovorodino—China and Russia crude oil pipeline construction and operation of the agreement in principle	Sino-Russian energy negotiations

Continued

Date	Key figure or event	Vital document	Achievement or significance
2008	China National Development Bank, Russian oil companies and oil transportation company	Loans for oil	China agrees to provide $25 billion in loans to Russia who will feed back oil supply to repay the loan
2009.4	Sino-Russian energy negotiation (fourth meeting)	Sino-Russian oil cooperation agreement between the governments	Reached a package of cooperation agreements
2009.10	Sino-Russian energy negotiation (fifth meeting)	Memorandum of understanding on cooperation in the field of natural gas	Entering the long-term strategic cooperation stage
III The third stage (2009—now) implementation			
2011.1	Medvedev's visit to China		Sino-Russian crude oil pipeline begins operation
2012.6	Sino-Russian energy negotiation (eighth meeting)	Sino-Russian energy negotiations on behalf of the eighth meeting minutes	
2012.9	Sino-Russian energy negotiation (ninth meeting)	Four documents between China and Russia	
2013.3	President Xi Jinping visited to Russia	Implementation of the Sino-Russian treaty of good friendship and cooperation between China and Russia (2013 to 2016)	Multi-domain cooperation
2014.5	Xi Jinping and Putin	Joint statement on the new stage of the comprehensive strategic partnership between the people's Republic of China and the Russian Federation	Further deepens cooperation in the oil field
2014.5		Sino-Russian gas cooperation project memorandum	The end of the ten years of natural gas supply negotiations between the two countries
2014.5	China and Russia's natural gas company	China-Russia eastern gas purchase and sales contracts	Russia will begin to supply in the East gas pipeline through Russia to China in 2018
IV Belt and Road Stage			
2015.9		Russia's second-biggest gas producer, Novatek, signed a framework agreement for China's Silk Road Fund to obtain a 9.9% stake in its Yamal liquefied natural gas project, the company said in a statement.	

Source: CNPC, China Daily

339

The timeline exemplifies one thing: whenever it encounters difficulty not only economic but also political, Russia moves closer to China, such as during the financial crisis (2008—2009) and the Ukraine crisis (2014—2015). IHS senior Vice President Carlos Pascual, former U.S. ambassador to Ukraine and Mexico and founder of the State Department's Bureau of Energy Resources, when he discussed the global political and economy implications of the decline in oil price on August 13, 2015 at the IHS blog, referring to Russia, he wrote:

> The collapsed oil price has been combined with international sanctions that preclude the oil exporters from access to capital markets and a way to finance itself out of its financial crisis. For Russia, the critical issue has been its extreme dependence on oil for export revenue. Oil constitutes 70% of export revenues, and together oil and gas make up 52% of the budget (the data could be re-calculated for confirmation). The combination of sanctions after Ukraine Crisis that has deprived Russia of access to new technology and to capital markets, as well as the collapse in oil prices, has put Russia in a dire financial position. The exchange rate lost 50% of its value. People have lost 50% of their real income. Businesses have lost 50% of their real income. Businesses have found it extremely difficult to operate because they cannot afford to bring equipment and foreign inputs into the country-and then translate those into local currency rubles costs and still have competitive products.

On the other hand, moving closer to Russia is a strategic option for China, one China cannot avoid. First, because Russia is a very big country bordering her; second, because China has the same economic transition as Russia experienced before; and third because, China and Russia are located in the same position in the international political and economic system, suffering fierce competition from the western bloc countries, and as we know from their history, both countries belonged to the socialist eastern bloc.

In short, apparently the oil and gas cooperation between China and Russia is a successful marriage of the resources and the markets. To China, the sort of oil and gas cooperation is more of strategic consideration, however, to Russia, it is both economic and strategic.

6.2.3   The Geopolitical Impact

Inside Asia there has gradually formed a complete, circular demand and supply (DS) system. The system is composed of three sorts of countries, the exporters, the importers and transit countries, which can help reduce the Asian gas premium and high oil prices. The exporters mainly include Russia and Central Asian countries (Kazakhstan, Turkmenistan and Uzbekistan) and Australia, the importers include China, Japan, Korea, India and Singapore, and the transit countries include Myanmar and Central Asian countries. As mentioned earlier, on May 21, 2015, after about ten years of negotiation, China signed a thirty-year gas contract with Russia. According to the contract, starting from the year 2018, Russia will export gas to China through the Sino-Russia gas pipeline.

A robust and effective demand and supply network has been established with Russia's oil and gas through the Sino-Russia oil and gas pipelines, Central Asia's oil and gas through the Sino-Kazakhstan oil pipeline and Sino-Central Asia gas pipeline, Myanmar's gas and the Middle East oil transported through the Sino-Myanmar oil and gas pipelines and the Australian liquidized gas through shipping. The oil and gas pipelines effectively connect the exporters, importers and transit countries in the Asia-Pacific region. For the other two big consumers in East Asia, Japan and Korea, a comparatively affluent energy supply in the region is also good news to them, as they can also enjoy the Russian oil and gas through the Sino-Russia oil and gas pipelines, with an expected cheaper gas price. Recently, a trilateral agreement took effect to facilitate investment among China, Japan and Korea, strengthening the cooperation among the three countries, despite the territorial and political conflicts between China and Japan.

Russia will be continuously competing with the U.S. in all of its major markets just as it did in the nineteenth century. Whilst the E.U. market may not be very attractive for U.S. LNG exports for various reasons, Asia, with its major energy consumers such as Japan, Korea, China and India is certainly a target market. The gas agreement successfully entered between China and Russia in May 2015 gave a good answer to the question of whether Russia can secure Asian markets before the U.S. LNG infrastructure has been built.

The gas agreement may also show that a robust and effective internal energy supply and demand circle has already been established in the Asia region. Now there is the possibility for a future Asian LNG hub. Establishing an LNG pricing mechanism responsive to Asian gas and LNG demands and LNG prices at a more competitive level compared to JCC are both desirable and enduring goals from the policy perspective of Japan, Korea and China. The challenges in creating an LNG hub price for Asia will have to be faced at some point in the medium term. However, it is clear that with reference to the experiences in North America and Europe such a price formation transition will not be a smooth one.

The gas agreement also means a huge change in world geopolitics. The Eurasia region demonstrates its geopolitical power through the energy requests from major energy consumers including China, Japan, Korea and India. The regional integration supply and demand helps Eurasia regain its importance as described by Sir Halford Mackinder's heartland theory of the "pivot area". In this concept, the "World Island" or "Core" comprises Eurasia and Africa, which contains sufficient natural resources for a developed economy.

6.2.4 Conclusion

Russia benefits greatly from oil and gas cooperation with China. While oil and gas prices have been dropping, Russia has secured China's huge market and energy investments. Therefore it transpires that China acts cushion for Russia against pressure from Western countries.

6.3 Expected Benefits and Potential Risks of Energy Cooperation under the Belt and Road Initiative

When Chinese President Xi Jinping visited Central Asia and Southeast Asia in September and October of 2013, he raised the idea of jointly building the Silk Road Economic Belt and the twenty-first-Century Maritime Silk Road, usually referred to as the Belt and Road Initiative. At the China-ASEAN Expo in 2013, Chinese Premier Li Keqiang emphasized the need to build the Maritime Silk Road oriented toward ASEAN, and to create strategic propellers for hinterland development. According to the initiative, accelerating the building of the Belt and Road can help promote the economic prosperity of the countries along the Belt and Road and regional economic cooperation. This section tries to use the energy cooperation as a case study, decoding the expected benefits and potential risks through economic evaluation.

6.3.1 The Background to Energy Cooperation in the Belt and Road Region

Energy is one of the five essential resources for the survival of human beings, and the strategic material for a nation's economic development. With globalization, energy security has been transiting from seeking independence after the oil shock in the 1970s, to the current trend of accommodating interdependence. It has transitioned more from emphasizing supply security

① Just as David J.C. Mackay wrote in his book, Sustainable Energy without the Hot Air (2009), two thirds of GHG are from energy consumption.

to achieving a balance of economic growth, energy sustainability and environment acceptability. Nevertheless, because of the close relationship between the economy and the environment, ① energy security has become a common security challenge to the globe and the focus of all economic activities.

By now, the initiative has been developed into a Chinese foreign strategy and gained a response from sixty-four nations. Therefore, there are now sixty-five countries under the cooperative Belt and Road framework, and these are categorized into six areas plus China: The Southeast (eleven countries), CIS (six countries), South Asia (eight countries), West Asia and North Africa (sixteen countries), Central and Eastern Europe (sixteen countries) and Central Asia (five countries). In consideration of the importance of their reserves and their geo-economic implications for China, the initiative lists two countries separately, Mongolia and Russia.

6.3.1.1   The role of different regions under the Belt and Road scheme

Among the sixty-five countries, we find there are three types of energy nations. The first group is composed of the energy exporters, mainly in the Southeast, West Asia and North Africa and Central Asia regions, such as Russia, Mongolia, Kazakhstan, Saudi Arabia, Iran, Indonesia etc.; the second group is composed of the energy importers, mainly in Central and Eastern Europe and South Asia regions, such as China, India, Poland, Czech Republic, etc. The third group is composed of the countries who are along the pipeline routes, which are mainly CIS countries such as Ukraine and Azerbaijan.

② BP (2015). *Statistical Review of World Energy June 2015.* Available at http://www.bp.com/en/global/corporate/energy-economics/statistical- review-of-world-energy.html.

From the BP data, we have the following tables to describe the regional role of each Belt and Road energy sector by fuel type ②.

The four tables (28-31), show the roles of different regions under the Belt and Road scheme. For instance, in Table 31, the countries of South Asia are the largest coal importers while Southeast Asia's countries are the largest coal exporters. It should be noted that all three energy types show a surplus when China is not taken into consideration. We discuss the situation including China in Table 32.

Table 28　Regional classification of Belt and Road countries

Region	Country
Central and Eastern Europe	Albania; Bosnia-Herzegovina; Bulgaria; Croatia; Czech Republic; Estonia; Hungary; Latvia; Lithuania; Macedonia; Montenegro; Poland; Romania; Serbia; Slovakia; Slovenija
Central Asia	Kazakhstan; Kyrgyzstan; Tajikistan; Turkmenistan; Uzbekistan
China	China
Commonwealth of Independent States	Armenia; Azerbaijan; Belarus; Georgia; Moldova; Ukraine
Mongolia	Mongolia
Russian Federation	Russian Federation
South Asia	Afghanistan; Bangladesh; Bhutan; India; Maldives; Nepal; Pakistan; Sri Lanka
Southeast Asia	Brunei; Cambodia; East Timor; Indonesia; Laos; Malaysia; Myanmar; Philippine; Singapore; Thailand; Vietnam
West Asia and North Africa	Bahrain; Egypt; Iran; Iraq; Israel; Jordan; Kuwait; Lebanon; Oman; Palestine; Qatar; Saudi Arabia; Syria; Turkey; United Arab Emirates; Yemen

Table 29　Oil in Belt and Road regions in 2014

Region	Role	Oil (Thousand barrels daily)		
		Production	Consumption	Surplus
Central Asia	Exporter	2007	480	1528
Russian Federation	Exporter	10838	3196	7642
West Asia and North Africa	Exporter	28342	7842	20500
CIS	Transit	848	545	304
Central and Eastern Europe	Importer	85	1240	-1156
South Asia	Importer	895	4419	-3524
Southeast Asia	Importer	2463	5722	-3259
Total (not including China)		43015	17721	25293

Table 30   Natural gas in Belt and Road regions in 2014

Region	Role	Natural Gas (Billion cubic metres)		
		Production	Consumption	Surplus
Central Asia	Exporter	146	82	64
Russian Federation	Exporter	579	409	170
Southeast Asia	Exporter	221	157	64
West Asia and North Africa	Exporter	593	469	124
CIS	Transit	36	66	-30
Central and Eastern Europe	Importer	16	53	-37
South Asia	Importer	97	116	-19
Total (not including China)		1687	1352	335

Table 31   Coal in Belt and Road regions in 2014

Region	Role	Coal (Million tonnes oil equivalent)		
		Production	Consumption	Surplus
Central Asia	Exporter	57	37	20
Russian Federation	Exporter	171	85	86
Southeast Asia	Exporter	310	126	184
CIS	Transit	32	34	-3
West Asia & North Africa	Importer	18	45	-28
Central and Eastern Europe	Importer	84	87	-3
South Asia	Importer	245	366	-121
Total (not including China)		915	780	135

We can see that although China, in 2014, was a pure importer under the Belt and Road energy sector, all three types of fuel had a surplus in Belt and Road countries. In particular, there was still a surplus of oil and natural gas, which was one of the key motivations for China to develop the Belt and Road scheme. Such surplus would enhance China's energy security for its economic development.

6.3.1.2 Different energy security strategies

Each type of energy nation has its own specific understanding of energy security. Take the first group to start with. To the energy exporters, the nations who rely on the revenue procured from the selling of energy resources and products such as Russia, Saudi Arabia, Kuwait, Indonesia, Kazakhstan, Turkmenistan etc., energy security means enough market and favorable energy prices to cover their budget; to the energy importers such as China, India, the Czech Republic, Poland, Tajikistan etc., energy security means enough economical and environmental energy to sustain the national economy. To the countries which energy transits through, such as Ukraine, Georgia etc., energy security means they can fully enjoy returns from the energy transported through them. Some countries like China, are an energy exporter, importer and also a transit nation. China has now become the largest oil importer, largest energy producer (68% coal) and second greatest consumer of energy. China also has the highest amount of carbon emissions, and conversely the greatest investment in, installation and consumption of renewable energy.

Table 32 China' s situation in the Belt and Road energy sector in 2014

Energy sector		Production	Consumption	Surplus
Oil ('000 barrels daily)	Total (from Table 29)	43015	17721	25293
	China	4246	11056	-6811
Natural gas (Billion m³)	Total (Table 30)	1687	1352	335
	China	135	186	-51
Coal (Mtoe)	Total (Table 31)	915	780	135
	China	1845	1962	-118

That is the reason why it is China who takes the lead in the Belt and Road Initiative, China feels the economic security challenges suffered by most of the Belt and Road countries, especially the energy security challenge. This section takes energy cooperation as a case study, decoding the expected benefits and potential risks through the economic evaluation.

6.3.2 The Prospective Landscape of Energy Security under the Belt and Road

6.3.2.1 Great changes in world energy development

In the past few decades, two regions have been significantly reshaping the global energy landscape. The first one is the North America region, the impact of which on the global energy landscape is highlighted by its success in the shale gas revolution, which mainly occurred in the United States. The other is the Asia region, which has been growing dramatically and is now the fastest growing energy consuming center of the world. It is commonly anticipated that the region, comprising mainly China, Japan and Korea together with India, will continue to play a key role in the energy consumption market in the coming years. Among the four countries, China and India are two newly emerging players, unlike Japan and Korea who have long been recognized as big energy consumers. The recent development in the two regions has given a clear message to the world that the global energy market has experienced a drastic reshaping and such reshaping will continue.

On the one hand, the influence of unconventional oil and gas resources in the global scheme has been increasing day by day; there is a very clear trend that the center of export of oil and gas is moving from the Persian Gulf to the Gulf of Mexico; while at the same time, energy exploration in the African continent has also attracted lots of interest around the world. On the other hand, the continuous growth of energy demands in China and India have caused the Asia region to become the dominant energy consumers, which means the main oil and gas import market has also been gradually shifting from the Americas and Europe to the Asia region. These changes have had a direct impact on the global energy order.

With the development of energy technologies, the world has entered into a real energy era. ① Energy geopolitics will never be the same as oil geopolitics, though currently oil and gas are still the priority. With the major energy consumers' unceasing efforts in developing unconventional and renewable energy, the current global energy consumption structure may undergo a huge adjustment. The conventional energy structure of energy consumption is facing a challenge from unconventional energy, which will influence both global energy supply and demand.

> ① Here, energy refers not only to the conventional energy such as the coal, oil and gas, but also the new energy such as shale gas and oil, tight oil and the nuclear energy and renewable energy.

On the supply side, the conventional oil and gas group is highly integrated and forms a strong market influence, which is an important feature of the post-World War II global oil and gas resources supply order. However, along with the commercial maturity in the development of unconventional oil and gas resources, conventional oil and gas resources are facing a threat from external forces. In order to maintain its competitive advantage, it is necessary to pay more attention to the consumer end, and make timely adjustments to their strategies.

On the demand side, emerging economies such as China and India, with their proportion of global energy consumption increasing, have become the big buyers as well as important game players in the global oil and gas market in the new era. Their enterprises will play a more important role due to their growing buying power, market influence and a strengthened international enterprise status. Their import choices will have a major impact on the future development of the world energy industry.

6.3.2.2 Influence of the Belt and Road region on the global energy order

Of the sixty-five Belt and Road countries, there are forty-eight Asian countries (the sixteen Central and Eastern European countries and Egypt not included). In other words, Asian countries constitute 74% of the total Belt and Road countries. Therefore, the Asia region (Belt and Road countries plus Japan and Korea) and the other Belt and Road countries have changed the global energy order in many ways.

Firstly, their continuously growing demands for oil and gas have made the Asia Region the largest contributor to the recent boom in world energy consumption. Taking oil as an example, in 2011, China and India imported from the Middle East a total of 137.8 million tons and 110.7 million tons of oil respectively. If Japan (175.1 million tons) is included in the calculation, the amount of oil imported by these three countries accounted for almost half of the whole oil export volume (979.4 million tons). At the same time, the volume of oil imports by North America and Europe was only 226.8 million tones. Detailed figures are given in Table 33 for comparison.

Table 33   Oil Imports from the Middle East

country \ year	2006	2007	2008	2009	2010	2011
U.S.	113.2	110.4	119.7	86.9	86	95.5
Canada	6.8	7	6.3	5	4.3	5.3
Europe	159.3	146.6	127.6	105.9	116.7	126
China	73.9	78.8	92	103.2	118.4	137.8
India			107.6	110.1	129.6	110.7
Japan	209.1	199.9	196.9	179.4	179.9	175.1
Total Middle East	1001.3	975.3	1000.7	913.8	935.9	979.4

Data source: BP (2015)

As shown in Figure 37, the contribution of these four countries (China,

Japan, South Korea and India) accounted for 59% of the total increase in the world primary energy consumption from 1993 to 2013 and the share of these four countries of the total world consumption in 2013 was almost 35%. This demonstrates the significant and growing impact of these four countries on the world's energy market.

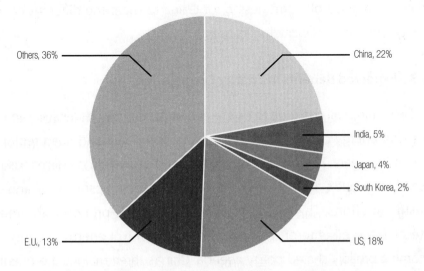

Others, 36%

China, 22%

India, 5%

Japan, 4%

South Korea, 2%

E.U., 13%

US, 18%

Figure 37   Share of world primary energy consumption in 2013

Starting in 1993, China first began to import oil products and has since become more and more reliant on oil imports. China's energy policy in this period has put much emphasis on the process of going out. In other words, it has gone through a journey of globalization, changing its policy focus to meet its fuel demands by using overseas' fuel markets while it still relies heavily on its own domestic resources. Due to its significant domestic coal production, China still has a relatively low level of dependence on foreign hydrocarbons (11%). However, its reliance on imported oil and gas is significant and has been growing continuously. China is now the largest energy producer, but at the same time also the largest energy consumer in the world, consuming 22% of the world's primary energy in 2013. India has faced a similar experience in expanding its energy demand to support its

351

economic development.

In summing up, the greatest changes in the world's energy development have brought to China both opportunities and challenges in ensuring its own energy security, while playing the role the second-largest economy should to meet the world's economic growth needs. Therefore, the Belt and Road Initiative is a good platform design for China to meet the different energy security requirements including its own.

6.3.3 Expected Benefits in Energy Cooperation

First, China will continue to be the engine for energy cooperation among the major energy consumers and suppliers of the Belt and Road region in the coming years. The prospect for continued growth in oil demands has pushed the world's oil and gas companies to increase upstream oil and gas investment efforts. This phenomenon is particularly pronounced among state-oriented oil enterprises as the enhancement of energy security has become a broadly shared policy agenda. China's three major state-oriented oil enterprises (CNPC, Sinopec, and CNOOC) are often considered to be global leaders in such efforts because of their visibility in a recent surge to acquire overseas upstream investment stakes and because of the sheer size of future Chinese petroleum demands.

In 2015, natural gas consumption reached 193 bcm (National Bureau of Statistics of the People's Republic of China), which cannot be met by its national supply of 100-150 bcm (National Energy Administration, People's Republic of China). Therefore, there is a need to increase its import volume through increasing the sources. Liquefied and pipeline natural gas are now the main import targets. In 2011, China imported liquefied gas from Australia (5bcm), Qatar (3.2 bcm) and Indonesia (2.7 bcm), giving a total of 10.9 bcm. China also started cooperating with Central Asian nations (Kazakhstan, Turkmenistan and Uzbekistan), Myanmar and Russia to complete its international NG pipelines in the Northeast and Southwest regions. In 2009, the China-Central Asia pipelines started to transport gas. In October 2013, the China-Myanmar pipeline (12 bcm/year) also commenced operation.

Second, the common interest of energy supply security promotes cooperation among Belt and Road countries like China and India, between Belt and Road countries and non-Belt and Road countries like with the U.S, Japan, Korea and Western European countries. India has developed its economy rapidly in recent years. This has resulted in a dramatically increasing demand for energy, as China also faces. It is predicted that India will need to import more than 250 million tons of petroleum in the year 2020, and will surpass Korea to become the fourth largest energy-consuming country following China, the U.S. and Japan. The IEA projects that by 2040 India will replace China to have the largest increase of energy consumption in the Asia region [1] . Back in May 2005, the India National Congress stated that if India could not find new oilfields in time, the currently proven oil deposit would be depleted by the year 2016. Hence, India has adopted protective gas-exploiting measures, and made a comprehensive supply plan for overseas energy expansion.

[1] IEA: *World Energy Outlook* 2015

India has made a "T" pattern in its diplomatic energy exploration strategy: trying to obtain the exploitation rights to Russian oilfields to its north; to build a secure oil transportation channel from Iran to India to its west and to gain the largest quota of Myanmar's oil exports to its east. In addition, India has also extended its reach to Africa and Latin America. The same foreign energy strategy has pushed India and China to move together. For example, the two countries have collaborated in exploiting petroleum in Kazakhstan, and jointly entered into the Sudan Petroleum Exploitation Project.

Third, the role played by the energy enterprises of these Belt and Road countries will affect their national energy security through an abundance of capital investment not only in energy infrastructure construction but also in energy trading and so on. Direct investment is the main way of energy cooperation in the Belt and Road region and the main player will be the enterprises not the government. The investment will be floated to the oil and gas fields, and also new and renewable energy industries, like wind, solar, geothermal and the NRE technologies.

Belt and Road countries such as China and India, with the increase in their global energy consumption, and the anticipated continuous trend of increasing energy demand to meet the development need of their national economies, have already joined Japan and Korea as big buyers in the energy market. It is anticipated that they will continue to grow and become even bigger and bigger in the energy market, their influence will increase will increase and sooner or later they will become some of the key game players in the global oil and gas market. Because of the diversification of choices for energy imports at the consumer end, it will undoubtedly have a direct impact on the global energy competition in price, import resources and conventional or unconventional energy development.

After the 2008 financial crisis shook the global capital market, the energy enterprises in Europe and the United States went through serious difficulty in financing, which greatly affected their business activities. Under such changes, the high market entry barriers to the energy resource market for Chinese, Indian and other Belt and Road countries' capital-abundant national energy enterprises began to loosen, and merger and acquisition activities by the Belt and Road countries increased. For example, with the going overseas process, China and India, as Japan and Korea had been doing before, have been accumulating lots of international experience in the process. Through in-depth cooperation with leading global enterprises, Chinese and Indian enterprises have already achieved a certain degree of international competitiveness and have acquired the basic quality of a top global energy company.

6.3.4 Potential Risks in Energy Cooperation: Investment and the Non-interference Principle

First is the geopolitical risk. Inside Asia there has gradually formed a complete demand and supply (DS) circular system. The system is composed of three sorts of countries, the exporters, the importers and the transporters, which can help reduce the Asian gas premium and appease the oil high price. The exporters mainly include Russia and Central Asian countries (Kazakhstan, Turkmenistan and Uzbekistan) and Australia, the importers include China, Japan, Korea, India and Singapore, and the transporters include Myanmar and Central Asian countries.

Russia's oil and gas through the Sino-Russia oil and gas pipelines, Central Asia's oil and gas through the Sino-Kazakhstan oil pipeline and Sino-Central Asia gas pipeline, Myanmar's gas and the Middle East oil transported through the Sino-Myanmar oil and gas pipelines and the Australian liquidized gas through shipping, all form a robust and effective supply and demand network. The oil and gas pipelines effectively connect the exporters, importers and transporters not only overland by the Silk Road (i.e. Belt) but also by the maritime Silk Road. For the other two big consumers of East Asia, Japan and Korea, the comparatively affluent energy supply in the region is also good news, as they can also enjoy the Russian oil and gas through the Sino-Russia oil and gas pipelines, at a cheaper price. A trilateral agreement took effect to facilitate investment between China, Japan and Korea; it has strengthened the cooperation between the three countries, despite of the territorial and political conflicts between China and Japan.

The geostrategic competition among world powers in the Belt and Road region, and among the major energy importers of the world for the energy resources is increasingly fierce. Multinational corporations from Western countries, compared with Chinese corporations, which control a large number of high-quality oil fields, can exert more influence on the region.

The possibility of political power instability in most Belt and Road countries which have rich resources and social conflicts deep-rooted in these regions between ethnic groups and religious sects, formed various geopolitical risks to China.

China's growing demand for oil is significantly changing the international geopolitics of energy, especially in the Asia-Pacific region. China's attempts to increase and diversify its oil supply and transport routes may also lead to serious conflict with Japan and other Asian countries. However, enhanced cooperation among the big East and South Asian economies (China, Japan and ASEAN), India and Russia, especially the Belt and Road countries is also a possibility. A move towards one scenario or the other will largely depend on China's strategic decisions in the coming years. The mission of the Belt and Road initiative is to turn hostility into friendship.

Second is the risk of conflict between China's foreign energy investment and its diplomatic non-interference principle. Conflict may arise when the non-interference principle will prevent China from acting on its growing demand for foreign energy investment, as well as its energy security concerns. The principle was instated by Chinese former Premier Chou Enlai in 1953 during the negotiations between China and India over the Tibet territory conflict. It was introduced as a part of the five principles of peaceful coexistence as the basis for negotiations: mutual non-aggression, non-interference in other countries' internal affairs, equality, mutual benefit and peaceful co-existence, which form the basis of China's contemporary diplomacy and energy diplomacy today.

China, together with the six other major nations has reached a historical agreement on Iran's nuclear program, which is likely to result in lifting the sanctions on Iran's crude oil exports. According to RAND, China's need for energy is one of the most important factors shaping Iranian-Chinese relations. Chinese NOCs are expected to invest heavily in Iran's oilfields to boost energy cooperation, as well as non-energy infrastructure, like railways, to boost Iran's integration into the global energy market. Furthermore, Iran might play an important role in China's Belt and Road foreign strategy implementation, due to its geographical position and abundance of natural gas and oil. Considering the rise in foreign energy investment in order to protect its overseas energy benefits, will we see any change in China's non-interference? Given the scale of investment in Iranian infrastructure, as well as the potential role it might play in China's Belt and Road Initiative, it is possible that China will take a more proactive stance to defend its long-term interests, if the necessity arises. In the near future, however, China is more likely to forebear from getting involved in Iranian internal affairs. The case of Iran shows that there is a conflict risk between large-scale energy investment and China's diplomatic non-interference principle.

参考文献

Chen J., Fleisher B.M. *Regional income inequality and economic growth in China. J Compar Econ*, 1996; 22(2):141–64.

Hu J.L., Wang S.C. *Total-factor energy efficiency of regions in China. Energy Policy*, 2006;34(17):3206–17.

Gelb C., Chen D. *Going west: a progress report. China Business Review*. March–April 2004. <http://www.chinabusinessreview.com/public/0403/chen.html>.

Muñoz Delgado, B. (2011). *Energy security indices in Europe.* Paper presented at the Economic Challenges for Energy workshop in Madrid, 7–8 February 2011.

Yukari Yamashita, *Asia/World Energy Outlook 2011.* lecture paper of Baoao Forum Global Energy & Resources Roundtable, November 5 2011, Qingdao , China.

APERC. *Understanding Energy in China (2008): Geographies of Energy efficiency.* Asia Pacific Energy Research Centre,2008

APERC. *Understanding Energy in China (2009): Geographies of Energy efficiency.* Asia Pacific Energy Research Centre,2009

Skeer, J. and Y. Wang.(2007). *China on the move: Oil price explosion? Energy Policy* 35(1):678–691.

Robinson, D. and Qinhua, Xu (2013). *Implications for China of North American Energy Independence, OIES*, 27 March 2013.

Chung, W., and Zhou, G.(2013). *CO_2 emissions analysis of China's regional thermal power. Working paper, Department of Management Sciences.* City University of Hong Kong, Hong Kong, January 2013.

Ang, B. W. (2005). *The LMDI approach to decomposition analysis: a practical guide. Energy Policy* 33(7):867–871.

Zhang, Z. X. (2010). *China in the transition to a low-carbon economy, Energy Policy* 38(11):6638–6653.

Dua, L., Mao, J. and Shi, J. (2009). *Assessing the impact of regulatory reforms on China's electricity generation industry. Energy Policy* 37:712–720.

Xu, Q., Chung, W. *China Energy Policy in National and International Perspectives—A Study Fore-and After 18th National Congress.* Hong Kong: City University of Hong Kong, 2014.

读石油版书，获亲情馈赠

　　亲爱的读者朋友，首先感谢您阅读我社图书，请您在阅读完本书后填写以下信息。我社将长期开展"读石油版书，获亲情馈赠"活动，凡是关注我社图书并认真填写读者信息反馈卡的朋友都有机会获得亲情馈赠，我们将定期从信息反馈卡中评选出有价值的意见和建议，并为填写这些信息的读者朋友 **免费** 赠送一本好书。

中国能源政策解读：能源革命与"一带一路"倡议

1. 您购买本书的动因（可多选）

☐ 书名　　　　☐ 封面　　　　☐ 内容　　　　☐ 价格
☐ 装帧　　　　☐ 纸张　　　　☐ 双色印刷
☐ 书店推荐　　☐ 朋友推荐　　☐ 报刊文章推荐
☐ 作者　　　　☐ 出版社　　　☐ 其他＿＿＿＿＿＿＿＿＿＿＿＿

2. 您在哪里购买了本书（若是书店请写明书店地址和名称）？

＿＿＿＿＿＿＿＿＿＿＿＿＿＿＿＿＿＿＿＿＿ 购书时间 ＿＿＿＿＿＿

3. 您是怎样知道本书的（可多选）？

☐ 报刊介绍＿＿＿＿＿＿（报刊名称）　☐ 朋友推荐＿＿＿＿＿＿
☐ 网站＿＿＿＿＿＿（网站名称）　　　☐ 书店广告＿＿＿＿＿＿
☐ 书店随便翻阅　　　　　　　　　　　☐ 其他＿＿＿＿＿＿＿＿

4. 您对本书的印象如何（可多选）？

封面：☐ 新颖　　☐ 吸引眼球　☐ 一般，没创意　☐ 不适合本书内容
内容：☐ 丰富　　☐ 有新意　　☐ 一般　　　　　☐ 较差
排版：☐ 新颖　　☐ 一般　　　☐ 太花哨　　　　☐ 较差
纸张：☐ 很好　　☐ 一般　　　☐ 较差
定价：☐ 太高　　☐ 有点高　　☐ 合适　　　　　☐ 便宜

5. 您对本书的综合评价和建议（可另附纸）。

＿＿＿＿＿＿＿＿＿＿＿＿＿＿＿＿＿＿＿＿＿＿＿＿＿＿＿＿＿＿＿
＿＿＿＿＿＿＿＿＿＿＿＿＿＿＿＿＿＿＿＿＿＿＿＿＿＿＿＿＿＿＿

● **您的资料：**

您的姓名＿＿＿＿＿　性别＿＿＿＿＿　年龄＿＿＿＿＿　职业＿＿＿＿＿
学历＿＿＿＿＿＿＿　电话（写明区号）＿＿＿＿＿＿　手机＿＿＿＿＿
电子邮件＿＿＿＿＿＿＿＿＿＿＿＿＿＿＿＿＿＿　邮编＿＿＿＿＿＿
通信地址＿＿＿＿＿＿＿＿＿＿＿＿＿＿＿＿＿＿＿＿＿＿＿＿＿＿＿

● **我们的联系方式：**

地　　址：北京市朝阳区安华里二区1号楼309室　刘文国
邮　　编：100011　　　　　E-mail: lwgpip@126.com
图书营销中心：010-64523633　　编辑部电话：010-64523602